...shire Hunt?

"...d, or tho sheep leave a stain,
_ again & again ! "

[Whyte Melville]

Memories of the Shires

With best wishes

With Jaffray

21 November 2012

Memories of the Shires

Hunting with the Quorn
in late Victorian & Edwardian England

by J. Otho Paget

Introduction and Epilogue by
Anne, Lady Jaffray and Sir William Jaffray, Bart

ESPERE ET PERSEVERE

Methuen

Published by Methuen & Co 2012

1 3 5 7 9 10 8 6 4 2

Copyright in the text © 2012 Anne, Lady Jaffray and
Sir William Jaffray, Bart

Copyright in the Introduction and
Epilogue © 2012 Anne, Lady Jaffray and Sir William Jaffray, Bart

Copyright in the Foreword © 2012
Lt-Gen Sir Barney White-Spunner KCB CBE

ISBN   978 0 413 77756 0

First published in Great Britain in 1920 by Methuen

Methuen & Co
35 Hospital Fields Road
York YO10 4DZ

Methuen & Co Ltd Registered number 5278590

A CIP catalogue record for this book is
available from the British Library

Typeset by SX Composing DTP, Rayleigh, Essex
Printed by CPI Group (UK) Ltd, Croydon, CR0 4YY

Author's Note

I am indebted to the proprietors of the *Field* for permission to insert extracts from articles I wrote for that paper, and here with acknowledge gratefully the favour granted.

Except in those few instances where I have thought it best to make extracts as originally printed, all the accounts of runs have been rewritten, but confess that I had to refresh my memory by a perusal of articles which were paid for by the *Field*.

J. Otho Paget

The Times

J Otho Paget 1860 – 1934

A link with the palmy days of hunting is severed by the death
of Captain J Otho Paget, a friend and colleague known
world wide for half a century or more as the writer on the
sport he loved so well and served so faithfully under the
nom de plume of 'Q'. Born seventy-four years ago at Thorpe
Satchville Hall, Leicestershire, he passed away on February
4th, and was buried on the 7th, his last resting place being
on Quorn territory, at Thorpe Satchville. Regarded as a
writer of great charm and knowledge on all matters
connected with the chase, the many volumes of which he
was the author are classics for the guidance of successive
generations. It may be said that Captain Paget died in
harness, for what proved to be his farewell contribution
relating to sport with the Quorn appeared in *Horse and
Hound* two days before his death.

As a Master, huntsman, breeder and judge of beagles the
late Captain Paget won lasting fame, for the Thorpe Satchville
pack was founded in 1890 and was hunted by him regularly
until illness last Christmas prevented him taking any further
active part. The kennel possesses the choicest strains of blood,
big winners at the hound shows, and [is] much sought after
by those seeking improvement. Last summer the Thorpe
Satchville kennel did not compete at Peterborough, as their
Master was judging the beagle classes, a long and arduous
day's work of five hours.

Brief hunting experiences trace the outline of a useful life spent in the service of sport, and turning to one of our late friend's volumes the following extracts are of interest and encouragement to aspirants of today.

'*Occasionally, as a small boy, I was taken in a carriage to see hounds, and perhaps had the pleasure of sitting on the sharp hoop of a crinoline. But I always hated wheels, and much preferred wandering across country on foot, in the oldest clothes I could find. Fortunate to hire a good pony at a small figure, I had a few excellent days with the Quorn, and in a crush at a gateway the pony jumped a big fence at the side. Brooksby shouted "Boy, you will kill yourself!"*

I carried the memory of those happy days to sea in a windjammer of the merchant service, and often lived them over again when keeping night watch beneath the Southern Cross. During two years aboard ship the rat was the only animal I had a chance to hunt, and having no terrier I was obliged to catch them by hand. On leaving the sea, the love of country pursuit and sport made me take to the fascinating but unprofitable business of farming; but I commenced hunting regularly in 1880-81 with the Quorn and Cottesmore.'

A bold rider, determined to be with hounds, he never spared himself or his horse, on a memorable occasion jumping locked railway gates at a crossing, clearing the first, and getting over the second with a fall, but alone with hounds. Captain Paget took part in the memorable midnight steeplechase at Melton in 1890, finishing second to Major A E Burnaby, with Mr Charles McNeill close up. The daring party of riders jumped a three-mile course near Marshall's Spinney, the fences being illuminated with oil lamps, and it was providential that no bad accident resulted. When the Great War came, Captain Paget joined up, though over age, and served with the Royal Sussex Yeomanry, winning the Military Cross.

Happily married late in life to a lady who proved to be a

real sporting partner, our friend leaves a widow and young daughter, and his presence will be greatly missed in the hunting Shires.

Contents

FOREWORD

Memories of the Shires

J. Otho Paget

All hunting people have their own idea of a hunting idyll. For some it may be a distant point over open moorland; perhaps for others it is jumping a line of great banks but for me, and I suspect many of us, it is a run over the best of English grass and fly fences, able to take your own line and hopefully getting to the end before anyone else. Sadly this does not happen very often and we have to content ourselves with imaginary hunts instead, and for me these are very like the great days enjoyed in the Shires at the turn of the last century and captured for the readers of *The Field* and for posterity by that great sportsman John Otho Paget.

Paget was writing when a combination of factors meant that fox hunting found its golden age in the English midlands in the late nineteenth century. The development of the railways in the USA and Canada in the 1870s led to cheap corn coming onto the European market, with consequent agricultural depression and land reverting to pasture. At the same time the Industrial Revolution was creating some very rich men who were determined to enjoy all the countryside had to offer, and hound breeding was becoming an art. From 1880, when Paget writes that he started hunting regularly with The Quorn and Cottesmore, until the outbreak of the First World War, fox hunting enjoyed a sustained purple patch.

Paget's great luck was to live and hunt in the Shires from 1860 and his great skill was to be able to convey the excitement of it. It is impossible to read his descriptions of the Quorn bitches racing, of galloping over the sea of grass and hedges in the open vale of Belvoir, or of Tom Firr's inspired cast to save a hunt on a darkening afternoon without your stomach tightening and mentally transporting yourself back to that wonderful and extraordinary sporting world where hunting was everything.

What is also so remarkable and enjoyable about this beautifully produced reproduction is the Introduction by Anne Jaffray, Paget's daughter. Not only does she bring an immediacy to his stories, but, now in her nineties, she brings the history, and particularly the sporting history, of the last 150 years together in the story of one family. Her father was born in 1860, and her grandparents lived through Queen Victoria's accession, the revolutions of 1848 and the Crimean War. Talking to her as we discussed this project, and hearing her recollections and those of her father, has been a remarkable privilege.

I feel a keen link to Paget, having latterly also been hunting correspondent to *The Field*, although sadly I cannot pretend to have enjoyed so much or such good hunting, nor to have acquitted myself to his high standards in the hunting field. I feel though that I can relive something of the excitement of his days through this wonderful book, and I hope you can too.

Barney White-Spunner

Acknowledgements.

What fun it has been to edit this New Edition of *Memories of the Shires* with so rich a seam of anecdotal history! Colin D B Ellis' masterly book on *Leicestershire and the Quorn Hunt* is an invaluable source of period material; particularly since many of the principal characters were within living memory at the time it was published in 1951. Towering personalities bestrode the rural stage when foxhunting was deemed the epitome of a life well spent, a vocation no less. Certainly, Lady Augusta Fane qualified as instigator of the famous Melton Midnight Steeplechase of March 1890, and her memoir *Chit-Chat* contains many contemporary anecdotes, some of which I have included in the appendices; equally, the American, Eugene Reynal, who beat a path to Otho Paget's door to improve his Millbrook pack. I am indebted therefore to Peter Devers for kindly consenting to include his written portrait of Reynal at Appendix III, and for his assistance in procuring the illustration of Reynal's prize harrier, 'Monarch' presently hanging in the American Kennel Club in New York.

Of other illustrations, I am indebted to Alexandra Davy of the Leicestershire C C collections for the image of Capt. Burns Hartopp by Sir Arthur Stockdale Cope RA. Courtesy of www. quornmuseum.com, Sue Templeman kindly provided the fine photographic image of Tom Firr on his retirement, and took a photograph of his grave in the quiet Quorn churchyard. Cuthbert Bradley, evidently a talented man,

Acknowledgements.

penned *The Reminiscences of Frank Gillard,* and drew the cartoon of Otho Paget beagling. The description of Otho Paget jumping railway gates is found in Gillard's memoirs; likewise, Julie Kemper Foyer kindly provided the photograph of Gillard from the original edition. For the paintings of Lord "Hoppy" Manners and Mary Fitzgerald, formerly Forester, their descendants have been most generous with their time. The illustration of Mrs. Otho Manners, Otho's maternal grandmother, is from a photograph in family possession. The original painting by Mary Martha Pearson hangs in the Royal Pavilion, Brighton.

Our family had very little information about Otho's Great War experiences until spring 2008, when I began corresponding with the late Mr. John A Baines of the Royal Sussex Living History Group. For the new introduction, he kindly provided me with extracts from Neville Lytton's book on *The Press and the General Staff,* published by Collins in 1921. Lytton was a fellow officer in the First Southdowns Battalion of the Royal Sussex Regiment, and John wrote as follows: "I think Lytton's final comment on the officer he knew expresses perfectly the esteem in which he held Capt. Paget and I hope will make both your mother and you extremely proud".

Michael Clayton and Countryside Alliance have been a tower of strength throughout, their unwavering support invaluable in bringing this New Edition to fruition. Whereas many typographical errors in the original text were caught by Methuen, I must hope my additional text has not increased the tally! And though I may not aspire to his literary heights, I am indebted to Hugo Vickers for his appreciation.

A new Epilogue brings this history up to 1950. My mother, of course, has provided many family recollections stretching back to the 19th century- both from her father, and personally from 1930 onwards, many of which might otherwise have been lost.

Bletchley Park historian, the late Dr. Brian Oakley CBE, was a fount of information about BP, and it is to him that I end this note. "Your Mother has had a difficult life" he said, "but she is indomitable".

Sir William Jaffray Bart.
London 2012

Introduction: The Golden Age.

In these memoirs, my father recounts the golden age of hunting over a span of thirty-five years with the Quorn, Belvoir, and Cottesmore, through till the onset of the Great War. He reserves particular affection for the Quorn, England's premier pack, in the days when Tom Firr carried the horn for twenty-seven seasons until his retirement in 1899; and where he draws on first-hand accounts in articles he submitted to *The Field* under his pseudonym Q. It is those articles, written at the end of each day out with the Hunt, that convey such a thrilling sense of immediacy to the reader, who in turn gains a sense of being in the thick of the fun.

My father, John Otho Paget was born on 21st May 1860, the second son of Edmund Paget and his wife Martha known as Patty, née Manners, at their family seat of Thorpe Satchville, near Melton Mowbray, in Leicestershire. Otho's great-grandfather, Joseph Paget, had built the house in the mid 18th century, no doubt when the previous dwelling had outlived its usefulness. The family had long-established roots in the locality dating back to 1409; later, in 1458, Henry VI awarded the manor of Ibstock and the right to bear Arms to Thomas and John Paget, the king desperate for support in the civil war engulfing the Houses of York and Lancaster, better known to history as the War of the Roses. Under the more settled times of Queen Elizabeth I, one descendant, Valerian, a French protestant refugee born in Rouen, judged it safe to return to his roots in 1563 to found a distinct line of Pagets of Ibstock, thereby distinguishing them from the many collateral branches of this fecund family.

Otho's more immediate relations led colourful and distinguished lives. His uncle, John Paget, a soldier, traveller and writer, and, rather surprisingly, a graduate surgeon of Edinburgh, left Thorpe Satchville in the 1830s on a grand tour of Europe, accompanied by the artist, John Herring; he also brought with him a pack of fox-hounds; meticulous for their care, each hound was provided with its own set of leather boots to protect their feet. When he reached Rome in 1836 he met and fell in love with Baroness Polyxena Wesselenyi Banffy, then followed her to Hungary, where they were married. Shortly afterwards, he adopted Hungarian citizenship.

European-wide unrest in the year of 1848 found him appointed ADC to General Bem at the head of the revolutionary armies, but he was forced to flee to London with his wife, staying en route in Dresden, from where he corresponded with his publisher, John Murray. His entry into Germany was confirmed by no less a personage than Bismarck, who endorsed his passport. Returning to his adopted country in 1855, he helped to manage his wife's estates; here he gained a high reputation as a scientific agriculturist, and as a beneficent landlord, by introducing an improved breed of cattle and taking a keen interest in viniculture. His travels throughout Hungary and Transylvania were published by Murray as early as 1839; yet it is through his notable political efforts in wresting independence from Austria that he came to be regarded as a founder of modern Hungary, the government somewhat belatedly recognizing his achievements with the erection of a plaque in Thorpe Satchville church in 1969.

Otho's maternal grandmother, Ann Singleton, married

Otho Manners, a grandson of the third Duke of Rutland. She was evidently a rare Regency beauty, as can be seen from her portrait by Mary Martha Pearson, now hanging in the Brighton Pavilion. She had died tragically young, and her grief-stricken husband kept her embalmed body, draped in all her jewellery, at home for eleven weeks, until her mausoleum was built; evidently, he was reluctant to part with her, even in death. Her funeral was a lavish spectacular, judging by the breathless report in the *Lincoln Rutland & Stamford Mercury*, 11th January 1828 edition.

'On Monday night last, at 6 o'clock, the funeral of Mrs. Manners, the wife of Otho Manners Esq of Goadby Hall took place at North Witham, in this county, in the churchyard of which parish a noble mausoleum had been built for the occasion. The funeral procession of course took place by torchlight, and it was most splendid and imposing in its effect. In addition to the usual attendants on similar solemn occasions, twenty-four javelin men and eight bearers on horseback preceded the hearse, the former wearing black cloaks, and two of them displaying armorial standards; the hearse was drawn by six horses, and was followed by four coaches and six, one coach and four with attendants in state liveries, a chariot and four, and a barouchette and pair, the whole of the horses of which were covered with black velvet housings.

The principal mourner was Mr. Otho Manners, followed by the five children of the deceased- a son and four daughters- the three brothers of Mr. Manners, the Rev. J. and Mrs. Singleton- father and mother of the deceased-Mr. Singleton, and other members of the family. The coffin, covered with crimson velvet richly ornamented, was deposited on a canopy bedstead in the mausoleum, decorated with escutcheons. From the roof of the building was suspended a beautiful ground-glass chandelier, having the armorial bearings emblazoned on the sides; and the vault – which is of sufficient capacity for a large number of coffins- was warmed by a stove, the fire of which, and the lights of the chandelier, we understand, are still kept up.

The cavalcade moved in funeral procession the whole way from Goadby to Witham, the bells of the twelve intermediate or neighbouring parish churches tolling during the interval. The church at Witham was lighted up and hung in many parts with black cloth, and the whole funeral was conducted in the most magnificent style.'

But that is not all. As can be imagined, the mantle of family history lay heavily on my father's young shoulders; he was expected to make his mark in the world. Not for him, the antics of a distant and more racy collateral branch. Sir Henry Paget, after becoming 2nd Earl of Uxbridge, distinguished himself at the battle of Waterloo when one of the last cannon shots of the day took off his leg. Turning to the Duke of Wellington, he remarked, "By God, Sir, I've lost my leg," to which the Duke replied, "By God, Sir, so you have!" before riding off into the mist.

Wellington was still resentful of Paget's conduct, when the latter abandoned his wife and eight children in 1808 to elope adulterously with Lady Charlotte Wellesley. And when Henry's daughter, Lady Caroline, became engaged to the Earl of March, it was the last straw for Jane Austen. In a letter she wrote to her niece, Fanny Knight from her house in Chawton, Hampshire on 13th March 1817, she acidly observed: 'If I were the Duchess of Richmond, I should be very miserable about my son's choice. What can be expected of a Paget, born and brought up in the centre of conjugal infidelity and divorces? I will not be interested about Lady Caroline. I abhor all the race of Pagets.'

Such excitements were a world away for my father, who, in the 1860s was brought up on a family estate that was self-sufficient in all produce save tea, sugar and wine. An early interest in field sports soon beckoned, and, as he recalled: 'Occasionally, as perhaps a small boy, I was taken in a carriage to see hounds, (in Patty's gingerbread cart), and perhaps had the pleasure of sitting on the sharp hoop of a crinoline. But I always hated wheels, and much preferred wandering across country on foot, in the oldest clothes I could find. Fortunate to hire a good pony at a small figure, I had a few excellent days with the Quorn, and in a crush at a gateway the pony jumped a big fence at the side. 'Brooksby' shouted: 'Boy, you will kill yourself!'

'I carried the memory of those happy days to sea in a windjammer of the merchant service, and often lived them over again when keeping night watch beneath the Southern Cross,' recalled Otho of his two-year stint on a training ship, HMS *Conway*, a wooden battleship incorporating a naval training school. The hymn 'For those in peril on the sea' was sung every Sunday, at Patty's insistence, until he returned home in 1879 when still only 19 years old.

Thorpe Satchville, just outside Melton Mowbray in Leicestershire placed Otho in the midst of the finest hunting country England had to offer: "On leaving the sea" Otho wrote, "the love of country pursuit and sport made me take to the fascinating but unprofitable business of farming; but I commenced hunting regularly in 1880-81 with the Quorn and Cottesmore." And, as he readily admits in *Memories of the Shires*, an irresistible pastime beckoned the young man: "perhaps it was that the joy of youth was then at its zenith, and to get on the right side of a fence was more important than the chances of a fall." Yet, in so many parts, this book is a tribute to Firr, and he gives us, the reader, a ringside seat in watching something quite out of the ordinary take place; a sense too of history in the making that has become a legendary part of hunting lore. It is his unstinting admiration for Firr and this huntsman's intuitive art in getting the best out of his hounds which Paget finds truly inspirational, and for us magical: "Tom Firr always kept in touch with his pack whilst in covert, and to see them flying out in reply to his cheer was a sight not to be forgotten when once seen."

The memoir is noteworthy for its absence of any criticism of the personalities of the day, and Paget's generosity in seldom missing an opportunity for praise; nor is he above admitting a certain sense of self-deprecating humour, which draws one to his strength of character; not surprisingly, his company was much in demand, not just from his contemporaries, but also from the rising generation.

It would be wrong though, to leave the reader with the impression that *Memories of the Shires* is primarily concerned with my father's days out with the Quorn. Indeed, it is not. One of Otho's more thrilling accounts is about a memorable day out with the Belvoir on Saturday 20th February 1886, and he imparts the thrill of an historic run in inimitable style.

'Now then, reader, if you wish to see the fun you must hustle through the first gate or two and gallop your hardest. Check not your steed as you reach Clawson Thorns, for the pack touch not the cover, but are racing like distraction up the narrow ride and out beyond. A short turn on the hill, and then down we go into the vale. The village of Long Clawson is in front, but a bend to the right leaves it a quarter of a mile on our left. The vale *par excellence* is now before us; good sound grass, bounded by fair, leapable fences that may be taken anywhere and everywhere. The pack are 'streaking it' across the level like pigeons, and two hundred horsemen are thundering in their wake. Already grief is general; loose horses are careering everywhere, and the cracking of timber is heard on all sides. A field of plough, over which hounds skim and horses flounder, is quickly left behind; and then we turn to the left and gallop down the road for Hose. Skirting the village the pace increases, the fun becoming fast and furious. In and out of a lane, some quick, recurring fences and an ugly bottom bars the way. One division is wide on the right, and hit the bottom, where a friendly bridge solves the difficulty. A hatless horseman is to be seen with a clear lead of his followers, cutting out the work in the rear of the pack, and an army of 'top-sawyers' comes crashing on behind him. Hold hard, gentlemen! Hounds are at fault, and here we are at Hose Gorse twenty minutes from the find.'

Hunting, and as a pastime, beagling, was my father's way of life, freely acknowledging in the book that 'it is possible to compress a lifetime of mad excitement into a few seconds, when you are on the back of a good horse and hounds are racing away.' And he was on the back of a good horse on Monday 10th March 1890 for the famous Melton midnight steeple-chase, won by Mr. Algy Burnaby, but which he himself would have won save for a contested wrong turn at the finish line. As I recall, forever afterwards, he would cheerfully complain he was wrongly deprived of the winner's cup.

The idea of a midnight steeplechase was not exactly novel: a previous event had taken place in 1837, when two officers from the Dragoons had raced by moonlight in their nightshirts and caps. High time to establish a tradition, thought high-spirited guests at the birthday party held for Lady Augusta Fane at the Old Club in Burton Street the previous Friday.

On the Monday evening of the chase, twenty-five dinner

guests were entertained, once again at the Old Club. Guests included the eleven competitors- Count Zborowski, a New Yorker of Polish extraction; Willie and Gerald Chaplin; Sidney and Otho Paget; Algernon Burnaby; Gordon Wilson; Capt. Rawlinson; Mr. Heneage; and Charles McNeil; Quorn MFH, Capt. Warner, was also present.

'The dining-room looked so gay,' recalled Lady Augusta, 'the men in red evening coats and white breeches, and the women in smart day dresses. At about 9.30 our groom sent in word that heavy clouds were obscuring the moon. No one would hear of the race being postponed, so Colonel Baldock (starter and judge of the race) came to the rescue and offered to go to the Midland Railway station to borrow lamps and a van, which he succeeded in doing through the obliging assistance of the station-master, Mr. Bedlington.'

On the important matter of attire, Lady Augusta offered a willing hand: 'In the meantime, we were fitting out the eleven competitors with white nightshirts to be worn over their red coats. Some had brought their own shirts, some had not, and they had to be supplied. I lent a pink gossamer nightie, beribboned and frilled, to Algy Burnaby, which caused much laughter and merriment as he struggled to get into it.'

Otho takes up the story: 'Shortly before midnight the horses were brought to the door, and their iron-shod hoofs clattering on the cobblestones awoke the vicar from his sleep. (The vicarage abutted the Old Club). Someone must have made a mistake with the almanac, as instead of a full moon, which we had been told to expect, it was a pitch dark night.' Ironically, once the race was finished, the clouds cleared and the countryside was bathed in clear moonlight.

The *Melton Mowbray Mercury* reporters were working overtime that night, as their report makes clear: 'Near upon 11 o'clock, unmistakable signs were observed, when heavily laden drags, an omnibus, the parcel vans of the two railways, carriages with their fair occupants, and flaming lamps, and men on horseback, rattled down Sherrard Street on their way to Gunby's Lodge, near the Melton Spinnies. In a trice, the foot people turned out in their hundreds. The traps of the butcher, baker and publican were requisitioned, and to the refrain of "We'll all go a-hunting today", they proceeded to the scene of the action.'

Unfortunately for Otho, his horse had wheeled away, out of earshot, as Colonel Baldock gave fresh instructions that the finishing line had changed to avoid the prospect of danger in the event of a close finish. As a result, Algy Burnaby won, Otho's horse following hard behind, one of only four of the eleven competitors to complete the course.

Otho continues his description of the action: 'It sounds rather silly now, but the race itself was very good fun, and quite exciting. The most noticeable feature to me was the galloping top speed across ridge and furrow without being able to see which was the up and the down it gave you an extraordinary feeling. And I can only tell what befell me in the race, as the white gowns of my fellow competitors was all that could be seen from the start to the finish.' 'I was able to catch up with the others before we reached the turning point and then commenced to draw ahead. I knew exactly the location of the gateway, and, as the finish was uphill, I could send my steed along best pace without fear of his 'dicky leg'. Although it was impossible to see, I could hear the other horses and all were well behind me on my right, so that after pulling up on passing through the gateway, I naturally imagined I had won. The whole affair was just for the fun of it, and there was no prize except for a cup that Count Zborowski gave, so that of course, I did not say anything, but must admit was very disappointed.'

Inevitably perhaps, the Reverend Karney was quick to rebuke

the 'unrighteous crew' in his sermon the following Sunday, still smarting, no doubt, from his rude awakening. 'The whole congregation was convulsed with laughter,' recalled the splendid Lady Augusta, who admitted, 'I had difficulty in preventing some of those who had taken part in the race from going round to the vestry and giving the parson their opinion of him and his works. I pointed out that he was not worth the trouble, as a man who could make such a fool of himself in the pulpit must be past redemption.'

In a sad postscript to the event, Count Zborowski, who later became a pioneer racing driver, was killed whilst competing in the 1903 La Turbie hill climb near Nice; his son, Louis, also died when competing in the 1924 Italian Grand Prix at Monza. Louis had raced his vintage cars at Brooklands, later inspiring Ian Fleming to write the children's book, *Chitty Chitty Bang Bang.*

For the five seasons, 1893 to 1898, Lord Lonsdale was a most mercurial Quorn MFH. The field found his dictatorial manner irksome; yet he was a great sportsman and possessed of enough self-assurance to enjoy a joke at his own expense. Before 1914, Hugh Lonsdale had entertained Kaiser Wilhelm II at Lowther Castle on many occasions. When reminded of this friendship after hostilities had broken out, he replied: 'Well! It only shows how careful one should be about picking up acquaintances when abroad.' In later years, his showmanship earned him the epithet 'the yellow earl' for his penchant for collecting motorcars painted in his trademark yellow. He also collected Lily Langtry, with whom he had an affair, provoking the Prince of Wales, later King Edward VII, to famously remark that the earl was 'almost an emperor, not quite a gentleman!'

By 1900 and no longer 'in extreme youth' Otho conveys his own sense of fin de siècle when it comes to the Quorn mastership of Capt. Burns-Hartopp: 'No man ever worked harder for a hunt or had more misfortunes to contend with.' Worse followed when Tom Firr, arguably the greatest huntsman to ever carry the horn, was obliged to retire; after his burial in Quorn churchyard in December 1902, Paget offers a touching farewell: 'Hunting men are not a class who give much outward expression to their feelings, but as the earth rattled down on the coffin-lid and we turned away they were few who did not feel some emotion and whisper, 'God rest his soul.'

At the outset of the Great War in August 1914, my father was so anxious to enlist that he joined the first regiment that would take him- the Royal Sussex, understating his age in the process. Neville Lytton was a fellow officer who wrote a book - *The Press and the General Staff.* Lytton describes the train journey from regimental headquarters to Southampton prior to shipping to France. 'There was the usual 3 am start in pouring rain and this time Captain Paget surpassed himself; not only did he carry the full equipment, which in all conscience is heavy enough, but in addition he had a frying-pan, several bird-cages, sponge racks, and other impedimenta, so that by the time he arrived at the station he was in a fainting condition. However, he was completely consoled as soon as he got a fire going in the carriage and fried some bacon, very much to the annoyance of his brother officers.'

The company landed at Le Havre, and marched to Abbeville and St Pol, eventually reaching a little village called Morbecque, several kilometres from Hazebrouck.

And it was here that Lytton appreciated how incredibly fierce soldiers become once in the line for some time. A German soldier apparently went mad with shell shock and stood up on the parapet with his arms raised, shouting 'Gott mitt uns'. 'Got mittens 'ave yer,' cried one of the Tommies, 'well, 'ere's socks,' and promptly shot him. Lytton resumes his account. 'We rested here for a few days and then marched to Estaires; once again Captain Paget relieved the monotony of the route. We were informed that Divisional corps and Army Commanders would be standing at a certain corner to sample the new division. We were warned to look to our march discipline, but not to pay compliments. Paget, among his many antipathies to conventional attire, could not bear to wear boots; his favourite foot-gear was sand-shoes, and, thinking himself at last in the battle zone, he cast all effort to appear like a soldier, and wore his favourite shoes. The route from Morbecque to Estaires is entirely paved with cobblestones and, long before we reached the corner where the distinguished Generals were standing, Paget's shoes were a memory, and his heels were showing bright pink on the frosty stones.'

No sooner is the company billeted in the trenches, then Lytton hears an amusing story from fellow officers in A Company: 'during the night Paget had appeared shortly after dinner in a striped (hoop-wise) bathing suit and had proceeded to pick his way through our wire, and was half-way across no-man's-land before he ran into one of our patrols and was fetched back.' In this eccentric disguise, Otho hoped to take prisoner a German who had information about the order of battle. He won the Military Cross in 1918 for wiping out a nest of German machine gunners with a cry of tally-ho to his men. As the writer of the account remarked, Paget was fearless and had nothing but contempt for death: ' I am sorry that circumstances prevented my following this officer's career throughout the campaign, but I am glad to know that he has survived and that his splendid courage has been awarded with a M.C.'

In autumn 1918 my father met and married my mother, Gertrude Williams (née Talbot-Butt); she was some thirty years younger and had recently been widowed. His duty had been to deliver Williams' personal effects to her, and perhaps to the surprise of them both, a whirlwind romance blossomed. Certainly, my father never expected matrimony at the age of 58, having previously been a bachelor all his life. 'In life, we can find little corners of happiness' he once said to me, to explain how things can take unexpected turns.

Whereas *Memories of the Shires* is his account of the golden age of fox-hunting up to the onset of the Great War, the post-war years saw him devote much of his time to the breeding of hounds, which he would ship to his American friends, a number of whom had travelled to England and first made his acquaintance when taking part in the Melton Hunts. The American people have a long and noble interest in foxhunting and hound work; indeed, George Washington was an avid rider to hounds in his home state of Virginia, and took a keen interest in their breeding long before he became President; a passion that was noted when he was invited to join the Gloucester Hunting Club in New Jersey. For Thomas Jefferson, pursuit of that wiliest quarry, the wild turkey, proved a greater challenge.

Thus, Otho happily followed a long-established tradition of a shared passion in field sports between the two nations. Although he provided hounds for Mr. William Iselin of New York, it was his beagles that were most in demand; among recipients of the latter were Mr. James Kernochan, Mr. Reynal, Mr. Newell Bent of the Western Beagle Club, and Mr. Appleton, acting for the National Beagle Club. By all accounts, Eugene Reynal was quite a character. He paid my father several visits to Thorpe Satchville, the first in 1908, to improve his beagle bloodline for his Millbrook pack; in later life however, he appears to have had a drinking problem. One day, in August 1931, his car overturned while he was trying to light a cigarette with both hands, a habit he had formed when astride his horse; his arm became pinned under the vehicle with multiple fractures, until someone righted the vehicle and extracted him. A passerby declared Reynal would die. Incensed by the remark, Reynal hauled himself out of the car seat, then hit the fellow in the mouth, saying "You first!"

From my earliest memories, I remember my father was someone very special, not just in family, but also with his many friends; and though my mother was wont to grumble that she had married the most popular man in Leicestershire, he was an iconic figure in my early life, of whom I was inordinately fond and remain so to this day.

I can recall one day in the 1930/31 hunting season, when I was eleven years old, watching the Quorn from my Welsh mountain pony, Midge, as they crashed past, into a field at Thorpe Satchville. The huntsman was casting the pack so hounds could pick up the lost scent, when I rushed up to one of the two whippers-in and pointed excitedly to where the fox had dashed into a low hedge to the left of a tree. "She knows nothing, she's just a girl" hollered the whipper-in to the huntsman, George Barker, who looked back at me and then corrected him: "that's alright, she's Mr. Otho's daughter." And to my relief, hounds soon picked up the scent and away they went. As can be imagined, I positively reddened with pride, and was thrilled George Barker had recognized me; George, of course, had a long connection with our family, as his grandfather had been Patty's coachman throughout Otho's formative years.

One of my last memories of my father was dancing with this silver-haired gentleman at the children's Hunt Ball held at Craven Lodge; to the tune of Sir Roger de Coverley, my father, splendidly attired in his red Quorn evening coat, danced towards me, then took me by the hand down the line. I was so proud.

Strangely, my mother kept his memory alive. Albeit from

a younger generation, she lived to extreme old age, and enjoyed reminiscing about the old days to my son in the 1970s as if these events had happened yesteryear, so sharp was her recall. After the Great War, Otho acquired a vehicle and trailer to take his horses to more distant meets. Wary of the new-fangled machinery, whenever his vehicle struggled uphill, invariably he would utter the exhortation, "Gee-up!" Of other anecdotes, there was a time when he truncated a parson's over-long sermon with an alarm clock at the church in Thorpe Satchville; the priest soon learnt to be succinct, and kept a beady eye on the clock habitually perched upon the pew.

About another incident, my father was at pains to claim, at least in part, to be apocryphal, though other writers support it. At one meet at Quenby, and after collecting the Quorn 'cap'- a duty he frankly disliked- everyone set off at a smart pace, but his horse slipped on the bank of a brook, and he tumbled into it, the gold sovereigns in his pocket sent scattering. Two bystanders held him upside down by his legs so he could recover the coins. For years afterwards, the locals would search the spot in the streambed they nicknamed 'Klondyke' in hopes of treasure!

My father died on 4th February 1934, his passing announced on the Radio. I did not attend his burial in the family vault at Thorpe Satchville on the 7th because I was away at school at the time, and my mother chose not to tell me till I returned home from Langford Grove in Essex. Perhaps she believed she was doing what was best for me, but I have harboured a smouldering resentment ever since; after all, the funeral rites allow mourners an opportunity to pay last respects, yet I was denied a sense of closure. My son, Will Jaffray, unknowingly stepped into the void created by my antipathy and formed a bond with his grandmother, relishing the retailing of old anecdotes at the end of his own day out hunting with the HH.

Otho Paget wrote a number of books and his writing ranks alongside Somerville, Beckford and Surtees. A museum in Melton Mowbray has some of his memorabilia on display. And though a century or more has passed since the events so movingly described in *Memories of the Shires*, those noble days are now an immutable part of hunting lore, a way of life for some, and a gold thread in the rich tapestry that runs through a very English tradition.

My father was a countryman to his fingertips, never failing to appreciate its beauty, of hares boxing on a spring morn, or a vixen enjoying a sunny spell with her cubs; among his many gifts, he learnt how to divine for water. And I recall very clearly, his remarking to me how fortunate we were to appreciate with our own eyes, our God-given landscape that so many painters had tried to capture. He established the Thorpe Satchville beagles in 1890, an additional pastime that allowed him the opportunity to study hound-work, a subject he was passionately interested in, having observed how Tom Firr got the best out of his hounds; thereafter, he took a keen interest in improving strains in their breeding. How he lived life to the full!

Let Frank Gillard, huntsman for the Belvoir from 1860 to 1896, have a last word. When relaying his reminiscences to Cuthbert Bradley, he paid tribute to my father's courage in the hunting field: 'The big day of the season occurred on Feb 8th (1888), with a regular flyer in the afternoon who went away from the west corner of Melton Spinney with sixteen and a half couple of the middle pack close at his brush. A hard-riding field were soon stirring up the mud in the brook, and then the railway with its locked gates confronted them. These Mr. Otho Paget boldly charged, got well over the first, but came an awful cropper at the second. Before the gates could be opened he was on his horse and away with a start of the flying squadron…..'

Since the passage of the controversial Hunting Act, a stain upon the Statute Book, there can be no better time to bring *this* book back into circulation. In the opening chapter of *Memories of the Shires,* he dismisses at once the pessimists who predicted the end of hunting after the Great War; and I think my father would be no less robust now, indeed perhaps delighted to know his work might play some small part in its glorious restoration.

Equally, I have little doubt dear Otho would have been saddened by the relatively recent rise in intolerance that has afflicted our country, an intolerance, he might suggest, borne of ignorance. Pursuit of the fox is but an aid to the ways of nature, a culling of the weakest, the quarry saved the indignity of death by far more cruel alternatives. If our countryside is not to be reduced to some ghastly 'theme park'- whatever that might be- then we need to be vigilant in preserving its traditions. After all, the Hunts we know today have histories stretching back 300 years, and they are as much a part of the English way of life as roast beef and Yorkshire pudding.

Anne, Lady Jaffray.
Sir William Jaffray Bart.
London 2012.

List of Illustrations

(Where no provenance is shown the illustrations are from the Paget/Jaffray family collection)

List of Illustrations

Endpapers are drawings by George Whyte-Melville from *With Horse and Hound in Worcestershire* published by Messrs Victor, 28 Albemarle Street, Piccadilly, London

Chapter I

Fox-Hunting and Melton

The war has created a gap in the history of time—events will be dated before or after. During the winter of 1914 a huge fissure was started in the affairs of fox-hunting which has gradually grown in width. Old customs, traditions and methods that were considered essential to the sport have been swept into the dustbin.

Pessimists with gloomy faces will tell you that hunting is at an end, and that the fox will soon be extinct; but I am firmly convinced that the sport will rise triumphant from the ashes of the past, and with a brighter future will become established on a broader basis. Although many good sportsmen have been killed, there are still plenty left, and many more growing up.

This appears to me to be the ideal moment to redeem my long-delayed promise to the publishers and to chat over the past—the five and thirty years preceding the war.

I think the love of hunting is inherent with most of us in a greater or less degree, but the degrees have a very wide range, and there are some in whom it is almost imperceptible. Those who have that love very strongly developed may consider themselves amongst the lucky ones of the earth, because they have an all-absorbing pursuit of which they will never tire. I have never yet met anyone who has said he was bored with a good run in which he had held a foremost position, but I have met many men, keen sportsmen, who have confessed to being sick of blazing away at pheasants for a whole day. I am saying nothing against shooting, but am merely pointing out that in one sport success is capable of palling on and satisfying the appetite, whereas in the other the most perfect run will only whet the appetite for more.

A well-filled purse, backed by a good gamekeeper, will generally ensure plenty of shooting, but riches do not command good sport in the hunting field.

One occasionally reads in a novel of the hero, who apparently hunts about once in a season, leading the whole field in an extraordinary run, and then turning homewards with the remark that it is an overrated sport. Such things, however, do not occur in real life, and the man who has been lucky enough to ride close up to hounds through a good run is brimming over with happiness at the time, and whenever he recalls the incidents his pulses will quicken with the remembrance of those exciting moments. Novelists, I regret to say, with a few exceptions, do not think it necessary to know anything about their subject when they write on hunting, and it is a sport they are very fond of introducing, to lend colour to their stories.

Since the time of Beckford it has been the custom of the literary brotherhood to look down with scorn on anyone connected with sport. It has always been sufficient condemnation for a man that he was known to be fond of hounds and hunting to be set down for all time as an uncultivated boor without a refined taste or a thought beyond the pursuit of a fox.

The easy and fluent style in which Beckford penned his *Thoughts on Hunting* a hundred and twenty years ago, would have earned for him ungratified admiration if the subject chosen had been aught else, but having confessed himself a sportsman, his work was considered unworthy of being read. Johnson, in his *Lives of the Poets*, grudges giving any favourable mention of Somerville, who committed the crime of writing on a subject—hunting—of which his commentator was ignorant. In referring to *The Chase*, Johnson says, "to this poem praise cannot totally be denied"; but in spite of such faint praise the poem has stood the test of time, and still appeals to every sportsman who reads it. There could be no better graphic description of hunting scenes set either in prose or verse.

Sporting literature is not always of a very high class, but there is no reason it should not be credited with what merits it possesses.

There must be very few hunting men who have not read *Handley Cross*, and still less who, having read, do not appreciate every line of the book, but I very much doubt our old friend being found in the library of any except those with sporting tastes. I admit that the vivid descriptions of runs and other technical matter would not appeal to an ordinary reader in the same way it does to a hunting man but the immortal Jorrocks is sketched in with the hand of an artist, and whatever your tastes may be you cannot fail to picture him a living character. His weak points, his occasional lapses from sobriety, and his little acts of meanness, are the frailties of a human being, and serve as a background to his many good qualities. The sturdy British merchant of that period stands before you when culture and polish were not considered necessary in a commercial education, but he acts the part exactly as we should expect him to do it, and never does anything inconsistent with our conception of his character. We love him for his keenness and his hunting proclivities, we sympathize with him in his troubles, and feel for him when he funks the fence. Fat and ungainly in figure, weak in his aspirates, and occasionally falling into vulgarity, he is yet the hero of the piece, and that is surely a triumph for the man who created him. His language may not be quite the right model for school or nursery, but the same may be said of Sam Weller, and no one has banished Dickens for that reason.

Surtees still stands at the head of sporting writers, and the caustic humour of his books retains its flavour to this day. He was perhaps a trifle too cynical, exposing the follies and foibles of mankind without laying to its credit those good points which always accompany the bad. *Handley Cross* is far away the best of his works, as Jorrocks is his best character, but his other books are all worth reading. It is, however, his women that have made him unpopular with the general public. They are sawdust dolls without life or meaning, and the stuffing of the sawdust does not command our admiration.

Most packs nowadays of any note have correspondents who send their reflections and impressions of the sport to one of the weeklies; but, with the exception of "Brooksby", I am afraid we are rather a moderate lot. Descriptions of runs are never satisfactory, they either leave too much to the imagination, or else go to the other extreme and attempt details that become tedious. However, it is easy to criticize, but it is by no means a light task to write a readable account of a run. In the first place, the man ought to have been in a position to have watched hounds from find to finish before he sits down to write his account. Then he must remember that accuracy of the main features is absolutely essential, and yet a mere statement of bare facts without a leaven of imagination is but dull reading. Though no two runs are the least alike, even with the same fox and over the same country, there must always be a repetition of phrase and expression which is wearying to the writer as it is to the reader. Truly the lot of the hunting correspondent is not altogether happy, but he has many things to be thankful for.

Whyte-Melville stands alone amongst writers of hunting fiction, and we can read his works to-day with as much pleasure as we did twenty years ago. They are interesting to read and they leave no nasty taste in the mouth, which is more than can be said for many writers of a later date. We are told Surtees is vulgar and Whyte-Melville prosy, but in default of these matters we are fed on stuff that has either no meaning or is questionable morality and thinly veiled indecency. This class of book may be popular for the time, but they are brilliant annuals that will die and be forgotten at the end of the year, whilst *Handley Cross* and *Katerfelto* will grow again every spring to claim a fresh batch of readers. In spite of this defence of sporting literature, I am bound to admit there are not many writers of the higher class who can be strictly called hunting men, but we have Beckford, Surtees and Whyte Melville of whom we may be justly proud.

Melton

Melton is the fox-hunter's Mecca, and he should make his pilgrimage there before he dies. Other parts of England have their bits of good country, but nowhere else is there a centre surrounded by glorious hunting ground.

An old-world market town, cosily nestling in the river valley, from which the gently rising hills roll away on either hand. The modern convenience of an excellent train service makes it possible now to return to London after a day's hunting from Melton, but railways have not yet destroyed the glamour of the past. We can imagine the gay bucks dashing out to the meets on their hacks, and the rattle of the post-chaise on the cobble-stones that brought a new arrival from town.

Many things have changed, but the beautiful old church must have looked much the same a century ago, and most of the houses clustering beneath its stately shades were in existence when George the Third was young.

The ancient character of the place has altered very considerably within the limits of my memory. There was a quaint, respectable air about the town, and each shop looked like a dwelling-house whose occupier sold articles over the counter only to oblige his friends. Nearly every shop had its bay window with small square panes, and every door was in two parts, the upper half opening independently of the lower. On market days keeping the lower half closed was a necessary precaution to guard against the possible incursions of unruly pigs and stray cattle, as at that time the farmers exposed their animals for sale in the open street. These queer old landmarks of the past have nearly all disappeared now, and glaring sheets of plate glass exhibit the latest novelties from the metropolis. At the beginning of the century Melton was rapidly becoming a fashionable hunting centre, and the men who assembled there were the cream of hard riders from other counties, but for several years previous to that date a few sportsmen had made the town their headquarters. In these early days, and for some years later, only bachelors visited Melton, and the married man left his wife at home. This will account for the mad pranks which history tells us were frequently played after dinner by the hunting men, such as painting signs, wrenching knockers and other wild freaks. When men get away from their women-folk and muster in any force, they are sure to behave like a lot of schoolboys; they feel at other times, I suppose, the necessity of preserving the dignity of the superior sex.

Even that most respectable body of men who make our laws, do sometimes forget themselves and indulge in playful antics which seem hardly in keeping with grey hairs. Individually and in the family circle it is impossible to imagine one of those legislators doing anything ridiculous, but we are told that collectively and when gathered together in the "House" they are capable of many strange things. It is good to be a boy again sometimes, and though we cannot get back our youth, we may at least play the fool and imagine ourselves young.

The ladies, however, gradually forced their way into Melton, and with their sobering influence the devilment of youth fled. Now the majority are married men, with snug hunting-boxes in and around the town. The bachelor element is still quartered at the various inns, but it is on its best behaviour, and goes meekly out to dine with Benedict, probably finishing up the evening with the all-absorbing "bridge." In the old days bachelors returned year after year to the same haunts, but now they either go elsewhere, or get married, and fresh faces appear regularly every season. These changes have destroyed the spirit of comradeship which formerly existed, but I think in other ways women's invasion has been a blessing to the Meltonian.

Without this controlling influence of the fair sex, the men of Melton, as I have said, were apt to do strange things, and indulge in practical jokes that would have delighted the heart of a schoolboy or an undergraduate. A certain lord—his name matters not—once played some jokes on the local doctor, and his victim determined to be revenged at the first opportunity. Not long afterwards a slight rick in the back caused by a fall out hunting delivered the playful peer into the hands of his enemy. The earl was a very keen sportsman, and, not wishing to miss a day's hunting, went straight to the doctor to be cured as quickly as possible. The patient bared his back, and after many unnecessary thumpings the injured spot was discovered. A strong blister—quite common in those days—was prescribed, and the doctor offered to put it on at once. The operation was performed, but then, I suppose, the temptation to pay off old scores seemed too good to be lost, and a liberal supply of blister was smeared to that portion of the human frame which is most intimately connected with the saddle. The doctor went away chuckling, having full confidence in the strength of the ointment he had applied.

A blister, as most people know, leaves a sore place for several weeks, and in consequence the peer was not only unable to ride for a considerable length of time, but finding the easiest chair unbearable, was obliged to lie in bed. The victim was, of course, unmercifully chaffed by his friends, but I am sorry to say he did not take the joke in good part, and on his recovery he administered a severe horse-whipping to the doctor.

With the exception of old prints, we have very little reliable evidence to go upon as to the styles of hunting-costumes adopted at different periods by the men of Melton; and if artists were as careless about details then as they are to-day, we must not place too much faith in their drawings. Before fox-hunting became fashionable, the long-skirted coat, the direct ancestor of the dressing-gown-like garment in which some masters now clothe themselves, was worn generally as most suitable and comfortable for the purpose; but it was not likely that fashionable young men would be content to hide a good figure beneath such an unsightly cloak. The consequence was frequent and rapid changes were made, and every year Melton came out with some startling innovation, that in the ages of the old school was more suitable for a ballroom than the hunting-field.

Mr. Dale, in his very interesting work, *The Belvoir Hunt,* makes a statement which, with all due deference to him, I do not consider is quite accurate. He tells us at the beginning of the century "leathers" were not worn at Melton, and were first introduced from Cheshire. I cannot conceive the smart Meltonian taking any hints in dress from such an out-of-the-way place. The majority of such who hunted hounds or who were not particular about their appearance, would probably find woollen cord most serviceable, but it must be remembered buckskin breeches were articles of everyday apparel with those who could afford them. In the country breeches and boots were the regular costume, and no self-respecting squire dressed otherwise except on Sundays or when he went to town. At what exact period whitened buckskins were first worn a-hunting must remain a matter for conjecture, but we know they were used in their natural state for riding long before the fox was an honoured beast of chase.

There is another small matter on which I disagree with Mr. Dale. In speaking of the early history of the Quorn, he says that the resident gentry of that county did not hunt, and that therefore the pack had not the advantage of local support. There were in the Quorn territory at the beginning of the century quite as large a proportion of hunting landowners as could be found in any other district, but they would, of course, appear in a minority, because their land happened to be favourable to the sport, and attracted men from every part of England. The visitors had the advantage of longer purses, which meant better horses, but still we know the locals held their own in the field. The sporting writers of that period catered for a public who were probably more snobbish than the readers of to-day, and they knew that the doings of the titled swells or those with a London reputation would be more acceptable than the names of unknown squires. Quite natural this, but it is as impossible to get a true account of men and matters at that date through such gossip as it would be to write a history of our own times from a modern society paper.

The face of Leicestershire must have altered very considerably since the beginning of the century, but I think there has been very little change in the last fifty years from a riding point of view. In the preceding half of the century the enclosing had all been done, and except for the occasional appearance of wire, 1900 found us in much the same state as

1850. I often hear people making assertions about the fences being stronger at certain dates, but these facts are gathered from unreliable sources, and their theories are based on an imperfect knowledge of the treatment of quickthorn hedges. It must be remembered that all the fences in Leicestershire were not planted in the same year. The history of the hedge is something like this. The quick, as the young thorn is called, was planted, and was protected by post and rails on each side with a ditch to carry off the water. Whilst the rails were new, this was a formidable obstacle to encounter, but time and weather speedily perish all wood except oak. In seven or eight years the thorn fence was cut and laid, and then, if properly done, a hedge grew up that would stop the wildest bullock from straying, and turn over any horse that tried to go through it. Cutting and laying a fence is an art confined to the skilled labourer of the Midlands. The thorn is cut half-way through as close to the ground as possible, and is then bent down between stakes, the latter being bound together by twisted briars or some other pliant wood. The thorn that is cut still lives and grows, whilst a wealth of young shoots are thrown out from the bottom. In ten or fifteen years the old layers would have commenced to die out, and the young shoots would have developed into a tall bullfinch. Every year after that the hedge would gradually be showing more daylight at bottom, and the fly-stricken bullock or the impetuous fox-hunter would have no difficulty in forcing a passage. The good farmer would then proceed to cut and lay again, so that the youth and vigour of the fence might be revived. In this way the hedge, in a period of twenty years, varies from the new-cut stake and bound to the high, straggling bullfinch. It is not the custom to lay all the fences on the farm in one year, but to do a length every winter, so that the fox-hunter finds the thorny obstacles in every stage of growth, giving him that pleasing diversity of jumps which is one of the greatest charms in riding across Leicestershire.

I have been tempted into this long explanation in order to show the absurdity of saying the country is more difficult to cross than it was twenty years ago, also because every man who hunts is not acquainted with agricultural details, and therefore might be glad of a little light on the subject. In the early part of 1830 I have no doubt fences were not as numerous as they are to-day, but then again very little of the land had been drained, and it must have been terribly holding in the winter. The ridge and furrow which is now a feature of Leicestershire pastures is a relict of the method of farming clay-land before subsoil draining had been thought of. On the flat, grass and corn would have perished during a wet winter, and the only hope of a crop of either was to throw the soil up in lands with the plough. Of course nothing grew in the furrows, but unless it was an exceptionally wet season, there were hopes of a crop on the top and sides of the ridge. Newcomers to the Shires now flounder across these little valleys, and, cursing the roughness of their horses' stride, wonder why nature thus seamed the face of the country. I am not very sure about my dates, but I think it was about 1840 or a little later that much of the grass was ploughed up, the price of wheat being then exceptionally high. I have a diary of my father's, dated 1835, in which he mentions riding across country from Ashwell— eight miles—to his own house, and he remarks, "a very pretty gallop; nice fencing, and not one ploughed field." There is not much arable in that line to-day, but it would not be easy to ride it without getting off the grass. I suppose in those days fewer people rode, and farmers did not mind their land being ridden over occasionally, but it would be a very unpopular thing now to go for a gallop over fences without hounds. In those times no one apparently objected, and, judging from several entries in the above-mentioned diary, it was my father's usual custom in getting from one spot to another to ride straight across country. The entry generally concludes with expressing satisfaction of the horse's performance, and elation of having discovered a new line. "Larking home" was also the usual finish to a moderate day's sport, and on one of these occasions a Meltonian challenged my father to jump some particularly high rails in Lowesby Park, with the result of a broken collar-bone to the latter. In these days we should say serve him right, but then hard riding was in its infancy, good riders and good horses both being scarce, so that we must not judge the youthful spirits of those times by the present standard. In spite of what one hears about the good sportsmen of past generations, I am quite certain there are a larger proportion of men now, who take an interest in the working of hounds, than there ever were before. The rather stupid and oft-repeated story of "what fun it would be were it not for these d—d hounds!" contains a sentiment with which few could agree to-day. I admit there is still amongst men who hunt a lack of knowledge on the details of the sport, which they might easily acquire, and which would enable them to appreciate a run with hounds more than they do now.

Referring again to my father's diary of 1835 I find the following passage: "Talked with Hartopp about fox-coverts; the county men think of taking them in their own hands, that they may have some influence on the masters of hounds." The Quorn country had always been hunted by strangers, and they probably made their arrangements without consulting the wishes of the landowners. I should imagine this was the moment at which the latter first began to assert themselves. Doubtless, previous to this date, the master had been an autocrat in the matters of fixing hunting days, whether or not it suited the men over whose land he hunted.

The argument is sound, that from a hunting point of view

a country is no good without a pack of hounds, but then it is equally true that a pack is no use without a country. It must always be a joint-stock arrangement, and though a master pays all expenses, he must not imagine he is thereby entitled to act in a way that is not conducive to the interests of his field. The master for the time being is the head of the hunting community, but when he shows himself incapable of conducting the hunt properly, or does it only in his own interests, he should then be made to abdicate the throne. In those few instances where the master is the principal landlord, and where the same family have kept the hounds for generations, the case is different; but even then the autocrat should consider the wishes of those whom circumstance has compelled to live within the limits of his territory.

The increasing popularity of fox-hunting has created a demand for more packs, and therefore more countries, with the result that there has occasionally been some friction when an old-established pack has been made to give up ground over which they claimed the right to hunt. There is no excuse for an individual starting hounds in another's country, even if he is a large owner of the soil; but if the existing pack cannot or do not hunt a district fairly, the residents should represent the case to the Master of Hounds' Association, and that august body ought to arrange a fresh division. Of course, all those who have the interests of hunting at heart see the necessity of giving their support to a hunt centre, which shall adjudicate on any dispute that may arise; but unless this ruling power base its decision on common sense, it cannot expect to have its dictates unhesitatingly obeyed. It may be laid down as an accepted fact that a country not fairly hunted will become short of foxes, will increase in wire, and, in short, will set up obstructions which when once established are very difficult to remove. Therefore it is important that the prerogative of hunting any part of a country shall not be allowed to lapse, and the residents are justified in taking whatever action may be necessary for preserving their privileges. We are all aware we have no legal right to gallop over another man's field for our own amusement, but custom has sanctioned the practice, and we must not give up what is really a birthright inherited from our forefathers.

I am not sufficiently versed in the mysteries of the law to give an opinion, but I had an idea that the original titles to all land came through the Crown, and that the sovereign reserved to himself the right, when the titles were granted, of hunting and sporting. If that were the case, there is no reason the king should not hand over his right temporarily to the recognized pack of each district, and then hunting would have a legal status. The erection of barbed wire would be an unlawful obstruction to His Majesty's right of hunting, and would entail dreadful penalties on the offenders. There was a little unpleasantness in the Quorn country a few years ago, but I will not do more than just refer to it, lest I rekindle smouldering fires. A portion of the country had been lent to the neighbouring pack, and when in course of time they were given up, it was claimed the rights for a separate kingdom had been established, and the majority of the residents invited a master to accept the throne. Many bitter things were written and said, but in the end the Quorn were obliged to submit to a slice of their country being taken from them.

Chapter II

Early Days in Leicestershire

My earliest recollections of fox-hunting are misty and indistinct. Occasionally as a small boy I was taken in a carriage to see hounds, and perhaps had the pleasure of sitting on the sharp hoop of a crinoline, but I always hated wheels and much preferred wandering across country on foot in the oldest clothes I could find. Then came the thraldom of school, and in the scanty holidays one pony amongst four boys did not mean many days.

I can, however, remember going out with Mr. Tailby's hounds, whilst Lord Lonsdale's figure and low crowned hat are distinctly imprinted on my memory. I think he had not come in for the title long then, and was better known as Colonel Lowther. Some of the Cottesmore country was at that time lent to Mr. Tailby, but I can't remember how it was divided, though I recollect going to a meet of his hounds at Tilton village.

Mr. Tailby was one of the pluckiest riders who ever crossed Leicestershire. No man had more bad falls or broke more bones, but none of these mishaps ever weakened his nerve. Though well over eighty he had several bad smashes, and I saw him riding over big fences, a few seasons before his death, that many young men would have turned away from. The squire of Skeffington never had a very firm seat in his best days, on account of being rather extra short in the leg, and naturally broken bones did not improve his grip.

Schooldays over and the stern realities of life loomed in sight. My father very wisely told me I should never be able to afford the luxury of hunting, and he was quite right, but still I have managed to ride to hounds without missing a season since I was twenty. Nothing to be proud of certainly, to have devoted my life and energy to my own amusement, for I imagine we are put in this world to work in the general scheme that is to advance mankind to a higher plane. Hardly the place this for moral reflections, but I do not wish a young man picking up this book to see in my life anything worthy of imitation. There is, of course, a pleasure in recalling the sport one has enjoyed, but there would be far more satisfaction if it were interspersed with work that showed some good result. Foxhunting and all sport should be looked upon as recreation—not as the business of life. The pursuit of the fox is the most fascinating of sports, and men are apt to devote all their energies to it, to the exclusion of everything else. They forget then that after all it is only an amusement, and the fox-hunter thus gains the reputation of being selfish.

The pony gone, or relegated to a younger brother's use, my only chance for a day's hunting in the holidays was to hire out of the slender resources of my pocket money. I was fortunate in hiring a good horse at a small figure and getting a few excellent days with the Quorn. Never having ridden anything above a pony before, I was delighted at being able to jump big fences, and imagined my mount's capacities in that direction was unlimited. I remember one day there was a crush at a small handgate and it seemed to me a good opportunity to jump the fence. At the first attempt my horse refused, and I have no idea whether the place was big or small, but as I was going at it again—probably riding very badly—"Brooksby" shouted out to me, "Boy, you will kill yourself." It was nothing to do with pluck, for I had not the faintest conception what was feasible, and my ignorance was only equalled by my excitement.

I carried the memory of these few happy days with me to sea, and oft lived them over again when keeping a night watch beneath the Southern Cross. Life in the Merchant Service is very well in its way, but the man with a love of sport will not find much opportunity for indulging his bent. During two years aboard ship, the rat was the only animal I had a chance of hunting, and having no terrier, I was obliged to catch them by hand. It was better fun than you might imagine, and the risk of being bitten lent a little extra excitement. In fair weather towards evening a rat would often go aloft for a little fresh air and then, unless he jumped for the deck, his fate was generally sealed. The rest of the ship's crew preferred to be spectators only in these hunts, and consequently I had a monopoly of the sport.

On leaving the sea, my love for country pursuits and sport made me think of fanning, and I have been engaged in that fascinating but unprofitable business ever since. I am not going to apologize for introducing these personal details, though I know they can be of little interest to anyone because I could not give you my hunting experiences without first tracing the outline of my life. It may seem bad form to dwell too much on the doings of a humble individual like myself, but I always think generalities bore one more to read than the minutiae of the humblest existence.

In the season 1880–81, I commenced to hunt regularly, and though I had only one animal, a mare about fifteen hands, she never missed her two days a week. I always hunted on Friday with the Quorn and the other day was either a Quorn Monday or a Cottesmore Tuesday. Mr. Coupland was then master, and Firr was in the zenith of his fame.

The Quorn had great sport that season, and very few Fridays

passed without a good run. One of the first days I rode my little mare we had a very fast burst from Ashby Pastures to ground in the railway bank near Kirby. The distance is not much, but I had never ridden in a similar gallop before and the pace astonished me. I was, however, more than satisfied with the mare, as I was fortunate enough to be one of the few to get a good start.

The previous season I had been only able to get two or three days' hunting, on which occasions I had hired the butcher's wonderful chestnut mare. Mr. Morris was quite a character, and was at that time the best known figure in the Melton Hunt. He always rode in his blue smock, and must have weighed eighteen stone; but when there was a stiff bit of timber to be jumped he was always ready to have first cut at it. Strangers then expected the timber to be knocked down, but the little chestnut was an extraordinary jumper, and generally carried her heavy burden safely over. The butcher had always a genial smile and a few cheery words to say, so that he was popular with every one in the hunting field. I shall ever feel grateful to him, as, I believe, knowing that I was keen and had not much money, he let his mare out to me at a ridiculously low price. It was from him I also bought my little mare.

The following season has left no very certain impression on my memory, though I know we had some excellent sport. Hunting was stopped for several weeks after Christmas by frost and snow. One Tuesday the snow lay thick over the country, but the farmers had no difficulty in getting to Melton market in the morning. At midday, however, a gale of wind sprang up, and in two hours' time the drifts in the roads were level with the top of the hedges, so that those who had delayed their departure from market until late in the afternoon were forced to spend the night at Melton.

I believe that it was the October of this season that an

incident occurred which perhaps Firr would not feel grateful to me for recalling. This great huntsman was very particular about having his pack free from riot of all kinds, and it was very seldom you ever saw one of his charges transgressing; but in this instance they forgot themselves, and Firr had to put up with much chaff afterwards when he met a brother of the horn.

Cub-hunting had not long commenced, and the young hounds had only been entered to their legitimate quarry a few times. I believe John o' Gaunt had been drawn blank, and a small ash plantation called Large's Spinney was being tried on the way to the next covert. Suddenly there was a crash of music, and we watched expectantly to view a fox away, when to our amazement a big black buck came bounding out of covert with the young entry clamouring at his heels. I don't think any of the older hounds took an active part in the proceedings, but they followed the lead of the juveniles, no doubt to ascertain what animal they were hunting.

I was young then, and did not consider the feelings of the huntsmen as I should do in a similar case now, but was keenly alive to the possibilities of a gallop. I happened to get a good start and had every intention of seeing the end of the fun. Luckily for the credit of the hunt, and much to my disappointment, the buck made a sharp turn into John o' Gaunt on reaching the railway. The young sinners flashed over the scent, and, of course, the old hounds would not help them in their difficulty, so that before they could go any farther down the path of wickedness, the hunt officials were able to cut them off. I must confess that my feeling at the time was one of disappointment that such a promising gallop should have been nipped in the bud.

It is difficult to imagine what would have happened had the buck continued the course he was pursuing, and gone straight over the railway, as a good eight miles of beautiful grass lay between him and the park from which he had strayed. The older hounds would probably have dropped out when they found what they were hunting, but the young ones and a few second season hunters, I imagine, would have continued the chase to the bitter end.

These little accidents will happen to the best-trained packs, but huntsmen will always make merry over the discomfiture of one of their profession, and the more celebrated the hunt, the more likely is the event to become public.

The historic gallops of the past have had their share of notice, and I am not going to bore you with what has already been written. The most interesting and instructive feature of a great run is an exact account of hounds' work, the individual exertions, and the pedigrees of those that were leading at the finish. This unfortunately was not considered worth noting by the hunting scribes of that time, and we get instead long stories of the fences that were jumped, but we know now these are not reliable, as the writer was generally not in a position to speak from personal observation.

The run which my father always put down as the best he remembered was from Thorpe Trussells to Vowes Gorse. I am very much afraid my parent thought more of the riding than he did of the hounds. I have no notes by me, and must trust to my memory to recall the story as told me some years ago now. It would be at the time Mr. Greene had the hounds, because I can remember my father saying, "Old Greene was behind, cursing and swearing at me for over-riding his hounds, whilst in reality it was all we could do to keep near them." It was one of the biggest foxes ever seen, and the second fence from the covert, a good four feet, he cleared in his stride. The first point was to Dalby windmill—a moss-grown millstone now marks the spot—on the brow above Burdett's covert, and here the fox turned right-handed. This was the only turn, and practically the only check. The farther the hounds ran, the faster they went, and on leaving Tilton to the right they began to forge ahead of their field, and though a few men were just able to keep them in sight, no one was really near them when they reached Vowes Gorse. The fox, I believe, was killed in the covert. Lord Gardner remarked to my father at the time, "I did not believe before that hounds could beat horses." I should think it was quite possible that hounds were neither as fast nor as fit as they are to-day; if they had been it would not have seemed wonderful for them to outstay horses, though it must not be forgotten that nearly every one rode clean-bred ones in Leicestershire.

Now that it is too late, I wish I had drawn further on the same storehouse and had jotted down a few notes, but all I can remember now are scraps without head or tail. Mr. Little Gilmour, Lord Gardner and Lord Wilton were contemporaries of my father's, and were three of the best men who visited Melton; but the honour of the county was worthily upheld by Mr. Cheney of Gaddesby, Mr. Tom Heycock of Owston, and the Rev. John Wilkinson of South Croxton. Of course, during the years my father hunted, Melton saw many fresh faces, but though some shone brilliantly for a time it was very seldom their light lasted longer than a season.

Lord Wilton was one of the quickest men to hounds; but he again was, I think, another of the school that thought more of the riding than the hunting. My father remembered the occasion when he beat them all in a fast gallop, I believe in the Belvoir Hunt. There was only one way out of the field, a foot-stile with an impenetrable bullfinch on either side. Towards this stile a mob of cattle were converging with all the speed that clumsy animal is capable of for a short distance. Lord Wilton took in the situation at a glance and with equal promptitude raced for the stile, just beating the leading cow by a horn. The next second the place was effectually blocked by the cattle, and before they could be driven away the Earl had established a lead and was not overtaken until the cream of the gallop was over. There is an excellent likeness of him in Sir Francis Grant's picture of the "Meet at Melton" at least I imagine it must have been good at the time, because I could pick him out from what I remembered of him many years later. Touching this same picture, I read in my father's diary already mentioned, "Went to the Academy and saw F. Grant's picture of the Melton Hunt—very good likeness of both men and horses." We may therefore take it that, apart from the artistic merits of the picture, the portraiture was true to life.

Colonel Forester (the "Lad") must have been ten or fifteen years younger than my father, and his was a familiar figure in the Shires up to a few years ago. I believe he was always short-sighted, but he could not have ridden harder if his eyes had been good. I remember my father told me one day there was a very dense fog, when he and two or three others got away with hounds in a very quick thing from Adam's Gorse. Knowing the country perfectly, the fog made little difference to him, and he was without difficulty able to keep in touch with the pack. Just as he was going through an open gateway at the bottom below Burrough, Colonel—I don't think he had attained the rank then—Forester came sailing down the hill, blind and heedless of what he might be charging. It was no small place, for in addition to the wide ditch that lay beyond, a post and rail with ample margin guarded the fence, but the horse must have been a wonder, as my father said he cleared it without an effort. Some forty years later I can recall an afternoon gallop with the Cottesmore, or at least one incident in it. I think we had found a fox in Berry Gorse, and having left Leesthorpe to the right, hounds were running fast up hill with the Oakham turnpike a field to the left. In spite of his sight, which had not improved, the Colonel was gallantly taking his own line, away to my right, but too far to warn him of the trap that lay before him. It was an innocent-looking hedge, but unfortunately had a ditch on either side, and the horse, landing with his forelegs in the farther ditch, over he went. A nasty fall for a young man, but the veteran never let go of the bridle and was soon going again.

It was in conversation about dancing, hunting or some other amusement—I forget really what now—that a lady was remarking to the "Colonel" she would soon have to give it up. His reply was, "Never give anything up, my dear, wait till it gives you up, you will find things give you up quite soon enough." This seems to me very excellent advice, and the man who gave it certainly acted up to the principle to the very last.

Touching that double ditch, you must not imagine that it is an obstacle often met with in the Shires. I only know of one other besides this, and you might hunt from Melton many seasons without coming across either, so that they come as an unpleasant surprise to both horse and rider when met with. Of course, if your misfortune condemns you to hunt in Northamptonshire or other barbarous counties, you must expect these traps and ride accordingly.

Mr. Little Gilmour is the only other light of the past whom I remember, and his hard riding days were over when I arrived on the scene, though he had always a kind word for a boy commencing his hunting career. He was the acknowledged prince of heavy weights, and I have often heard my father endorse that opinion. It was said of him he was "a lion in the field and a lamb in the fold."

In speaking of heavy weights, I should think Colonel Wyndham was the man of most stones who ever attempted to hunt across Leicestershire, but I don't think he ever tried to be in the first flight. I believe he was comparatively a poor man, but was very keen, and used to see a lot of sport with two strong cobs. My father said he was a very active man, and would run up the hills to relieve his horse of his ponderous weight.

Lord Grey de Wilton, like his father, was an exceptionally quick man to hounds, and in a fast run was nearly always to be found in the first flight. Although of a very charming personality and extremely kind-hearted, in the hunting field he was afflicted with the curse of jealousy, a disease that has spoilt the pleasure of hunting for many good men.

Mr. Cheney of Gaddesby had given up hard riding when I knew him, but though no longer a member of the thrusting crowd, it was easy to note the perfect horseman. Exceptionally good hands and a seat almost entirely by balance, were, I think, his chief characteristics. Mr. Tom Heycock of Owston and "Parson" Wilkinson of South Croxton were both under the turf before I arrived on the scene, but my father always said they were very hard to beat across country.

"Parson" Bullen was a light of other days when I remember him, but though he must have been nearly eighty he still liked having a jump. "Spurting Bullen" described his methods of riding to hounds; but in extenuation it should not be forgotten that he was a poor man, and probably never owned a sound-winded horse in his life, so that his only hope of enjoying the excitement of a gallop was to participate in the first few minutes. On a good jumping whistler and not scaling much over six stone, little Bullen could hold his own for a time with the best of them. Report said that he would always give the leading hound pride of place, but was averse to allowing other members of the pack to be in front of him. He began his career as a curate in Lincolnshire, and even in those early days had developed his dashing tactics of riding to hounds. These methods are not looked on favourably by masters and huntsmen, so that it is not surprising to hear that the Lord Yarborough of that day was anxious that little Bullen should exhibit his prowess in pastures new. The Master of the Brocklesby was, however, a kind-hearted man, and possessing a sense of humour he was able to do the little curate a good turn, have a joke on a neighbour, and rid himself of what his huntsmen considered a nuisance. He wrote therefore to the Duke of Rutland to say that having heard the living of Eastwell was vacant, he could supply him with a hard-riding light weight curate who would doubtless make an excellent vicar. Belvoir soon discovered his peculiarities, but the little man was allowed to retain the living to his death. I believe "Parson" Bullen was the original of a story which has become rather an ancient chestnut. He was galloping alongside of a gilded youth from Melton one day, the Parson as usual riding a roarer and the other an expensive purchase from Toynbee or some well-known dealer. The Parson exclaimed, "Your horse makes a noise" and the youth replied, "Yes! by Jove, so he does." Whereupon the little man tried to buy the animal; but history does not state whether he succeeded. When two horses are fairly close it is not as easy to detect which makes the noise as anyone would imagine.

Chapter III

Ancient History

The next generation of hard riders began before my time and were in their prime when first I entered the hunting field, though I would back several of them to hold their own over a stiff country against young men to-day. Amongst first-class men it is difficult to say who was the best, but there was certainly none better than Capt. A. (Doggie) Smith. Not only was he a good man to hounds, but he was also a very fine horseman. It was an education in itself to see him humouring that fiddle-headed chestnut into the belief that there was no necessity for running away and then steadying him up at a stiff bit of timber when the beast was in one of his mad fits. He was, however, an undoubtedly good horse, and carried his owner brilliantly through many good runs, though in previous hands he had proved to be quite unmanageable. Capt. (Bay) Middleton was also a very fine horseman and equally good across country. If alive he would doubtless be still showing us the quickest way to hounds, and taking the lead where the fences were strongest. He was always keen, whether it was dancing, foxhunting or steeple-chasing, and he did everything with a boyish enthusiasm that did one good to see. There was one slight weakness he possessed which must have made him lose a good deal of pleasure in riding to hounds. Unfortunately for himself he was jealous, which meant when hounds were running he could not fully enjoy the companionship of those equally well placed. Capt. (Sugar) Candy was one of the hardest men across country in the early days of Mr. Coupland's reign, and in addition was an excellent horseman with first-rate hands. The best man I ever remember for getting a bad horse over Leicestershire was Capt. (Brooksby) Elmhirst, and he was always to be seen in the first flight with hounds. He was always keen, and was ever attentive to what was going on at the covert side, so that it very seldom happened he was left at the start.

Many other men have sparkled brilliantly for a season or two, then their lights have faded, and Melton has known them no more. With fair nerve and a good stud of horses anyone can take a place in the front rank, but few are able to retain that place after some heavy falls have calmed the exuberant rashness of youthful valour. Capt. Boyce was one of the quickest men to hounds, and never rode a "cocktail." He and Capt. Riddell are familiar figures in our earliest recollections of the hunting field, but they had passed the zenith of their fame when I appeared on the scene.

Capt. Molyneux also had earned his reputation as a hard rider before my day, but could still go to the front when he wished. His hands were perfection, and he fully understood the art of using them. Mr. Ernest Chaplin of Brooksby flourished somewhere about the same date, and could hold his own with the best.

In those days there was no better man across country than Tom Firr, and then twenty years later we find him still in the same position, ever ready to face the stiffest obstacles when necessary, but never jumping for the sake of jumping. I remember an occasion in his last season but one that impressed me very considerably at the time. Hounds had been hallooed away from Botany Bay, and the huntsman, being in the covert, made what haste he could to follow them. Arriving at the gate out, which had always previously only wanted a push of the whip to open, he found it chained up. Most of us in a similar position would have been disconcerted, and lost time in fumbling at the hinges, but Firr never hesitated a moment, and turning his horse round, popped quickly over the gate as if it had been a gap. The performance was a masterly exhibition of nerve, quickness, and horsemanship, a collection, I may remark, that is not often found in men who have reached the ripe age of fifty-eight. There is a story of Firr and two Melton bruisers that is worth telling, though, as I was not present, I will not vouch for the truth of it. Capt. A. and Mr. B. were rather jealous of one another, and each probably watched his rival's proceedings more carefully than the hounds, but they were generally in a prominent position during a run, unless the desire for jumping an extra big fence brought them to grief. One day Capt. A. happened not to be out, and during the run Firr found himself confronted by a piece of timber in the corner of the field as the only means of getting to hounds. The timber was extra high and stiff withal (promising a fall to the man who first essayed to charge it).

It is a general rule in the Shires that if a huntsman wants first cut at a fence, he must make use of his opportunity, or others will be over before him; but this was an occasion when no one seemed anxious to usurp the huntsman's right of going first. Firr turned his horse half round and exclaimed, as if to himself, "Ah! I wish Capt. A. was here; he would soon show us the way over." The remark had the effect it was intended to have, and Mr. B. dashed gallantly at the timber, levelling it to the ground, and taking a heavy fall. The huntsman then rode on after his hounds, whilst the fallen sportsman gathered himself together and remounted his horse. These men had probably often been guilty of overriding hounds, so that it was a masterly stroke of Firr's to make use of their jealousy to further his own progress.

Coming down to my own time, I find it difficult to speak of men critically who are still taking their part in the hunting field. The "Bell" at Melton sheltered a party of young men who always held a foremost position when hounds ran. There was Mr. (Buck) Barclay, who is still one of our leading lights, Count Charles Kinsky, Count Kaunitz, and Mr. Alfred Brocklehurst, the latter a finished horseman and a very quick man to hounds; but they were all first rate. I think the hardest and most determined man across country of that period was Mr. Edmund Leatham, for when hounds ran there was nothing big enough or strong enough to stop him; but though he possessed a firm and graceful seat, his hands were heavy. This did not prevent him from following the pack wherever they went, and nearly always getting to the end of a run; but lacked that delicacy of touch which is essential to the comfort of a horse.

A little later, but well within the eighties, Count Zbrowski was always in the front rank when big fences wanted jumping or wide ditches negotiating. He was an exceptionally fine horseman in every sense of the word, and though he was rather at sea for his first year, he very soon trained his eye to watching hounds. He introduced the red ribbon into Leicestershire as the sign of a kicker, and I remember being repeatedly asked what it was for. This will seem curious to those who have only commenced hunting lately, and have been accustomed to look on the ribbon on a horse's tail as a recognized danger signal. About this period the 10th Hussars were strongly represented in Melton, and when hounds ran fast, you might be pretty certain there was one of that regiment in the front rank. Now they all seem to have drifted away into other countries, and the Shires see them no more; but for aught I know they are generals now, and the grey hairs are creeping into the brown.

The two Bentincks, Lord Henry and Lord William, were at that time members of the select band of hard riders from Melton, but the young brother, Lord Charles, had not then developed the talent for riding to hounds which he has since shown. I should have no hesitation in saying that the youngest is now the best of the family. I can remember poor Edmund Leatham riding home from hunting one night, saying to me, "I'm afraid that young Charlie Bentinck will never ride like his brothers; he does not seem to have any dash." I quote this conversation merely to show that parents need not despair of their boys going well across country because they do not exhibit much excellence at first.

I have seen Mr. Beaumont Lubbock in a fast gallop ride brilliantly to hounds, but he was too courteous and unselfish in a scramble for a start. His horses were always good and his horsemanship perfect. I have had the pleasure of hunting with him for twenty seasons, but have never seen him lose his temper or speak crossly to anyone. The man with this record, who hunts and who is also a martyr to the gout, is the nearest approach to a saint that I can imagine.

These are a few of the Melton men whom I can remember, but there are many others, just as good riders, whose names I cannot recall and who were only with us for a season or two. Beyond Melton, out in the country and round Oakham, men lived who, we expected to see regularly every Cottesmore Saturday, and usually with the Quorn. The best all-round man I always considered to be Mr. Cecil Chaplin, as he not only rode well, but knew what hounds were doing.

Before I became correspondent to the *Field*, I generally hunted with the Cottesmore on Tuesdays. Neal was then huntsman, and though he was not a great artist, he showed some very good sport. The Goslings were familiar figures at every meet, and were all real good sportsmen. We have some of the family with us still; but the ever cheery "Colonel" we have not seen for years, and the "Old Goose," I am sorry to say, is dead. Mr. Henry Callander and Mr. Granville Farquhar were hard men to beat, but it was a pleasure to ride a run in their company, as they were always cheery and keen. In those days Sir Bache Cunard was master of the country south of Billesdon, but I don't remember hunting with him more than two or three times. His brother, Mr. Gordon Cunard, was the best man with that pack then, though Mr. Logan was almost equally good!

I am not quite certain about the date, but it was either in '82 or '83 that the vicar of Waltham made his first appearance in Leicestershire. Many seasons have slipped away since then, but Parson Seabrook up to the season before his death in 1913 was always in the front rank when hounds ran fast. His horses had generally a weak spot in their tempers, but with a resolute heart and a strong pair of legs they were made to compete successfully with the best mounted field in England. Mr. Hatfield Harter hunted from Melton in the eighties, and was one of our very best men. Sometimes he now pays us a flying visit, and we see then he has lost none of his dash or quickness in riding to hounds. There are hosts of other men whom I can remember as going well and who with a lead would go anywhere, but those I have mentioned were all capable of cutting out the work and finding their way across country unassisted. I have known men who were quite willing to ride first at a fence if they had someone alongside of them, but directly they found themselves alone with hounds were hopelessly at sea and utterly incapable of retaining the position they had won. Mr. Hugh Lowther—Lord Lonsdale now—I remember hunting with the Cottesmore, but in those days he was seldom out with the Quorn. I have elsewhere stated that I consider him one of the best horsemen and one of the best men to hounds that I know.

Judging from the stories that have been handed down to us, I should say there is less competition in riding now than was the case forty or fifty years ago. Still there has always been a little harmless jealousy between Grantham and Melton, when both towns were equally represented in a Belvoir field. Hounds then were generally over-ridden and the sport had to suffer, but the hard men gain some extra excitement in their struggles for supremacy. Some years since a large landowning baronet* on the Grantham side was one of the quickest men to hounds, and when the Belvoir met near Melton his was a foremost figure in a fast burst.

One day Melton Spinney was being drawn, and the brook below swept down the valley a muddy, swollen torrent. The railway that now lies beyond had not then been thought of, and as foxes generally run a line towards Welby, the first men over the water were not easily caught. On this occasion the brook had overflowed, the ford was almost impassable, and the banks being invisible a horse could not see where to take off, so that there was every chance of a ducking for the man who risked a jump. To every one's surprise and annoyance the fox faced the stream, when how to get over became the burning question of the moment. The gallant baronet grasped the situation and rode straight down with every intention of getting across wet or dry. Fortune favoured him, for a young hound having waded through the shallow water, was standing hesitatingly on the brink of the stream. The man saw his opportunity at once and rode directly at the hound, so that the horse taking off at this hound guard-fence landed him well on to the other side. The hound naturally did not wait

*Sir Thomas Whichcote.

to be made use of again and the baronet was thus alone with the pack; but his brilliant exploit met with scant reward, as the fox ran only one field and then turned back to recross the brook. I give this as an instance of quickness and decision in grasping an opportunity, which is the characteristic of a good man across country, but I do not advise the beginner to try and emulate the feat, as it is not a method that would commend itself to a master of hounds.

Some five-and-twenty years ago, a man came to Melton for whom the biggest fence in Leicestershire had no terrors, and though he may not have been popular with masters of hounds or huntsmen, he was undeniably brave. On one occasion that season hounds were running smartly from Prior's Coppice and two first-flight men having noted the newcomer's ambition, thought the opportunity well timed for a joke. In the valley was a brook that was almost unjumpable, but a handy ford made the feat unnecessary. The newcomer suddenly found himself sandwiched between two well-known men, racing downhill at the brook, and this at once awoke a desire to be first over the water. Fast as he went his two attendants kept beside him until within a length or two of the banks, when they dropped back and the next second splash he went into the water, whilst the others rode quietly through the ford.

A Leicestershire field has the reputation of being rather averse to open water, but those who have hunted in that country for any length of time have generally found by experience that the brooks are much easier to get into than to get out of. The banks are of clay, and the bottom is usually of the same material, so that the former get washed away and undermined, whilst the latter have a tenacity for holding a horse in the water which often means a cart team to pull him out. The first flight are, however, always ready to ride at a brook when one comes in their way, a combination of boldness in horse and man then generally carries them safely over. If either is vacillating or half-hearted in making the attempt, they are pretty certain to come to grief. There is a certain amount of satisfaction in sailing down at a brook and flying over without having to look at the place first. The satisfaction is considerably enhanced when the next man makes a hole in the water and then crawls dripping up the bank. The streams that divide the different valleys in Leicestershire are very deceptive, and one place may be only six feet wide, whilst a few yards right or left it is quite likely to be twenty feet. I remember one day we came down to the Twyford brook; hounds were not running very fast, and a friend said, "Where can we get over?" "Come on," I replied, and digging in my heels rode confidently at a place I thought was quite small. My memory was, however, slightly at fault, and the horse, thinking the jump beyond his powers, tried to cut it in the last stride. In we went with a splash, much to the amusement of the others, who, finding the spot I had misjudged by a few yards, were able to cross without difficulty.

Firr tells a story which I have no doubt is true, and which he considers the best example of coolness he can remember within his varied experience. Hounds were running fast, and down they came to a brook. On one side of Firr and a few lengths in front, a stranger was riding gallantly at the stream. His horse, however, was not quite of the same mind, and on reaching the banks swerved suddenly to one side. The man went on, and turning a somersault in the air, disappeared under water. The celebrated huntsman could not check his horse and sailed over, but while he was in the air a hatless head bobbed up out of the water directly beneath him, and a voice cried "Cuckoo." The remark may not have been very witty, but I think most of us under the circumstances would have been too much afraid of the flashing hoofs above our heads to have said anything. This reminds me of rather an amusing incident which happened to the same huntsman, though it has nothing to do with Leicestershire, but the story borders on the indelicate, and ladies are therefore requested to turn the page unread.

At that time this huntsman was with some pack in Scotland, and it was their custom to exercise hounds along the seashore in the early morning. It was a wild part of the coast, with no habitation near, and three ladies thought it would be an excellent place to bathe without costumes. The tide had gone out for fully half a mile, and leaving their clothes on shore the ladies proceeded to dip themselves in the sea. In the midst of their splashings, one of the mermaids turned round and to her dismay saw a pack of hounds with hunt servants advancing along the water's edge. Their first idea was to rush to their clothes for protection, but they had misjudged distance, and found they would have to pass in full view of the cavalcade. The three nude figures then dropped on to the sand, and squatting down, turned their backs on the hunt. All would have been well had not the curiosity of an old hound been aroused by these strange objects, and wishing to find out what they were, he left the pack and advanced silently with cautious steps across the sands. "Solomon" had never before seen the human form divine unclothed, and knowing his eyesight occasionally deceived him, he meant to ascertain by sense of touch or smell what the pink statues were made of. "Solomon" crept nearer and nearer, but the ladies heard nothing, and no doubt thought their ordeal was nearly over, when one of them suddenly felt the hound's cold nose in the middle of her back. There was a yell of terror, and, oblivious of the men in scarlet, the frightened women rushed screaming to their clothes.

Chapter IV

Mr. John Coupland

1870–1884

Before dipping into the storehouse of memory for incidents and sport in my own time, I must give you a few personal details.

After nearly two years in the Merchant Service, I came to the conclusion that if I continued in that profession I should never have an opportunity of indulging my love for sport. The previous two years' training on the *Conway*, and subsequent time at sea, were not what the Americans would describe exactly as "a picnic", but the discipline and hard work certainly did me a lot of good, as well as proving useful in after life.

My father strongly advised me to go into business, but I hated towns and loved a country life, so that it did not take me long to decide on farming. A very pleasant occupation for those who have a natural bent that way, and the soil can always be depended upon to give a fair return for outlay, if judiciously expended. Although I can claim that my efforts on the land nearly always met with success, I have to admit that I squandered my gains on illegitimate objects, such as speculating in hunters and backing horses on the race-course.

If the love for an occasional bet is in your blood and you also are keen on racing, it is a very difficult matter to abstain altogether. There is no harm in having a bet if you always make it a rule never to risk more than you can lose without inconvenience to yourself or to anyone who is dependent on you. Remember that backing horses is a losing game, and though you may win at first, you are certain to be out of pocket in the end. The immoral side appears to me to be contained in the attempt to make money without working for it, and as we are all meant to work, by doing otherwise we try to defeat the ways of providence.

If you must have a bet, you might satisfy your conscience by making it a rule, that in case of loss you are prepared to sacrifice some luxury you usually enjoy.

It was in the autumn of 1879 I left the sea, and it was some time during the following winter that I bought from Morris, the Melton butcher, a little bay mare, who carried me many seasons. During the two following seasons I hunted her regularly two days a week—usually Friday with the Quorn and either the same pack on Monday or the Cottesmore on Tuesday.

Being one of a large family I never had much money, and, of course, with no prospects of inheriting any, I ought to have settled down to hard work. That I have been able to hunt from that time until now was due entirely to being fortunate enough to get the job of hunting correspondent.

It is from these weekly contributions I propose to cull any news or other matter which I think may prove of interest. Although my duties as correspondent covered days with the Cottesmore and Belvoir as well as the Quorn, I lived in the latter country, and shall therefore date my yarns by the different periods of mastership. Actual dates are, of course, very useful in a book of reference—this is not—but I think to the ordinary individual they are dry and unpalatable.

Mr. Coupland was a real good sportsman, and there was probably a better average of first-class runs during his reign than have been seen before or since. The Quorn were in want of a master and his offer to take the hounds was accepted, though almost practically unknown in Leicestershire. When business allowed, I believe he had been a fairly constant attendant with the Cheshire packs. To the average hunting man, unfamiliar with business, the mere fact that the new master was an owner of ships spelt riches with a capital R, and he had no idea of the large share which credit frequently plays in such undertakings. Mr. Coupland was a clever man without a large amount of capital at his back, and at the time he took the hounds, he was apparently on the high road to fortune. Unfortunately for him there came a slump in shipping a little later, and freights were reduced to a minimum.

Having the control of an important country like the Quorn, with the numerous and unavoidable expenses attached thereto, with a large business that was threatening every day to collapse, it will be seen that he had a heavy load to bear.

At that period the master settled damages and paid compensation for poultry, etc. I am quite sure that Mr. Coupland would have paid all claimants handsomely if his private purse had not been so severely taxed at that moment, but as it was he paid only the most pressing and thereby was subject to some rather hard cricitism on leaving. My idea is that he not only deserved our warm thanks for the excellent sport he had shown, but that he should have had our sympathy in his difficulties. He was very keen and did all in his power to maintain the glories of the Quorn, and, I feel sure, would never have resigned had it not been for his financial troubles, which almost to the last he hoped would be overcome. Let it not be forgotten that he brought Firr to the country, found a very moderate pack in kennel, and left one that earned itself a great reputation.

My first introduction to hunting journalism appeared in

Mr. John Coupland

Bell's Life above the signature of "Corde Chasse," and I always remember with some pride that my earliest efforts came out beneath the sleepless eye of that ancient sporting weekly. Being only a beginner, I followed the lead of well-known correspondents and always gave a full list of those present at a meet—no doubt the fact that I was paid for quantity made the addition of names a consideration.

It was on 11th November 1882 that my maiden article appeared in the above-mentioned paper, and being a first attempt at literary composition of any kind, the effusion probably cost me much anxious labour. I was considerably indebted at this period for assistance and encouragement I received from "Brooksby", who was then, as now, the king of hunting correspondents.

In the list of names at Kirby Gate, 1882, I see that of the Rev. Bullen, who was then in his eighty-fifth year, and, according to my account, "looking as well as ever". His hard riding days were over, but I can remember him going well a year or two earlier, though his style did not get him often to the end of a long run.

The best day we had in November of that season was on the 17th of the month, but on looking through my account I find we did not kill a fox. I remember the occasion well, and can see now the dull, leaden sky as we rode to the meet at Rearsby. There was a great scent, and hounds raced from Brooksby Spinney to Barkby Holt. Somewhere near the Gaddesby brook another fox jumped up, and part of the pack went in pursuit. The Duke of Portland, Mr. Walter Peake, Downes, and the writer happened to find themselves following the erring division. It was too late to join the main body then, and we therefore determined to make the most of our mistake. The run fox had gone straight on, whilst ours bore left-handed, and I remember took us over a very stiff country by Barsby to South Croxton. I think we only had about five couple of hounds, but with a burning scent and the fox hardly out of sight it took us all our time to live with them. Naturally we did not say much about it at the time, but my companions will probably remember that stirring little gallop now.

Mr. Walter Peake—Colonel is, I believe, his title now—belongs to Leicestershire, and is the possessor of exceptionally good hands, an article which many of our best riders lack. Downes was rough-rider to Mr. Julius Behrens, and an accomplished horseman as well as a very quick man to hounds.

Frost and snow came early that season, and for the first fortnight in December there was practically no hunting. The weather suddenly changed, and the Meltonians, who had all gone away, could not get back to meet the Quorn on Monday, 18th December, at Six Hills. Foxes were rather hard to find, but we eventually found one at Ella's Gorse and he gave us a first-rate gallop. In those day there was no bridge over the stream that flows below the covert, and getting over was not an easy matter. There was one place close to the covert where fence and brook could be jumped together but it wanted a fairly bold horse to face it. On this occasion the only man who rode at it was Capt. Elmhirst, with his arm in a sling, but he either had not enough steam on or his horse funked it, and dropping its hind legs, fell back into the water. Hounds turned sharp to the left, and we did not catch them until we were close to Willoughby Gorse. From thence on we had a most enjoyable gallop to Bunny Wood, eventually losing our fox in the sticky ploughs near Leake, after taking him through Stanford Park. The fast part of the gallop was twenty-eight minutes with a five-mile point.

In December and January sport was very meagre but it was not from the want of moisture, as I think we had more rain that winter than I ever remember since. The last Tuesday in

Mr. John Coupland

January gave the Cottesmore a very fast five-mile gallop from Prior's Coppice. It was late in the afternoon, and as there appeared no scent, nearly every one had gone home. Hounds raced the whole way, and horses had difficulty in living with them. I did not see this gallop myself, but those who were in it said it was the quickest thing of the season. This afternoon burst was the preliminary to some very excellent sport, of which the Quorn had, I think, the lion's share. On 2nd February that pack, finding a fox in Gartree Hill, raced across the Burton Flats by Wild's Lodge nearly to Stapleford, and then, swinging left-handed, ran into Burbidge's covert. Here was the first check, and possibly a change of foxes, but the pace was equally good across that stiff line to Guadaloupe and down to the river at Eye Kettleby. After crossing the river it was only slow hunting, and the fox was lost near Sysonby. Mr. Arthur Pryor had the misfortune on this occasion to kill his old favourite chestnut in jumping a gate. The horse was noted for his timber-jumping qualities, and had carried his owner safely over many a high-backed stile, but he had reached his twentieth year, and the activity of youth had been replaced by the stiffening joints of age.

On the next Monday the same pack had about the best run of the season with the old bob-tailed customer who had set both the Belvoir and Quorn at defiance for some time. We found him in Holwell Mouth, and getting away on good terms, hounds ran fast to Little Belvoir, where they turned left-handed up the hill and ran at a modified pace to Cant's Thorns. Here our bob-tailed friend waited for us, and, relying on his cunning rather than his speed, laid down in the covert, and, getting up after the pack had passed, slipped away to Kettleby village. Firr was not to be beaten by these tactics, and getting his pack clear of the village they settled down to race. Past Old Hills and Scalford Spinney the pace was so good that few men were able to keep near hounds. Then came some plough, which brought the pack to their noses; but Firr held them forward on to the grass, and leaving Melton Spinney on the right they ran straight away to Freeby Wood. The fox evidently meant going on, but unluckily one sportsman was a little too forward and turned him back into covert. The remainder of the run was slow hunting, and it was only by an exceptionally fine bit of science that Firr was able to hold on to his fox. Back we went across the valley of the Melton brook and past Chadwell, then between Scalford and Goadby a halloa put us on better terms. The pace increased again, hounds were bristling for blood, and the next two miles it was all we could do to keep them in sight. Leaving Clawson Thorns just on the left, the pack running from scent to view rolled over one of the stoutest foxes I have ever seen hunted. It was two hours and fifteen minutes from the find, and most of the time hounds had been running fast. I remember there was a general exclamation of "Of course, it is not the same fox." Firr said nothing, but held up a three-inch stump of brush. We had started with a "bob-tailed" fox and we finished with one; but there are people who will always say there has been a change, and had not they been silenced by the short brush, the huntsman's triumph would have been disputed by their loud-voiced opinions.

I have mentioned this run because it is one of my earliest impressions of Firr's wonderful skill and patience. There was a good scent on the grass, but very little on the plough, and I know no other man who would have brought that fox to hand under similar conditions.

On the following Friday, 9th February, the Quorn had again another first-rate day's sport, though without killing a fox. Finding at Barkby Holt, they ran round by Queniborough and then straight away to Ashby Pastures—very fast. The quickest thing of the day, however, was a streaming gallop from Thorpe Trussells, in which hounds were always a field ahead of horses. This was a ring, but so fast had it been that most people had no idea such was the case until they found themselves back at the starting-point. Fresh foxes in every direction and a bad scenting covert saved the life of the one that had staggered back in front of hounds. This was perhaps an unsatisfactory day for hounds and huntsmen, but for the hard riding section of the field I think it was the best day of the season.

There was little more sport in February, and then came a first-rate scenting day on the 2nd of March. Foxes were getting scarce on the south side of the Quorn Friday country, and the good scent was wasted. There was, however, a very fast forty minutes from Lord Morton's, and hounds fairly raced their fox to death; but it was a twisting sort of gallop, and did not commend itself to the hard riders.

The following Monday the Quorn had very indifferent sport in the morning at Lodge-in-the-Wolds, though they managed to kill their fox. Then Curate's Gorse and several other coverts were drawn blank until late in the afternoon, when Mr. Coupland decided to go home. The field may perhaps have misunderstood him, or in a momentary fit of weakness he may have been persuaded to change his mind, but certain it is that only those whose route home lay with the pack saw Ella's Gorse drawn. The result was a five-and-thirty minutes' racing gallop, and there are men in Melton now who bewail that lost opportunity. This was the end of a fortnight's beautiful spring weather, and before the middle of the week the ground was covered with snow, there being at least six inches of it on Friday, 9th March. I suppose the country to the north of the Wreake was getting short of foxes as the Quorn met at Great Dalby on Monday, 19th March. There was some frost and snow still left, but the "going" on the whole was very good. We found a capital fox in Gartree Hill, and had one of the most enjoyable days of the season. Hounds ran fast through the Punchbowl, and leaving Somerby to the left went nearly to Owston village, but bearing to the right they crossed a beautiful line and lost their fox in between Tilton and Skeffington. A good six-mile point.

The next Monday provided us with one of the fastest gallops of the season. The morning had been spent in walking after a fox in the neighbourhood of Lodge-in-the-Wolds, and as there did not seem much chance of sport, very few went on to see Ella's Gorse drawn. A fox went away at once with hounds close at his brush, and for twenty-eight minutes they raced him without a check. Another few seconds would have sealed his fate, but the main earths in Shoby Scoles were open and he just reached them with not more than a yard or two to spare.

We were bothered with both frost and snow at intervals nearly up to the end of March, and then the weather became suddenly warm again. The Quorn finished the month by running a fox very smartly from one of the Gaddesby coverts and killing him in Beeby village. The same pack had their last day of the season on the following Monday, when they met at Lord Wilton's house, Egerton Lodge, Melton. This was a huge meet, with visitors from all the surrounding hunts. I remember it was Count Charles Kinsky's first appearance amongst us after his success in the Grand National, a few days previously, on Zoedone. He had left us a month before to ride gallops and to get himself fit; but before going he had told me he thought he had a good chance, and being a great admirer of his horsemanship. I invested my modest sovereign at 20 to 1.

With the ground dry and a hot sun, this last day did not promise much sport. A fox managed to get a long start from Gartree Hill, and it was slow hunting by Little Dalby and Pickwell to the Noel Arms. Firr, however, wanted to finish the season with blood, and sticking to his fox eventually managed to get on better terms, when hounds increased their pace and killed close to Stapleford Park. The Cottesmore finished their season the next day with a very fast seventeen minutes and a kill from Stapleford.

Season 1883–1884

October of that year brought us some capital sport. Towards the end of the month the Quorn had a very fast gallop from Gaddesby Spinney, and I do not ever remember hounds running better for thirty minutes. It was not very straight, but we went over a beautiful country and there was not a sign of a check. I have a vivid recollection of the gallop, and the stiff line we had to cross that bright autumn afternoon. The fences had lost none of their leaf, and the ditches were overgrown with grass. Men and horses were steaming with perspiration when hounds marked their fox to ground in a drain beneath the turnpike close to Brooksby Hall. The pack deserved blood, and Firr meant to have it; but for once in a way he made a mistake in not trying forward. The fox had gone right through the drain, and whilst we were sending for terriers, he was putting himself at a safe distance from the hunt. The same pack had another capital afternoon spin the following Monday. This was from Ella's Gorse. A brace of foxes went away, and only a small portion of the field realized that Firr was intent on following the one which had crossed the brook. There was never any difference of opinion on a question of this sort between the pack and their huntsman. He would give two or three cheers and they were after him as quick as lightning. Hounds after one fox and huntsman after another was a thing unknown in the Quorn country.

On this occasion they were streaming up the grass beyond the brook before most people were aware a brace of foxes had gone away, and those who had thus lost this start never saw the hunt again that day. A thick fog came on, hounds ran very fast, and it was impossible to catch them up if once you got behind.

It was on the 15th of November that the Barkby-Holt customer was first found. I give him that title because it was by that name he was known, but on this occasion we found him at Baggrave. Hounds ran very fast by Carr Bridge and across the Ashby valley to Thorpe Trussells. The sky then clouded over and scent entirely disappeared. I have no doubt in my own mind that this was the same fox we found the following Friday at Barkby Holt when he gave us an exceptionally good run, but there was not much covert in the Prince of Wales' then, which was perhaps his reason for seeking fresh quarters. I remember the events of the day distinctly. We had killed a fox from Gaddesby after a smart scurry and then went on to draw Barkby Holt. Firr asked me to watch the down wind side, so that I had a good opportunity of seeing this extraordinary fox as he went away—a big dark coloured fellow with, I believe, hardly any white on his brush. It was in the gorse he was lying and not in the wood, though we generally speak of the whole covert as the Holt. My lungs were pretty strong in those days, and though I was down wind of the pack, they were all out of covert before the huntsman could get round. From the Holt to Large's Spinney near Loseby Station is a five-mile point, and hounds never checked or hesitated a second. The fox ran through the Prince of Wales' covert and pursued the same line he had done the previous Friday as far as Carr Bridge, but he then kept to the brook-side by Lowesby Hall and until he had baffled us at the station. If I remember right, I think there were not more than half a dozen men who were actually with hounds up to this point, and they were glad enough of a check as their horses could not possibly have galloped up the hill to Tilton. When the line was recovered, scent seemed to have changed and our fox eventually beat us at Owston Wood. A fortnight later we again found our old friend at Barkby Holt, and through the field being drawn up on the side he wished to break, he was obliged to take a turn round Croxton village before he could get on his favourite track. The pace was good at the start, but soon degenerated into a slow hunting run, and was a very poor imitation of the great gallop over the same line. On this occasion the fox was lost soon after passing Tilton, though he no doubt went on to Owston Wood. Now comes the sad part of the story. The following Friday the meet was at Beeby, and Mr. Coupland could not resist the temptation of having another try at the old customer. There was a strong wind blowing, and hounds drew the Holt up wind. The gallant fox, who had already given us three good runs, was resting from his exertions of the previous week, and hounds were upon him before he knew they were in covert. His stiffened limbs refused to act, and in this ignominious fashion died the hero of the season's best gallop.

On Monday, 10th December, we had a very good run from Ragdale Wood and killed our fox at Clawson village. The first five-and-twenty minutes to old Dalby Wood were very fast. It was in the afternoon, and the field had assumed reasonable dimensions. I can see the hounds now as they raced over those flat twitch-grown fields that lie to the north of Shoby Scoles, and Mr. Beaumont Lubbock popping over a gate just before we crossed the Shoby Lane. What fun it was! This was one of the many good runs we had that season, but it would be difficult to say which was the best. Nearly every day produced a gallop, and I can recall no season in my experience that could boast such a record of good sport. Regularly every Friday and Monday the Quorn had a run that in these days we should call first-class, but there is not space here to give an account of all.

On Boxing Day we had a screaming fifteen minutes from Thrussington Gorse, and the following Monday's hounds had an extraordinary hard day. Finding a fox in Curate's Gorse they ran first of all to Widmerpool, and then swinging round to the left ran across the vale to Holwell Mouth. Here the pack changed on to a fresh fox, and all the efforts of the whip were of no avail to stop them. We then had a rattling gallop through Sherbrooke's covert and bearing left-handed round Upper Broughton, made straight for the hills again. There was rather a long check at Watnaby Stonepit Spinney, but the line was at length recovered and we went slowly on to Saxelbye Wood. Whether or no it was a fresh fox that went away from this covert, I could not say, but he managed to slip away with a long start and the pace to Ragdale village was very moderate. Hounds then spurted again and ran sharply down to the earths in the Hoby Vale.

I think we must have changed at Saxelbye Wood, as the fox that had been bustled in the vale could not have gone on, whereas the one we were hunting kept getting farther ahead. It was a real good fox, and finding the earths closed he went straight on, leaving Cossington Gorse and Seagrave to the left, passing Burton and finally beating hounds close to Wymes-would.

On referring to my weekly contributions to the *County Gentleman*, the Quorn appear to have had a good run nearly every day they went out. On 4th January they had a fine hunting run from Scraptoft, and killed their fox in Gaddesby Spinney. I recollect the occasion well, as it was one of those marvellous performances of Firr's that impressed all those who had the pleasure of hunting with him. Then on the following Monday we had two great gallops, neither of which, however, finished with blood. The first fox we found in Grimstone Gorse, and after a very fast forty-five minutes marked him to ground in Goadby Gorse. It was well for this fox that the covert was not half a mile farther, for he would assuredly never have saved his brush. There was no ringing or twisting at the start, and hounds went straight away from field to field, with very few people in attendance.

The leading lights on that occasion were Capt. Smith, Mr. Alfred Brocklehurst, and "Brooksby". Within the first two miles the line included three or four very awkward bottoms, and these helped to make the front rank the more select. The bottom is the most awkward obstacle we have to encounter in Leicestershire, and neither man nor horse may have a weak spot in his nerves if he hopes to negotiate it safely. A bottom is a ditch that divides a little valley, and is guarded on one side by a fence. The difference between a brook and a bottom is that the former contains running water more or less all the year round, whilst the latter is dry except when the heavy rains of winter rush down the little hills in haste to reach the sea. In their turbulent haste the waters are continually washing away and undermining the clay banks, so that what appears to be an innocent-looking fence may hide an unjumpable gulf that would hold half a dozen horses.

Later in the day the field found themselves at Welby Osierbeds, and the run that ensued was if anything better than the first. To Scalford Windmill hounds ran without a check, and again only a select few were in the same field with them. I think after that we must have changed foxes, and the remainder of the run was rather twisty; but hounds were still hard at work when failing light and tired horses made it necessary to turn for home. Those who took a foremost part in either or both of these two runs will, if alive, have a very distinct recollection of the chief incidents of the day, and I feel sure that the Duke of Portland, who was going particularly well,

will not have forgotten those exciting moments. At one time
we had crossed the Waltham road, but the fox soon turned
back again, and the remainder of the run was enacted in the
valley near Melton Spinney. Stirring gallops still crowded
one another, and we never had a bad day. The run that I can
remember enjoying more than anything in that season started
at Thorpe Trussells and finished at Burton. The morning had
been most uninteresting, and to all appearance there was
very little scent. Then matters did not improve much when
we first left the Trussells, but the ground had been foiled,
and the fox had got some distance ahead. It was one of those
moments when the field begin to lose interest at the prospect
of sport fading away to nothing, and the talk is of the shortest
way home. These were the occasions when Firr's exceptional
talents would come to the fore, and you might be certain that
if it were possible to retrieve the day, it would be done. The day
had been unproductive of any amusement for the field, and
it was plainly evident to us the fox was getting farther ahead
every moment. Not half a mile away was Adam's Gorse, and it
was then, as it is to-day, the home of good foxes; but at that
time it was a gorse only in name, and there was very little lying
in the spinney. Firr galloped on towards the covert to get on
better terms with his own fox or to cross the line of another.
A whip was sent on so that there should be no mistake, and
a minute later hounds were streaming up the hillside that
protects the covert from the east. There was not a great scent,
but it had improved considerably since the morning, and we
had got away on good terms. I remember, however, we had
to gallop best pace to keep in touch with the pack as they
swept down on to the old steeplechase course and then bore
left-handed towards Burdett's covert. The fox then for some
reason turned up the hill in the direction of Great Dalby, and
thereby took us over some very stiff fencing before bringing us

to the road by Gartree Hill. Hounds never entered the covert, but just skirted the boundary hedge to emerge beyond on to the Burton Flat. Here were one or two fields of plough, but scent had improved so much that hounds were able to cross it quicker than horses, and, of course, directly they touched the grass again they were flying along at top speed. We seemed to have only just left Gartree Hill and a few minutes later we were in the big field by Brentingby gate-house. If you know the country, you will know we crossed the best of the Burton Flats. The fox swung to the left on reaching the river, and entered Burbidge's covert; but he dare not dwell, and the pack drove him out, killing a few minutes later in Burton village.

This was exactly thirty-five minutes from the time of leaving Adam's Gorse to Burbidge's covert, with a five-and-a-half-mile point. Whether we started with a fresh fox from that little covert I am not able to say, but think not. It was the place to which the one we were hunting appeared to be going, and it was Firr's marvellous quickness in anticipating his intentions that gave us the gallop. Hounds were never touched after leaving Adam's Gorse. I looked back on this as one of the best gallops I ever saw. The date was 11th January 1884. There were several other good runs before the end of the season.

This was the end of Mr. Coupland's reign of the Quorn, and he was succeeded in office by Lord Manners.

Chapter V

Lord Manners

1884–1886

The season 1884–85 I was not writing for any paper, or, at least, not regularly, and I have no notes with which to refresh my memory.

Poor old *Bell's Life* ceased to be a weekly some time in the summer of 1883 and was, I believe, incorporated more or less with a sporting daily. In spite of the Motto and the eye that never slept, this ancient paper had been content to slumber on with its out-of-date journalism, allowing the *Field* to usurp its place and become an established favourite.

The season 1883–84 I wrote for the *County Gentleman*, which at that period was struggling to keep its head above water with, I fear, rather indifferent success. How many times it has changed hands since then I do not know, but it is still in existence, and much in the same style as when I knew it, but I understand it is now flourishing.

Even in its struggling days the articles were always printed in a bold, clear type, that did not try the eyes to read, which is, I think, a great recommendation to any paper. About twenty years later I wrote them a series of articles on beagles.

In the summer of 1885 I was offered "Brooksby's" post on the *Field,* which embraced the reporting of hounds' doings within the Melton circuit. This meant Monday the Quorn,

Tuesday the Cottesmore, Wednesday the Belvoir, Thursday Sir Bache Cunard's, Friday the Quorn again, and Saturday Belvoir and Cottesmore alternately.

My old friend "H. S. D.", who had taken on "Brooksby's" place in 1884–85, but who had found the distances too great from his home in the Billesdon country, asked me if I minded giving up Tuesday and Thursday to him. This, with the Editor's permission, I was very glad to be able to do, and readers of the *Field* will remember his signature under the heading of "High Leicestershire".

The hunting Editor of the *Field* was then Mr. Walsh, and I have no hesitation in saying that he was the best man for the post that the paper has ever had. This is said in no disparagement of my good friend, the present hunting Editor, who is an excellent sportsman, and probably the best man to be found for the job.

Mr. Walsh was, however, exceptionally brilliant, and possessed the knack of knowing exactly what his readers wanted. In my humble opinion the *Field* owes its success chiefly to him, and also in no small degree to Capt. Pennell Elmhirst ("Brooksby"). When the latter first began writing his articles, the style of the ordinary hunting correspondent and his methods of describing a run were both feeble and uninteresting. "Brooksby" began a new era, which raised the form of hunting correspondence on to a higher plane. From the time when he started to write for the *Field*, that paper rose rapidly in popular favour. Although it embraces many other subjects and phases of sport, hunting was ever its leading topic, and hunting men have always been its strongest supporters.

In the autumn of 1885 I began my duties as hunting correspondent to the *Field*, and have continued on without a break until hunting was temporarily put on one side by the war.

My stiff and halting contributions must have been poor reading after "Brooksby's" brilliant articles, for he would always describe a moderate day's sport in a manner to make it interesting. However, it is always better to write in your own moderate way than to try and copy the style of another. With the Editor's permission I instituted a radical change by omitting names of people at the meet, and, in fact, of not mentioning anyone—the custom has since become more or less general.

My predecessor had always headed his *Field* letters with a list of those who were out, and was exceptionally clever in adding colour to his narrations by inserting names of those occupying good positions in a run.

There are people who delight in seeing themselves in print, but I felt that to pander to such petty desires was derogatory to the character of the leading sporting weekly. I think we may leave the personal paragraph to the "society rags", which we all in reality despise, even though we read them. There were other reasons, also equally good, which influenced me in making the decision, and perhaps the soundest of all was that I did not feel it was in me to treat personalities with "Brooksby's" delicate touch. Whenever possible, I considered it my duty as well as pleasure to watch what hounds were doing, and with a field of three hundred, there is not much time to observe performers and pack. Then if you are riding to right or left—as you should be—well clear of hounds, it is very easy to miss seeing someone on the opposite side, and it is better to mention none rather than to miss out someone equally well placed.

Mr. Jorrocks, in one of his sporting lectures, remarks that "the finest receipt for making men ride is shaking a sporting hauthor afore them at startin'". I don't think that is quite the right spirit to encourage, and if the desire to see hounds as well as a natural wish to be first does not inspire to deeds of daring, they had better be content to ride in the ruck.

I look on the master and hunt servants as public men, but the field being composed of private individuals, who go hunting for their own amusement, it seems rather like taking a liberty to put their names in print. In the lecture aforementioned, Jorrocks, pointing out the difference between Beckford and a sporting writer he quotes, says the former is for the pack and the latter for the performer. I have tried to follow Peter's footsteps and endeavoured to record the doings of the pack.

Here, however, in these recollections of the past I do not hesitate to make use of names—a newspaper seems more public, and then a large majority of those I mention have stepped off the stage.

On Mr. Coupland's resignation the hounds were bought by three of the largest supporters of the Quorn for £3000. Firr's skill as a huntsman had probably earned the hounds a reputation rather beyond their merits. Although most people are of a different opinion, I have always thought that a new master should either take over the pack at a valuation, or that they should be put up for auction and he could then buy what he wanted. A pack of hounds can be made or marred in six years, so that though a master may take over a lot that are both good in looks and work, those he hands over on retiring may be useless for hunting and worthless on the flags.

Perhaps I ought to modify this statement that a pack can be altogether ruined in that period, because if the original blood is good the former excellence may be retrieved by judicious breeding. Unfortunately, it is the general rule for the retiring masters to hand over only the same number of hounds that he took in, quite irrespective of their breeding, so that it is possible in buying in drafts to have a pack that has none of the original blood in its composition. Of course, the same argument applies to a very moderate pack, which a good huntsman can convert into one of great excellence, and it is only fair he should reap the benefit of his improvement.

The purchase of Mr. Coupland's pack was done in the interests of the Quorn Hunt, and the intention was good, but whether it was a wise proceeding is another matter. There was some very good hunting blood in the pack then, and Quorn Alfred was a name that always stood for working qualities in a pedigree. At that time there were "lemon-pied" and "badger-pied" hounds in the kennel, colours you might be certain of seeing at the head of affairs while scent was bad or with a sinking fox. The craze for Belvoir tan was then beginning, and masters as well as huntsmen, who were bitten with the colour mania, were ready to sacrifice blood that had proved its worth in the field merely for the sake of pleasing the eye. I had such a profound admiration for Tom Firr that I hesitate to admit that he could have fallen a victim to the fashion for colour, but it appeared to me that the working qualities of the pack steadily degenerated after about 1890.

From what I can remember of it, the season 1884–85 was not very good, but there were occasional bright spots, though few and far between.

There were many pleasant days I can recall in the season 1884–85, although it was not considered good on the whole. Each of the three packs had their share of what sport there was, but frost interfered on several occasions, and for a fortnight in March the ground was covered with a foot of snow.

Amongst many other good men to hounds at that time I seem to see Messrs. Edmund Leatham, Alfred Brocklehurst, and "Buck" Barclay always in the first flight. Mr. Leatham was one of the hardest and most determined men across a country I ever saw—a great heart and a beautiful seat, but rather heavy hands.

If I remember aright, the two latter men had by this time joined the order of Benedicts, and had left the "Bell" for hunting-boxes in the neighbourhood. Marriage did not, however, quell their ardour for the chase, and when hounds ran fast, you might be quite certain of finding them amidst the select few.

The Rector of Waltham, known familiarly as "Parson Seabrook" hunted pretty regularly with all three packs, though his living was in the Belvoir country. I have had many a good ride with him, but never the privilege of hearing him in the pulpit, where I was told he was very good.

In the hunting field he was a man of few words, though those few always to the point. I have probably already mentioned him, as he was a prominent figure in my first few seasons, and was holding his own five-and-twenty years later. He rode his own horse in the Grand National under the name of "Mr. C. Brook," but I can't at this moment remember the year, though I believe it was before he came to Leicestershire, and about 1879. In his prime he was a very powerful man on a horse, and could squeeze unwilling performers into negotiating obstacles that few other men could have got them to look at. His hands were not too delicate, but he made up for that deficiency by the strength of his muscles, and he would frequently buy a hard-pulling brute that few others wanted to ride. If anyone reads these lines who hunted from Melton in those days, they will remember the grey he rode for several seasons.

The dear old Parson was the cheeriest of comrades to ride a run with, in spite of the infliction of jealousy; but you had always to remember he was out to beat you, and he hated anyone to get in front of him. With two couple of hounds on the line, he always considered the flag had dropped, and unless restrained by the master, away he would go in hot pursuit. Another little weakness of his was to imagine that hounds were on ahead of those that could be seen, and at the same time to persuade the huntsman to believe such was the fact. I do not think he ever tried this on with Firr, but that huntsman could start away with a few couple with perfect confidence that the remainder of the pack would thread the horses and be with him in less time than most packs take in getting out of covert. I cannot remember now when it was the Duke of Portland first came to Melton, but think it was about 1881. However, he was still a regular visitor to the town in 1885, and it must have been about then his half-brothers, Lord Henry and Lord William Bentinck, first appeared. The elder brother had the misfortune to be a heavy weight, and had therefore that difficulty of getting horses to carry him which all such men have to contend with, even when there is practically no limit to the purse. No one, I think, enjoyed his sport more, and I have been surprised that he never revisited the scenes which I feel sure he will look back upon as some of the jolliest in his youth.

Lord Manners, when he took the Quorn, was a very good man to hounds, and being a light weight, could ride blood horses. If he will forgive my saying so, I don't think he was ever what you call a "hound man", but was very keen on the sport, and was content to leave that part entirely to Firr. Financial embarrassments in the previous mastership, as I have already said, raised up rather strained relations with some occupiers of land, which required a liberal hand and considerable tact to remove. Lord Manners was most successful in pouring oil on troubled waters, and on his resignation after about two seasons he had gained every one's goodwill, and the country was sorry to lose him. For a man who does not make a business of steeple-chasing, and who only sports silk occasionally to ride in hunt races, to have placed his name on the roll of those who have won the Grand National is a great feat.

Lord Manners

Known to his own intimates as "Hoppy", Lord Manners was an exceptionally quiet man, and probably his greatest friends never credited him with the ability to win over the Aintree course. I do not suppose that a bad rider has ever won or ever will win that race, but I never considered him quite in the first class as a horseman, and rather strange to say, though a very light weight his "hands" were not good.

I was not at Liverpool that year, but have had the story told me many times. It was a pouring wet day, and as every one knows in a steeplechase under those conditions, a pair of woollen gloves are almost a necessity to get a firm grip on slippery reins. The owner and rider of Seaman had no thought of this, but a friend had grasped the situation, and insisted on lending a pair. This friend happened to be well over six feet four, and the gloves must have been many sizes too big, but they answered the purpose, and doubtless were an important factor in the ultimate success.

Leicestershire is always strongly represented at Liverpool, and Lord Manners' many hunting friends were there to wish him luck, though I think very few expected to see him win. Needless to say they were very enthusiastic over the result, and showered congratulations on the mud-bespattered hero. Every one was both excited and elated. I was told the only cool person there was the man who had come through that severe ordeal of four miles and a half in triumph.

This happened several years ago, and the story of how Lord Manners bought the horse only a short time before the race, will perhaps be new to the present generation.

Seaman was in a well-known Irish stable which had trained several Liverpool winners, and what they did not know about the business was not worth knowing. The horse was supposed to have had a very fair chance when he was sound, but he had developed a "leg" in training, and was almost broken down.

Under these circumstances his clever owners considered he would never "get the course," and were probably very glad to accept Lord Manners' two thousand for him, particularly as they had another horse in the stable almost equally good, and with the advantage of four sound legs, with an experienced jockey to ride him. A cool head and good nerves, backed by a strong determination, make, however, a very good substitute for that experience which can only be acquired by frequent riding.

An occasion in a race at the Melton Hunt meeting recurs to me, when Capt. "Doggie" Smith was caught by Lord Manners and just beaten on the post. I may be wrong, but always thought that his offer to take the Quorn was not from any desire to become a "M.F.H.", and was only because the country at the moment required a helping hand. The previous mastership had provided extraordinary [sic] good sport, and had been favoured with a succession of seasons that had few really bad scenting days. Scent is a problem that no one has yet satisfactorily solved, and the greater the experience the more difficult it appears, but there is no doubt Leicestershire gives better results when very wet.

Lord Manners came into office at the beginning of the dry time, and scent was very moderate during his first season, with only a slight improvement in the second. Some people may think that the showing of sport should be a master's chief consideration, but to my mind his first duty is to preserve harmonious relations between those who hunt and the occupiers of land.

Although this (1884–85) was considered very moderate, I come to the conclusion, after going through my old *Field* accounts, that it was much better than many we have had of later years. November was a particularly good scenting month, and there were some first-class runs. On the 6th of that month the Quorn had an exceptionally nice run in the afternoon from Barkby Holt over an ideal bit of country, but not very straight. About five-and-forty minutes, beginning not too well, but the pace increasing at every field and hounds running into their fox at the finish. The following day the Cottesmore had a brilliant twenty-five minutes from the Long Spinney, going through Burbidge's, skirting Melton, and killing near the railway short of Sanham.

I have a vivid recollection of the next Monday with the Quorn, and as I recall various incidents of the run, I begin to wonder if the foxhound of to-day has the working and scenting qualities of his ancestors. On this occasion I remember being filled with admiration at the hounds' performance. In the earlier part of the run they raced along with the dash and drive for which they were celebrated, but later on, with a failing scent and a beaten fox, they puzzled out the line until they ran him from scent to view. He was also an extraordinary stout old fox, though not very straight-necked, and a weaker member would have probably succumbed after the first twenty-five minutes.

Those initial minutes were, I remember, great fun, as after finding in Ragdale Wood and running through the gorse, we crossed the Fosse, swung left-handed and raced down the valley to Seagrave. Here the fox had hoped to find an open drain, but being disappointed turned back to his starting-point, and by some clever dodging managed to get well ahead of the pack. They, however, worked up to him and were on good terms again at Ragdale village, but he succeeded in giving them the slip, and made his last effort in the Hoby Vale.

It was not a really good scenting day, and the smell of a fox grows less as his strength weakens, so that hounds had to put their noses down and work hard; but they were ably assisted by their huntsman, and the final triumph was due to the combination—that mutual trust and confidence which always existed between Firr and his pack.

This was only one of many instances of the great huntsman's skill, patience and perseverance.

In later days I have heard men who had not enjoyed the privilege of hunting with Firr remark, "Of course he never stopped to hunt a fox, but directly hounds threw up their heads, galloped on to the nearest covert," and they will also innocently inquire: "Isn't it true that more than half the good gallops of the Quorn were after Firr and not after a fox?" These slanders have probably originated from men who had an occasional day with the Quorn, and were either too badly mounted or had not the ability to ride in the front rank. They would then return to their provincial packs, and speak in an authoritative voice of what they had never been in a position to see. Jealousy would seize eagerly on such baseless information, and use it in the endeavour to belittle the art of an acknowledged master of his craft. I think the silly idea that a run with the Quorn was frequently only a gallop after Firr, must have had its birth in one of his marvellous casts.

If a fox had evidently got a long way ahead, and with a moderate scent there appeared every likelihood of the gap growing wider, he would catch hold of the pack and make a forward cast of perhaps half a mile to a mile. In making these casts he would ride straight across country to the point he expected to get on terms with his fox again, and it was very seldom that he did not succeed in hitting off the line. I can imagine the visitor and what he would say on seeing Firr with his pack behind him, sailing over a succession of big fences.

It may perhaps have been quite true that on these occasions the bulk of the field and those who are content to ride across country with only the back of the man in front to guide them, never realized that hounds were not running.

When, however, a fox had been hustled sufficiently to make

it reasonable to expect he would be getting tired, Firr would never willingly relinquish pursuit, and would bring him to hand in the end.

The art of a huntsman is in knowing when to lift hounds and when to let them hunt. You may be quite sure that a pack which won't bear being lifted has no confidence in its huntsman.

The trust and sympathy which his pack had for Firr was plain to be seen; they knew they would not be deceived, and if he helped them, it would be help in the right direction.

A hound is a reasoning animal, which added to intuition or instinct enables him to gauge fairly accurately the capabilities of the man who presumes to assist him in hunting.

Anyone with a love for animals, and who also takes the trouble to make their acquaintance, can gain the affection of a pack of hounds, but it does not in the least follow that they will allow their love to blind them to his defects in the field.

I seem to be meandering from my text, which was a summary of Lord Manners' second and last season, but the subject of Tom Firr always works up the old enthusiasm and admiration I felt for the man when hunting with him. Having begun I may as well continue, although he carried the horn for many seasons afterwards. He was very quick, but never in a hurry. Very quiet, but had a beautiful voice, and his cheer would always put new life into a pack. In provincial countries where there is no crowd, you can perhaps afford to stand outside a covert and blow your horn until nearly all the pack are out, but in the Shires you must get after your fox as quickly as possible. My own opinion is that unless hounds are running another fox, they ought to be out of covert as quickly as the huntsman and should therefore never be waited for. A hound hates to be left behind.

Tom Firr always kept in touch with his pack whilst in covert, and to see them flying out in reply to his cheer was a sight not to be forgotten when once seen. He never looked back, but galloped on blowing his horn, and though he might have started with only one or two couple, every hound would be there before they were out of the first field. Perhaps it may have been in their anxiety not to be left behind that made the Quorn rather weak in the matter of drawing—it was the one bad point. Every huntsman has his own idea or feeling as to what quarter of a covert a fox is likely to be in, and the feeling is frequently influenced by previous experience in that covert; hounds will be inclined to search more diligently where they have previously found, and neglect a part where they have never met with success.

In the short winter days you cannot afford to waste time in drawing unlikely spots, and Firr was doubtless right in trying where he had found before, which, when blank, he would leave quickly to try elsewhere.

The finding of a fox always interested me, and if I saw that Firr had missed a spot which in my mind was likely, I frequently tried it myself. My success on these occasions was probably due to having studied the habits of the fox. I hardly ever remember finding in a covert after the Belvoir had drawn it. I recall one occasion with the Quorn when, had it not been for my officious interference, we should have missed a very good gallop.

It was a bright, sunny afternoon towards the end of March, and with only moderate sport in the morning the order was given for Burrough Hill Wood as a last chance. This covert has changed its appearance since then very considerably, the old trees on the hill above have been cut down and others planted below. At that time the new addition was in two stages of growth, one having been planted about five years, and the other only the previous autumn.

There was good covert in the wood above, and we had always found there, so that Firr confined his attentions to the thick covert above and left the lower part alone. Foxes are very fond of lying in the sun, and will often not move if they think they will not be observed. The young larch were barely three feet high, but the ground had been taken from an arable field, and there was good lying on the dry twitch grass. Firr had aready blown hounds out of covert, when it seemed to me he had missed the most likely spot, and I rode in to search amongst the young trees. A fox was there sure enough, and gave us a most enjoyable gallop before killing him at Owston Wood.

This is, however, getting ahead too fast, and we have not yet finished with Lord Manners' mastership. On 21st November the Cottesmore had another good run from the Long Spinney, and scored a seven-mile point, but on this occasion failed to catch their fox. They lost him eventually at Wartnaby, in the Quorn country, after running through a large slice of the Belvoir. It was a very unusual line, and I remember uncomfortably stiff, but the pace was very good for the first thirty minutes, and it takes an exceptionally awkward obstacle to stop a Leicestershire field when hounds are running fast.

That bit of country between Thorpe Arnold and Melton was, in those days, fenced with "Oxers", a type of fence that wants a bold and resolute horse to negotiate, with the same qualities in his rider.

The Cottesmore Saturday on the Melton side was as popular then as it is now, and always attracted a large crowd. For some reason the ladies favoured this day, and you could be certain of seeing them in greater numbers than at any other fixture of the week. Perhaps there may have been a little rivalry between the fair supporters of the three different hunts. Every one on that particular day was bent on getting as close to hounds as they could (men and women alike, but I recall seeing Mr.

"Granny" Farquhar frequently at the head of affairs, and sailing over the Melton Brook). He in those days hailed from the Cottesmore side, and though a fairly regular attendant on the Quorn Fridays, was seldom seen with the Belvoir.

No one enjoyed a ride more, and his beaming smile at the close of a fast burst in which he had participated did one good to see. I don't know that I ever saw anyone get hotter, when the hounds ran, and the man who does not get hot under those circumstances is either not keen, or has something wrong with him.

Whilst we are talking about the Cottesmore I should mention that Mr. W. Baird was then master and Neal huntsman. A very excellent master he was, and I regret to say that he has died lately. He was very quiet with his field, and for that reason when he did speak his order was immediately obeyed.

If he saw a gateway to which the over-eager and impetuous crowd were surging with the pack evidently about to throw up in the field beyond, he would block the exit with his horse and remain there sphinx-like until the situation was clear again.

I hardly think he cared much about competing with the hard riding crew in a fast burst, but he was a fine horseman and ready to jump a big fence when necessary.

Perhaps what he enjoyed most was to act as his own second whip, and by riding forward get a view of a beaten fox. His brother, Mr. Ned Baird—he may be a general now—was a first-class man to hounds, a good rider, with nice hands. He was one of the select few you could always be sure of seeing in the first flight, and at that time was a regular attendant at the meets in the Melton circle. Leicestershire has not seen him for some years, and I presume he has forsaken the hunting field.

November appears to have been about the best month of the season, and then sport shut down for a time, but the Quorn had a very fast gallop from King's Gorse on 21st December.

Lord Manners

Referring to my *Field* letter, which brings back the scene as it was, I read, "Dig your spurs in and hustle along if you want to see any of the fun. There is a ravishing scent, and the Quorn bitches are racing. Four or five smooth fields are skimmed over, and the half-dozen who get the best start jump into the road at Willoughby. A score or so of good men are flitting along in the wake of the pack. A bend to the right, and unless you are quick over the next fence you will lose your place. Monsieur is darting in and out of the small enclosures like a will-o'-the-wisp, whilst a well-known man between the flags is cutting out the work on a grey."

The first of these was Mr. Emile Deschamps, who had been a regular visitor to Melton a few years earlier and was a good man across Leicestershire, being also desperately keen. He must have spent a small fortune in silk hats, as whenever hounds ran fast you might be sure of seeing him bare-headed. I remember an old flea-bitten grey named "Bob Ridley" that carried him well in many good hunts. I believe this gallop was the last occasion he appeared in Leicestershire, but have no idea whether he is still alive.

The steeplechase rider was Mr. Charlie Cunningham, one of the hardest men and cheeriest of comrades to ride a hunt with. He was very strong and resolute, but with rather heavy hands, which, however, he usually neutralized by riding with a snaffle.

His strength and determination probably won him many chases, although when he first began to ride between the flags report said he caused amusement to the crowd. This, however, does him all the more credit, for it is very seldom that a man who has previously done little riding can take up the steeplechase game when past his first youth and become proficient at it.

I regret to say he is another of the good men who have "gone

West" and without attaining his highest ambition, which was to win the Grand National. My memory is very bad, but I think he was second on "Why Not?"

The last day of November—having given an account of a gallop in December it will be said I am "running heel"—the Quorn had a most enjoyable burst in their Monday country. Here is an extract from my account to the *Field*:

"Run number two, though short and ringing, was a very brilliant burst. Thirty minutes and a kill in the open afford sufficient eulogy and requires no further comment. The field had become scattered at the close of the first run—second horses, coffee-housing, and loitering, each occupying some attention. So that when Firr proceeded to draw Grimstone Gorse there was only a small mustering in the ride. The fox was soon away through Saxelby Wood and pointing for Wartnaby.

"If you are in the cover at starting you will have to gallop your hardest or be left a long way in the rear. Fortune favours you if you bear slightly to the right; the pack hesitate for a second, then swing down across your front. A post-and-rail fence stretches across the field, but it is low, and a score of horses clear or rap it in as many different places. A gap in the corner is the only possible exit from this field in the right direction, so there is nothing for it but to wait your turn in patience. The next obstacle is the well-known bottom which runs down the valley from Wartnaby. There is a bridge on the left, but to scramble through in the wake of hounds is feasible—both take about the same time. The pack reach the Asfordby Road by themselves and for a moment dwell there. A man with his hat up catches Firr's eye down to the right, and hounds are going again faster than ever. Over the tunnel and flashing by Saxelby village they race along the tree-belted brook for the Shoby Lane. Some turnip pullers have turned the fox a yard or two from his course, but the pack don't waver an instant, doubling short up the hedgerow as their quarry doubled and then chasing across the open again for Shoby village. Another second or two and fox and hounds are rolling and tumbling together in the ditch by the roadside.

"To run a fox to death in thirty minutes is a creditable performance, but particularly so in this case when there was only half a good scent. Mr. Simpkin, junior, on his grey pony was, as usual, well to the fore throughout; it is difficult to say which is the most wonderful—the pony or the rider."

The Belvoir were out of luck in the earlier part of the season, but they commenced getting their fair share of sport after the January frost and snow. On Wednesday, 17th February, they had a brilliant burst from Coston covert to Woodwell Head, where the fox managed to slip away unseen, and the run faded out at Saxby. Then they went on to draw Newman's Gorse, found and ran very fast to Goadby by Bullamore, from whence it was slow hunting to Harby Hills. Here most of the field were hopelessly left as the pack slipped down into the vale and raced away at top speed with only about half a dozen men in attendance. The canal between Hose and Harby was too much for a tired fox, and he turned back for the hills, to be eventually killed near Eastwell.

The following Saturday the same pack had a still better day. Fifty sterling minutes in the best of the vale with hounds racing, and it takes a good horse to live with the Belvoir when there is a scent. It was certainly only a ring, but it was over a perfect line, and if we had not landed back at Holwell Mouth with its unmistakable features, the majority would never have realized it was a circle. Here is a cutting from my *Field* article of the first twenty minutes:

"Belvoir in luck again! Wednesday was a good day's sport, but Saturday was better. Fifty merry minutes in the vale, a lovely country and a rattling scent. The maddening music, as it rose and fell from the throats of the descendants of Rockwood, Fallible, & Co., is still ringing in my ears, and I hasten to jot down first impressions ere the blood cools.

"Imagine yourself, reader, perched on the hill that commands the cover known as Holwell Mouth, your luncheon consumed, your second horse mounted, and you, 'full of beans and benevolence' for the world at large. A single hound gives the note that proclaims a find, followed very soon by a chorus from the pack. One turn round the cover, and the fox breaks away in view; hounds are out on his line in a twinkling, and dashing up the steep hillside.

"Now then, reader, if you wish to see the fun you must hustle through the first gate or two and gallop your hardest. Check not your steed as you reach Clawson Thorns, for the pack touch not the cover, but are racing like distraction up the narrow ride and out beyond. A short turn on the hill, and then down we go into the vale. The village of Long Clawson is in front, but a bend to the right leaves it a quarter of a mile on our left. The vale *par excellence* is now before us; good sound grass, bounded by fair leapable fences that may be taken anywhere and everywhere. The pack are 'streaking it' across the level like pigeons, and two hundred horsemen are thundering in their wake. Already grief is general; loose horses are careering everywhere, and the cracking of timber is heard on all sides. A field of plough, over which hounds skim and horses flounder, is quickly left behind, and then we turn to the left and gallop down the road for Hose. Skirting the village the pace increases, the fun becoming fast and furious. In and out of a lane, some quick, recurring fences and an ugly bottom bars the way. One division is wide on the right, and hit the bottom, where a friendly bridge solves the difficulty. A hatless horseman is to be seen with a clear lead of his followers, cutting out the work in the rear of the pack, and an army of 'top-sawyers' come crashing on behind him. Hold hard, gentlemen! Hounds are at fault, and here we are at Hose Gorse twenty minutes from the find."

Gillard was, of course, at that time huntsman to the Belvoir, and continued to carry the horn for another twelve seasons. Recalling this run to memory brings back to me Gillard's reply to my remark whilst I was riding alongside of him, "A good enough scent to-day, Frank." His answer was, "Oh, not too good, but the Belvoir hounds make their scent", which meant they had the nose and drive to make the most of what scent there was. This was rather characteristic of the man, for he loved his pack, and had a great belief in them. I do not think any man ever worked harder or lived a more strenuous life, for at that period he was hunting hounds five and six days, had the whole kennel management in his hands, and in addition was doing work usually performed by a hunt secretary. Sometimes he had very long distances to ride home, but however late he might be, he always wrote the Duke an account of the day's proceedings.

Every master and huntsman in England considered it a duty as well as a pleasure to visit the Belvoir kennels, but no one ever arrived there except to find hounds and kennels in first-rate order.

Gillard never spared himself, and though he was always considerate of the men under him, they had plenty of work to get through before they went to bed. As a huntsman he could not, of course, compare with Tom Firr, but I have never yet seen anyone who could. Still, I had many happy days with him, and have seen him hunt a fox very skilfully, more particularly in the late afternoon.

In those days the Belvoir—I am speaking of the Melton side—had what I consider a very bad practice. Every small covert had an artificial earth which was never "stopped" on hunting days, with the result that foxes almost invariably ran from one covert to another. This fact was probably responsible for the habit Gillard acquired of casting to a covert, when, if it was unsuccessful in hitting the line of his own fox, he was fairly sure of finding another in the earth.

When I say the earths were not "stopped", that, of course, means overnight, but they would be "put to" in the morning, so that any foxes using them would be underground. It is perhaps a custom that ensures a find, but it is not productive of real sport.

I have delved more than I intended into my *Field* contributions to show that this season had a very fair average of good runs, and, to continue, find the last fortnight showed capital sport for all three packs.

On 3rd April the Belvoir had a very good run from Sherbrook's covert to Lodge-on-the-Wolds, portions of which were very fast. Then on Friday the 9th, the Quorn had a first-class run from Scraptoft Gorse, and killed their fox close to South Croxton village. For some unexplainable reason I can recall every incident of that day in spite of the lapse of time, and can see now the big yellow fox as he went away in the direction of Houghton. It was near that village hounds commenced to run fast, and then after pointing for the Coplow they swung round by Carver's Spinney and raced down the valley under Ingarsby. Soon after passing this place they turned sharp to the right to cross the railway, and at that moment up came a train. The engine-driver promptly applied his brakes, and what looked like a certain disaster was happily averted, but it was a very near thing. In my account after this escape I read, "Garnet's dark sides are to be seen leading up the furrow in the big grass field rising from the brook to the Coplow-Keyham road." I recall that bitch Garnet, and remember to have frequently seen her at the head of affairs. She was a very dark-coloured hound, and, when going fast, her ears had a way of flapping up and down. The farthest point in the run was Queniborough from whence the fox turned back to meet his death.

I believe this day was the last occasion that my old friend Mr. Edward Frewen of Cold Overton appeared in the hunting field, and he lent his horse to Firr to finish the run. The ground was very deep that day, and any horse that had carried its owner near hounds was pretty well beat.

The Cottesmore finished the season on 10th April with two very fast gallops, fifteen minutes from Wild's Lodge to Burbidge's, and twenty minutes from Berry's Gorse to Cold Overton.

Chapter VI

Captain Warner

Season 1886–1887

I look back on this Mastership as being the period I enjoyed most, although I have had many happy days before and since.

Perhaps it was that the joy of youth was then at its zenith, and to get on the right side of a fence was more important than the chances of a fall. I can remember we had some rattling good gallops during the cub-hunting of that season in spite of summer-like weather.

On 2nd October the Cottesmore met at a very early hour to rattle up the cubs in Ranksboro Gorse, but for some reason they were not to be found. A litter was supposed to be at Knossington, but only an old fox was discovered and hounds were stopped from him near Pickwell. It was then about 12 o'clock, and with a hot sun the chances of doing anything seemed very remote; but after Mr. Frewen had given the hunt officials refreshment, every one appeared to become more cheerful, and as a litter had been bred in the earth near America Spinney, it was worth going there on the way back to kennels.

The master was not out, and the decision therefore lay with the huntsman, Neal. What the liquor was that the butler handed round I have no idea, but it appeared to put new life into poor old Neal, who had probably breakfasted about four o'clock.

Until that day I did not even know the Spinney was called America, and it is only a very little place, but being far away from roads it does not get disturbed. I do not think we were more than half a dozen, including hunt servants, but the irresponsible portion, of course, hoped for a gallop. If the cubs had been there as they ought to have been, good work would have been done, and probably one or two killed, but there was only an old fox. The spinney is on the banks of a stream, which further on helps to form the noted Whissendine, and the fox elected to leave on the opposite side to the whip, so that he had no chance of stopping hounds; he did his best, but he was never within a field of them until the run was over. It was one of the best and fastest gallops I ever remember. Hounds were racing for five-and-twenty minutes without the semblance of a check. What fun it was! The fox followed the stream nearly to Whissendine, and then swung up to the left. The leaf was still on, and I have a vivid recollection of many hairy obstacles at the back of Noel Arms before recrossing the turnpike, but there was no time to pick and choose your place.

At the end of twenty-five minutes we found ourselves at the Punchbowl, and unluckily with several foxes afoot.

Fortunately for me my horse was very fit from having spent his summer in drawing a grass-cutter. He was one that Mr. "Buck" Barclay gave me, and this was the first occasion I had ridden him in a gallop.

On 18th October the Quorn had a most enjoyable scurry from Baggrave to Hungarton by way of Carr Bridge, and the whole distance was accomplished in thirteen minutes.

The 25th of the month the same pack met at Gaddesby Hall, when, except for the absence of scarlet, it might have been a meet of the regular season. The trees and hedges were also still in their summer dress. I remember that morning thirty-three years ago as well as if it was yesterday. The morning was bright and pleasant, with just a touch of east in the wind. Every one was in the best of spirits and full of cheery good humour.

We found our fox in Mr. Cheney's Long Spinney, and for thirty golden minutes were racing over one of the stiffest lines in Leicestershire. It is a bit of country in which even when hedges are bare you must be in the same field with the hounds to see them, but with everything still in leaf, if you lose sight of the pack, you may never see them again. It was really a large field for October, and I think all enjoyed that gallop, but only a very small minority saw a hound from find to finish. The gallop was crammed full of excitement, incidents and fences. After all it was only a ring, and at the end of the thirty minutes we were back at the starting-point; but the delirious joy of riding to hounds when they run fast is not to be measured by the hand of time or gauged by the distance covered. On this occasion there were several Americans out, who had come to Melton for the season, and they were the forerunners of many welcome visitors from the same country. The Belvoir also in that same week had an excellent run from Sproxton Thorns. The fox was such a long time in leaving covert that every one made sure it was a cub, and after being well hustled it did not seem likely he could last long in the open. The result was several men rather took liberties with their horses and had to be content with a position in the rear before the end of forty-five minutes, when hounds killed. Saltby church, Buckminster Park and the finish at Coston does not spell out a very good line, but the beginning and the end was over as nice a country as the most fastidious could desire.

The cub-hunting season should always be looked upon as a time when the master's only consideration is the making of his hounds and the visiting of his coverts. We, the onlookers, are only there on sufferance, and these rehearsals are not for our amusement; but we can't be blamed if a run does come off occasionally, and, of course, enjoy it all the more for being unexpected.

There were some very cheery mornings that October, and I should like to see a repetition of those gallops; but suppose age might prevent me participating in them with quite the same spirit as of yore.

I had almost forgotten the last day's cubbing with the Quorn, which contained a really first-class run. An excellent country to ride over, hounds running fast with hardly a check, and a seven-mile point, are features that give character to a hunt at any period of the season.

The usual business-like morning, a litter roused, a cub killed, and others hunted in small circles, did not appeal to those who wanted a gallop, but the master elected to try Walton Thorns on the way to kennels. The litter here had been hunted on a previous occasion, and the fox we found this time I feel sure was a cub; but two or three fields away is Cradock's Ashes, and it was there I believe we changed on to an old fox. Up to that point hounds had run as if there was little scent, but they quickly changed their tune then, so much so that they were into Mundy's Gorse before the majority of the field knew they had gone.

A bend to the right gave those who were quick a chance of making up leeway, and then for fifteen minutes we were galloping best pace over an ideal country.

The remainder of the run was by no means slow, the pack occasionally having to put their heads down and then driving on again; but they were never at fault for long, and horses had all they could do to keep with them. He must have been an exceptionally bold fox, as he never condescended to enter a covert until, too weary to go farther, he turned aside and found refuge in the main earth at Welby Osierbeds, but I firmly believe that Melton Spinney was his point. From Walton Thorns to the plantation belt south of Ab-Kettleby, known locally as the Cat's Tail, the line was nearly straight, the only deviation being to avoid Lord Aylesford's and Grimstone Gorse. Such a good fox every one said deserved to live, and doubtless they were right, but I fear my sympathies were with hounds, and they certainly deserved their fox.

In looking over my account of the run I come across this sentence. "A momentary check below Wartnaby collected the scattered field, but Old Dorcas' feathery stern was seen disappearing up the opposite hedgeside, and the rest of the pack were soon with her." I remember that old bitch well, and she helped Firr kill many a fox. She was one of the light-coloured sort that the craze for Belvoir tan has almost made extinct, but in those days there were several of the colour in the Quorn kennel, and they always showed up when scent was bad. I imagine the crowd at Peterborough Hound Show would be shocked if any pack were bold enough to show a light-coloured hound now, but the Quorn "Dreamer" won the cup (1888), and he was that colour.

I walked "Dreamer" myself, but never quite liked him or his sire the Rufford "Galliard", in spite of the fact that he was out of "Dorcas". If my memory is not at fault both Gillard and Firr used the Rufford "Galliard", being attracted by beautiful legs and feet with great bone, but I fancy neither were pleased with the results.

Kirby Gate, the Quorn opening meet, does not appear to have been productive of much sport, but the Belvoir had a very fast gallop on the following Wednesday. It was, I remember, a typical Belvoir burst, hounds racing, a few happy men near them, and the rest of the field struggling to overcome the disadvantages of a slow beginning.

Captain Warner

Referring to my account, I read, "Count and Cornet are striving for the lead, and are cutting out the work for the rest." The former was Count Zbrowski, and the latter Capt. F. Forester—not a captain then—who has lately resigned the Quorn Mastership. This was, of course, before he had the accident to his leg, which affected his grip of the saddle, and he was very hard to beat across country. I hear he was going as well as ever last season, hunting hounds himself and always with them. Yet it is over thirty years since that day from Sproxton Thorns with the Belvoir.

I cannot remember now the exact year Count Zbrowski came to Melton, or how many seasons he was there before migrating to the Atherstone country, but can recall his face and figure in many good hunts during the next five years. His hunting education had been begun in America amid the stiff timber of Long Island, where the drag plays a prominent part. With all due apologies to my many friends across the water, I must here say that they begin the education of the fox-hunter from the wrong standpoint. The fence and the getting over it appears to come first, whereas they should only be looked upon as affording additional pleasure and excitement to following hounds.

Count Zbrowski in this school acquired the knowledge and ability to cross a country which with his naturally fine hands enabled him to find his way across Leicestershire. It was not known until he had gained considerable experience in the neighbourhood of Melton that he developed the habit of watching the hounds, and now let me say that no one can become a really first-class man without keeping his eye on the pack. Without providing anything sensational, November was a month of consistent good sport, and scent improved towards the end. There was one day when the Quorn hounds had a ring in the Hoby Vale practically to themselves, that is, no horseman was within a field of them; and there in the same week the Belvoir had a very fast gallop from Piper Hole Gorse.

It was an afternoon run, and I remember when the covert was drawn only an hour's daylight remained. The morning crowd had gone home to tea, and there were scarcely a score left, but I remember one lady, who, if my memory does not deceive me, was Lady Gerard—"Mrs." then.

How we shivered on that hilltop and wondered if we had been wise to remain, with perhaps a lingering lament for the poached eggs and buttered toast. "Gone away" dispelled the gloom in an instant, and the shivering onlookers were converted next minute into glowing performers.

For five-and-twenty minutes we were galloping over the vale, with the pack racing on and horses striving to keep them in sight.

The inevitable result of drawing late is that you have to stop hounds when they might kill their fox, and this is what happened that evening; but it was a hot and happy little band of sportsmen who rode back to Melton in the dark. Most of them are, I expect, dead by now, but if any are still alive they will easily recall that gallop. It is such a long time ago that I can't say now who they were, but Lord Henry Bentinck was one of the party, and he is still flourishing, though nowadays he appears to prefer a seat at Westminster to one in the saddle.

These memoirs will not contain the name of any lady who is still alive, but I shall reserve the right of mentioning those who are not now competitors on the stage of life. There are any number of women whom I have had the pleasure of seeing ride brilliantly across Leicestershire, and many of them first-rate riders, but very few who could keep their eyes on hounds and at the same time take their own line.

The only two I can think of at the moment are the Duchess of Hamilton and Mrs. Bunbury. Lady Gerard, although not attempting to cut out the work, was a very fine horse-woman and exceptionally keen. About this period I can recall seeing her nearly always one of the last to leave hounds, and a certain starter in a Belvoir late afternoon gallop.

Gillard was ever ready to draw a covert if there was any light left and anyone was anxious to go on. Frequently we found ourselves riding to hounds when it was impossible to see a fence until we were close to it; but these little things added to the excitement and fun. I fear we did not always consider that in thus giving us pleasure, he at the same time gave himself a much longer day, and whilst we could clatter home at a good pace, he had to collect his pack and jog slowly back to kennels.

I cannot explain it or give any reason, but the Belvoir hounds at this period always seemed in better form in the afternoon than in the morning, more particularly the big dog pack.

The Cottesmore had a very good run on 20th November from Ranksboro, killing their fox in an hour and twenty minutes.

Had the fox chosen a straight line this would have ranked as one of the great historic runs, and there would have been very few to see the end. In spite of being able to cut corners, there were hardly any horses could raise a gallop at the finish, and I remember hounds had it all to themselves for the last few fields to Brannstone village.

The run did not start until about three o'clock, and for the first half-hour hounds could only hunt, so that by the time we reached Oakham the fox had established a long lead; but Neal allowed his pack to work it out for themselves, and they gradually increased their pace.

It was somewhere between Lady Wood and Knossington that horses were asked to gallop fast. From that point up to Ridlington there was never a chance of easing up or drawing rein, and if you know the country you will realize there is not a more severe line in Leicestershire. According to my account, I estimated that though it was only a five-mile point, hounds must have covered at least fifteen.

These are items I have chosen haphazard from the November records of a season that was supposed to be only moderate, and each month brought some good gallops. Early in December the Quorn had an excellent hunting run from the patch of gorse outside the Coplow, and though they ran into the Cottesmore woodlands with several fresh foxes afoot, they stuck to the hunted one, and finally killed him in Brown's Wood. It was not a pleasant run to ride, as from the first the fox chose that rugged hillside which leads to Large's Spinney, and then after leaving Tilton, we became swallowed in the chain of woods. It was another triumph for Firr, and showed that his skill was as good in woodland as it was in the open.

Near the end of December there was a very fast scurry from Hose Thorns to Piper Hole Gorse—a real Belvoir burst. In the serious business of fox-hunting these bursts ought to be considered of no account unless they are the preliminaries to runs that attain definite ends; but whilst the blood of youth glows in our veins, we must indeed be miserable beings if a foremost position in a quick thing does not stir us up to frenzy. It is possible to compress a lifetime of mad excitement into a few seconds, when you are on the back of a good horse and hounds are racing.

I can't remember how or why it was that a hard-riding field were left, but on this occasion only four fortunate individuals saw the gallop, and by that I mean were in the same field with hounds. My recollections of leaving the covert are dim and indistinct, but recall myself one of a happy little band when some two or three fields away. The pack then suddenly settled down to run, and if the Belvoir go their best pace, it needs a good horse to keep with them.

Captain Warner

The chase had at first pointed for Clawson, which may have induced the crowd to keep the road instead of taking the initial plunge into the fields. It was just their misfortune that hounds should have suddenly started to run at the moment they were temporarily out of sight, but it was equally good luck for those who happened to be with them.

There was no time to pick your place in a fence and you had to accept everything as it came, for to diverge a yard from the straight line would have been fatal to your position. That brilliant amateur between the flags, Capt. Roddy Owen, mounted on one of Mr. Gardiner Muir's best, was thoroughly enjoying himself; Mr. Gradwell, a temporary visitor to the Shires, was having the ride of his life; whilst Downes, rough-rider to Mr. Julius Behrens and a superb horseman, was carving out a route with his usual skill. Each rode his own line and took his fences as fate presented them. After crossing the Hose-Clawson Road, hounds bore somewhat to the left, and shortly afterwards another road was encountered.

First one and then the other of the four would gain a slight advantage, but there was nothing in it. My good fortune enabled me to beat the others into the second road by a few lengths, and I marked my place out—the only place in a bullfinch. Whilst I was on the left the others were to the right of the pack, and before them the bullfinch became a low cut hedge. My joy and pride at the position I had secured met with the reverse it deserved, and I was doomed for the remainder of the gallop to a back seat.

At the moment my horse was about to jump out of the road, a hound slipped back into the ditch, which was both deep and steep. The two or three attempts to climb up before she succeeded could only have occupied a few seconds at the most, but it was sufficient to lose me my place, and I was thenceforth a good half field behind Capt. Roddy to Piper Hole Gorse. I think there was a slight element of competitive jealousy in the air that day, and the desire to be first into every field was very marked.

There was a lot of frost in January, and very little hunting, but a partial thaw during the last week gave hounds a chance of being taken out. Unfortunately the Quorn made a start from Barkby-Holt, and in that district found some hedge-sides with frost still in the ground. The result was a broken collar-bone for Firr, and hounds having to be content with the first whip for three weeks.

Fred Earp was a first-class whip, and assisted Firr for many seasons. He was always in the right place, and ready to turn hounds when wanted. I never had the pleasure of hunting with the South Notts, when in later years he helped Lord Harrington, and cannot therefore say what ability he showed, but a good whip does not always mean success as a huntsman. I always had a very high opinion of Fred Earp as a whip, but did not think that he would be equally good with the horn. He rather lacked initiative and dash, though no one could have been quicker in following Firr over a country, and it was very seldom that he was left behind. In the period referred to when Firr was laid up, I remember one very long day which I thought should have finished with blood; but it is hardly fair to judge a man by what he did on a solitary occasion. After two exceptionally hard runs in the morning, a fox was found in Ragdale Wood about three o'clock. There was a wide left-handed ring to start with in the direction of Wymeswould, and extending nearly to Burton. Most of the time hounds were running a good pace, but several fields of plough on the return journey reduced them to slow hunting. However, they worked up to their fox at the covert they had found, and set off again with renewed vigour. A short dip into the Hoby Vale and then the pack streamed away across the big fields to Shoby

Scoles. A few minutes in this covert and then away at the lower end. There was a temporary check, Fred had the hounds at his horse's heels, and not two hundred yards away the weary fox could be seen crawling up the opposite hill.

The dusk of a winter evening was already merging into darkness, and every second was of value. Had Fred rammed his horse through the fence and given the pack a scream, they would have got a view and killed at once. Instead, he dismounted to pull out a tied-up hand-gate, and a priceless opportunity was lost. No one else was there, and I was putting the hounds to him; but seeing him get off his horse at such a moment nearly gave me a fit. The result may be imagined—a fresh fox jumping up, and the pack being with difficulty stopped in the dark.

If Fred Earp should read this, I feel sure he will forgive the criticism, as it is such a long time ago, and he is not likely to be looking for a huntsman's berth. If he had been turning hounds to Firr, and that gap had barred his way, he would have crashed through without the slightest hesitation, yet when the initiative to act was his he failed.

Not only did the Quorn lose their fox that night, but also a hound. Getting on the ice in Shoby Pool, he broke through and was drowned.

It was somewhere near the end of January in this season that about half a dozen men, thinking hounds had gone, started off on a two-mile ride across country, with the idea of catching them.

Being one of the guilty party, I can vouch for having a very enjoyable ride, though feeling at the same time rather ashamed of myself afterwards. It was a late afternoon with the Belvoir, and whilst Gillard was drawing Brentingby Spinney, the field remained on the up-wind side. There was probably a certain amount of coffee-housing, and then it suddenly dawned on us, as the buzz of conversation lulled, that not the faintest sound of Gillard's familiar voice disturbed the peaceful quietness of the afternoon. Some one said, "They've gone away," and then a sudden panic seized the cavalcade. Off we went across the turnpike at top speed, and down the valley towards Thorpe, then straight away to Melton Spinney. I think the wraiths of former hunts must have walked abroad that day, or we were all in very imaginative moods, for first one and then the other would exclaim, "Yonder they go!" and that, of course, spurred us to greater efforts.

On reaching the Spinney I happened to look back, and there was Gillard with hounds at his heels trotting quietly on the bridle-road—they had not even found.

I cannot recall any fellow culprits now, but Lord Henry Bentinck was one and Mr. Weston Jarvis another.

Frost stopped hunting for several days both in January and February, but when hounds could get out, they had some very fair sport. The Belvoir had a capital forty-five minutes, and killed their fox on 5th March, whilst the other packs did equally well. Then there was another spell of frost and snow, so that it was not till the end of the month that hunting was again in full swing.

The last week or two—we went on to the second week of April—of the season were really brilliant, and made amends for the numerous stoppages in the previous months.

The last Friday in March the Quorn had a very good run from Ragdale Wood—fifteen minutes at top speed in the Hoby Vale and the remainder at a good hunting pace. After passing Thrussington village it was rather an unusual line, as the fox followed the river nearly to Syston, crossing and recrossing several times. Turning back by Ratcliffe, it looked rather as if the run would fizzle out, but Firr persevered, and getting up to his fox in Cossington Gorse, killed him in Thrussington village.

The Belvoir on 30th March, finding a fox in Newman Gorse, ran him hard for forty minutes and killed him near Sysonby. The start was in the direction of Garthorpe, and hounds had reached the hill overlooking that hamlet before they swung to the right past Freeby village. No coverts were touched, and the fox did not even condescend to enter Melton Spinney, but bore away to Scalford, and then went on past Old Hills to his doom. Those who know this country will realize that hounds must have run a great pace to do it in forty minutes, and it was probably the best gallop of the season.

The Quorn had a very good run late in the afternoon of the 1st of April from Mr. Craddock's celebrated covert, Waltham Thorns. The weather, wind with a cold rain, had been all against hunting during the greater part of the day; but it began to clear slightly about four o'clock. I think it must have been past five when the run commenced, the majority of the field having then gone home, wet and miserable. As for us, I remember there were only about a dozen men left, but they were all triers, and not easily turned aside by the stiffest fence. Hounds were away out of the covert on the back of their fox, raced down alongside of the bottom nearly to Burton, and then, swinging left-handed, went straight away to Hoby. Thirty minutes at top speed over the finest country in the world is something to have lived for.

Unfortunately the villagers of Hoby hallooed [*sic*] us on to a fresh fox, and though hounds ran on for another forty minutes they had to be stopped, as every horse was "stone cold" and it was nearly dark.

I remember that good sportsman, Lord Harrington, was going exceptionally well amongst the big fences in the Hoby Vale, which must have seemed enormous after the South Notts country. At that time he was hunting his own hounds four and five days a week, but he liked to get an occasional day with the

Quorn, and you could always be sure that on those occasions he could hold his own with the best talent from Melton. His is yet another face that we shall miss when the hunting world reassembles, though his death was not caused by the war. I hear it was blood-poisoning through a slight cut, and it seems hard luck to be laid low by such a small thing after having hunted for forty years with numerous falls and accidents.

I do not think I ever had a day with his pack; but have always understood they hunted very well and showed excellent sport. The last time we met he offered to mount me any day I liked to fix, and that was one of the good things I had promised myself after the war.

In addition to the South Notts country, which is rather straggling, Lord Harrington accepted a slice of Quorn territory from Capt. Forester on the Forest side. For a man over his "threescore and ten" to hunt six days a week, with portions of his country lying wide apart, is a genuine proof of his keenness and marvellous constitution. I wish there were more like him, and regret that he had not a son, for England can ill afford to lose the stock from such tough fibre.

The Quorn finished the season with a brilliant seventeen minutes from Ella's Gorse, the sun shining, and in clouds of dust. That was on the 9th of April, and two days later the Cottesmore had a very enjoyable wind-up from a meet at Langham.

This was a season that was universally condemned as bad, and yet it will be seen by the extracts I have made that there were many good runs. The truth is that foxhunters are like farmers, they love grumbling, and if their sport is stopped for a week or two they forget all the fun they have enjoyed in dwelling and thinking over the few days they have missed.

1. J. Otho Paget 1860–1934.
Photograph by Elliot & Fry 1900

2. Caricature of J. Otho Paget by Cuthbert Bradley.
From *Vanity Fair*, 30 January 1902

3. Otho Paget's maternal grandmother, Mrs Otho Manners, formerly Miss Ann Singleton from a painting by Mary Martha Pearson, (Royal Pavilion, Brighton). Ann bore five children before her death in 1827 at the tragically young age of 28.

4. Thorpe Satchville Village Street, August 1919.
A watercolour by Otho Paget's sister, Geraldine Needham.

5. Thorpe Satchville Hall. A watercolour by unknown artist, mid 19th century.

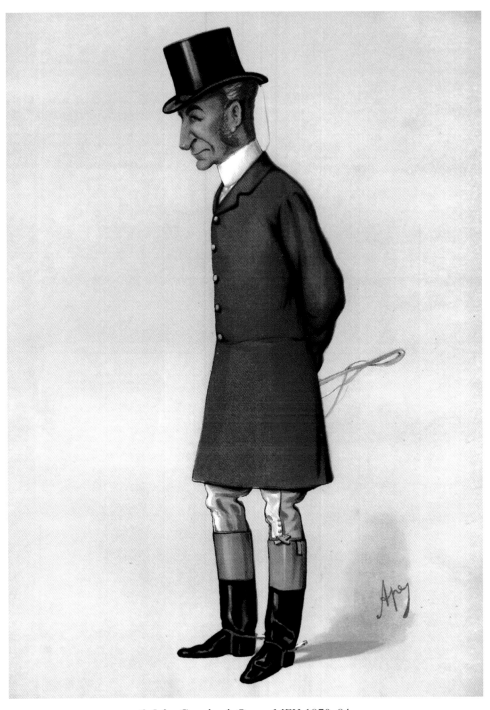

6. John Coupland, Quorn MFH 1870–84.
A caricature by Ape from *Vanity Fair*, 12 July 1884

7. Tom Firr, Huntsman of the Quorn, 1872–99.
Photographed for *The Stable* magazine 11 February 1899
Courtesy of www.quornmuseum.com

8. Tom Firr on Whitelegs. Contemporaries said he looked like a bishop and rode like a jockey.

9. Tom Firr's grave in Quorn churchyard.
Courtesy of Sue Templeman

10. The Quorn Meet at Baggrave Hall, 1881–82, hosted by the Burnaby family
Baggrave Hall still stands today, the sole surviving building of the mediaeval village of Baggrave.

11. Key to the Quorm Meet.

1   Viscount Downe
1a Miss Livingston
2   Sir Frederick Fowke, Bart.
3   Lord Manners
4   Mr. R. W. Johnson
5   Sir Frederick Johnstone, Bart., M.P.
6   Miss Burnaby
7   Mr. Evelyn Burnaby
8   Capt. Middleton

9   Mrs. Coupland
10 W. Little Gilmour, Esq., on "Forester"
11 Capt. Smith
12 Mr. Duncan Coupland
13 Earl of Wilton (the late), on "Giraffe"
14 Mrs. F. Sloane-Stanley, on "Nigger"
15 Capt. Whitmore
16 His Grace The Duke of Portland, on "Rook"

17 Major-Gen. E. S. Burnaby, M.P.
18 Capt. Boyce, on "Dove"
19 John Coupland, Esq., on "Forester"
20 A. C. Barclay, Esq., on "Ilston"
21 T. Turner Farley, Esq.
22 Tom Firr (Huntsman)
23 Earl of Lanesborough
24 Capt. E. P. Elmhirst
25 Earl of Wilton, on "Besique"

26 William Chaplin, Esq., on "Kathleen"
27 Miss Webster
28 Julius Behrens, Esq., on "Blue Ruin"
29 Ernest Chaplin, Esq., on "Grey Fox."
30 Isabella, Countess of Wilton, on "Snowdrop"
31 Countess of Wilton on "Hanky Panky"
32 Col. The Hon. H. Forester
33 Capt. The Hon. H. H. Molyneux

12. Capt W. P. Warner, Quorn MFH 1886–93.
From *Bailey's Monthly Magazine*.

13. Frank Gillard, Huntsman for the Belvoir 1860–98.

14. Lord 'Hoppy' Manners on Seaman. Winner of the Grand National 1882.
Quorn MFH 1884–86.
Artist unknown.

15. The Melton Midnight Steeplechase, 10 March 1890.
From an engraving by Mr H. Zigomala, published in the *Graphic*.

16. Lady Augusta Fane.
Instigator of the Melton Midnight Steeplechase, 10 March 1890.

17. Mr A. E. Burnaby.
Winner of the Melton Midnight Steeplechase.

18. Capt James Burns Hartopp.
Quorn MFH 1898–1905.
Painting by Sir Arthur Stockdale Cope RA
Courtesy of Leicestershire County Council Museums Service

19. Capt Frank Forester.
Quorn MFH 1905–18.

20. The Earl of Lonsdale, Quorn MFH 1893–98.
Photographed on retirement from the Cottesmore, 1911.

21. Mary Fitzgerald, formerly Forester, riding point on Dolly.
From a painting by Heywood Hardy, 1917.

22. Anne Paget (Anne, Lady Jaffray) being 'shown'
at a Quorn Meet in 1924.

23. Anne Paget with her late father's beagles, 1934.

24. Anne Paget at Cheltenham, 1940, shortly before going to Bletchley Park.

25. Sir William Jaffray on Star at Rosie Gammon's Gymkhana, near Liss, Hants, 1963.

26. Monarch, Eugene Reynal's champion Harrier.
By Edward Megarge
American Kennel Club, New York.

27. Eugene Reynal with his beagles.

28. Capt J. Otho Paget MC with some beagles, late 1920s. *Leicester Mercury*

29. Capt J. Otho Paget MC judging beagles at the Leicester Horse Repository as his wife Gertrude looks on. *Leicester Mercury*

Chapter VII

Captain Warner

Season 1887–1888

The first incident of this season was a lawn meet at Little Dalby on the occasion of Miss Hartopp's coming of age, a lady who was destined later on to become the wife of a Quorn Master. Little Dalby is in the Cottesmore country; but as the family have been intimately connected with the Quorn for generations, representatives of both hunts were there to pay their respects. It was this season that the Quorn took back that bit of country on the Donnington side which had been lent to Lord Ferrars, and here, I may mention, it was decided to revert to the old order of things by hunting the north side of the Wreake on Mondays.

The change had been made the previous season, with, I believe, the idea of decreasing the large crowds that always attended the Quorn Fridays.

There was a fair amount of sport in November, but nothing that is worthy of being retold. It was in this month that a former master of the Quorn died, Mr. "Jack" Chaworth Musters. I was too young to remember much about his mastership, but had always heard that he was a first-class huntsman, very clever with his hounds, and as quick as lightning in getting them away on a fox. I believe he hunted the dog pack and Gillard the bitches.

Apropos of that time I remember Gillard telling me a rather

curious story of a fox which had given them several good hunts, and was lost at a certain point without them being in any way able to account for his disappearance. As far as I can recollect the fox was always found in the Bradgate district, and ran into the Atherstone country.

The last occasion was after an exceptionally good hunt which, as usual, came to an end at the same spot others had done on various occasions. Mr. Musters tried everywhere, but could not solve the mystery, and had started for home with the pack at his heels. One hound, however, Gillard noticed, was very reluctant to leave the banks of a pond, and kept on gazing into the water. He therefore got off his horse to make a closer inspection, and then found that a drain emptied into the pond several inches below the water's surface. The other end of the drain was practically sealed, but, of course, it was soon opened while Mr. Musters was called back. A terrier was put in, and the fox bolted out into the pond.

My explanation is that this pond, like most others in Leicestershire during the summer, would be nearly dry, or at most half full and that the entrance then would be well above the water. The fox must have been in the habit of using it—perhaps bred there—in dry weather, and knowing its exact position would have no difficulty in entering it under water. Foxes, as a rule, object to getting wet, and it showed memory, as well as intelligence, to have recollected the drain sloped upwards, so that after making the dive he would be able to get on dry ground again.

Sport improved in December, and there were several nice gallops, short, sharp and generally ending with a kill. On the 9th of the month the Quorn ran from Curate's Gorse to Melton, a nine-mile point, but unfortunately scent was never too good and the pace was only moderate. The fox was viewed between Melton and Welby, evidently very tired, and his subsequent escape was due solely to darkness.

At the beginning of the season the ground had been exceptionally dry, and then after a deluge of rain there were several interruptions through frost. However, there were several days, both in December and January, when hounds ran fast, but no very good run. In the second week of February all three packs had good sport, and there was generally a useful scent, which was followed by more frost and snow.

The Quorn had a seven-mile point on 11th March, but the fox eventually beat them in the back gardens of Syston. The same pack did better the following week, as after a meet at Six Hills they had two good runs, in each case killing their fox.

I remember well the 26th of the month and the excellent run we had, an hour and five minutes with a kill in the open. The Quorn were advertised to meet at Twyford at twelve o'clock, and at eleven the ground was covered with ten inches of snow. About twenty minutes later the sun came out, and by 12.30 the ground was practically clear. The master, therefore, sent out a telegram to say hounds would meet at Gaddesby at one o'clock, but unfortunately by that time the majority of Meltonians had taken train to London and missed the sport. The run was by no means straight, but you could forgive that with hounds running fast the whole time, and only about a score of people riding to them. The two Bentincks thoroughly enjoyed themselves that day.

The next week a very good run from Thrussington Gorse to Welby Osierbeds brought the Quorn season to a close, and the Belvoir finished the following Wednesday with a very fast burst from Burbidge's to Freeby Wood. In spite of it being April, hounds ran faster that day than they had run the whole season.

Season 1888–1889

The Quorn opening meet at Kirby Gate is looked upon as a general holiday by the whole of Leicestershire, and I should imagine parts of adjoining counties. Every species of vehicle is requisitioned for the occasion and a huge crowd go on foot, so that a fox has not much chance of getting a clear course. The result is that there is not usually much sport for those who ride, but occasionally the difficulties are overcome, and a fox gets away.

This year, after a short run from Gartree Hill, in which the foot people were able to join, we had a capital run from Burrough Hill Wood. Hounds slipped away with very few in attendance, and circling round Burrough village, went on to kill between Sanham and Kirby. I happened to be one of the fortunate few, and have therefore a vivid recollection of the day. The crowd is usually much too keen on the opening meet, and in their anxiety to secure a good start ride rather closer to the pack than either master or huntsman approve; but on this occasion I expect the first run had given the impression there was very little scent, and they had consequently grown slack. If hounds had not swung round under Newbold and from thence on to John o' Gaunt station, the loiterers would never have caught them, but by making use of the hard road, they were able to cut them off before embarking on the fields for Adam's Gorse.

November continued to show good sport, and there was a fair amount of rain, so that the ground which had been exceptionally dry in October was in a rideable condition. I note that the Quorn had a good gallop on the Prince of Wales'—King Edward later—birthday, and from the covert that still bears his name. Probably the majority of those who stand at Baggrave covert-side nowadays waiting for a fox to go away, do not know that it owes the name to the illustrious godfather having sprinkled gorse-seed on the ground.

I am not sure about the date, but fancy it was somewhere about 1877, when Colonel Burnaby, father of the present Quorn master, was alive. Gorse, however, does not thrive on all soils, and in spite of the royal sower, it refused to grow with the luxuriance which is necessary to hold foxes, and then, in addition, many of the young shoots were cut down by a severe frost. In 1884 the gorse was replaced by blackthorn, whitethorn and privet, which, being well planted and carefully tended, quickly grew into one of the hunt's strongest coverts. Ever since then, it has always been a sure find, and has practically a better average for good runs in the last twenty-five years than any other covert in the Quorn territory.

Another celebrated fox covert that came into prominence either this season or the next, was Adam's Gorse, an ideal spot for a fox to lie and from which to start a gallop.

In the days of Sir Richard Sutton, though not considered a sure find, it bore the reputation of harbouring good foxes, and several first-class gallops started there. A small spinney and some straggling unenclosed patches of gorse were then all that constituted a covert, but Lord Manners in the last season of his mastership enclosed about three acres at his own expense. The expense, however, was not heavy, and including fencing only amounted to £40. I have a copy of the account now. The soil was favourable to gorse, and in three years it was a certain find. The success of my efforts and the low cost gave me considerable satisfaction, so that I have always patted myself on the back when recalling it. Naturally I took all the credit to myself, and did not take it into account that both soil and season were in the main responsible for the quick growth. Lord Manners had asked me to get it done for him, and I don't know which of us took the most fatherly interest in the place, whenever it was being drawn.

I fear now it has fallen on evil days, and I hear that foxes were seldom found there during the war. The family of Underwood, who had occupied the surrounding land for over a hundred years, have left, and with them the glories of Adam's Gorse have departed.

On looking over my notes I see that this was George Gillson's first season with the Cottesmore, and it will not be out of place to quote a paragraph written then.

"Gillson, the new huntsman, appeared always to be in the right place at the right moment, whilst he seems to know when to handle hounds and when to leave them alone." This was written on about the first occasion I hunted with the Cottesmore that season, and the opinion then formed was never changed; but I have always looked upon George Gillson as the best kennel manager I knew. His hounds not only worked well, but were always fit. In my humble opinion a good pack of hounds that are really fit should require very little assistance from their huntsman. Gillson, although, of course, not such an artist as Tom Firr, was a very good huntsman, but in the latter part of his time he suffered from ill-health.

The Cottesmore had been unfortunate on the Saturdays near Melton, but 22nd December made amends for previous disappointments, and was probably the run of the season up to that date. The fox was found in Wymondham Roughs, and was pulled down in the open near Woodwell Head after an hour and ten minutes. A big loop into Belvoir country had been made before hounds swung round by Coston to Severston, where practically the first check occurred. This run established Gillson's reputation on a firm basis, and also gave him the necessary confidence. Surtees hit the mark when he put into Jorrocks' mouth on the occasion of a "sporting lector" the sentence, "A fish-tag's ware is not more perishable than a 'unts-man's fame; his skill is within the judgment of every one—cleverest fellow alive!—biggest fool going!"

The Quorn wound up the old year with a really first-class, old-fashioned hunting run. The fox was found in Gartree Hill, and after starting out on the Burton Flats, bore to the right and went fairly straight to the Fish-pond Spinney at Cold Overton. From this point he turned back, running through the Punchbowl and Burrough village to be killed near John o' Gaunt station.

Gillson had the bad luck to break his collar-bone in January, and on the 17th of the month Mr. Baird hunted hounds from a meet at Leesthorpe, killing a leash of foxes.

Firr accomplished another of those marvellous performances on the following Monday, when he hunted a twisting fox from Thrussington Gorse for fifty-five minutes with extraordinary patience and under great difficulties.

Hounds then got on better terms, and running hard for another forty minutes, killed in the open.

The Quorn had a very good run on 18th February from Curate's Gorse to Scalford; the first part, up to Little Belvoir, hounds were racing over the cream of the vale.

It may be that the Belvoir found the same fox on the Saturday following at Hose Thorns, but after giving a good run he again beat hounds in the neighbourhood of Willoughby. In the afternoon of this same day a fox from Clawson Thorns took a similar line, and was run over by a train on the railway beyond Curate's Gorse—a rather unusual happening.

Sport was good all through March, and, in fact, I think this was a really good season, probably the best since 1883–84. The Belvoir had their last day on 10th April, and though they met at the Castle for the ostensible purpose of drawing the woods, Gillard managed somehow to drift to Goadby

Bullamore. Here, it so happened, a good fox awaited us, who chose a very nice line down Chadwell Valley, and then away by Old Hills nearly to Saxelbye Wood. A capital gallop and most of it very fast, which, of course, being unexpected, was very much appreciated.

I should like here to quote some remarks culled from my *Field* notes at the close of the season, as I have seen no reason to alter the opinions there expressed, and it may help to avoid friction with our friends the farmers.

"Fox-hunting in the spring is always unsatisfactory; and though we may not like bidding goodbye to hounds, it would be better if the last of March saw the last of hunting. One day in April will often cause more unpleasantness with the occupiers of land than would a dozen days earlier in the season. Fences have been mended, fields have been rolled, and the work of the farm is in full swing."

Chapter VIII

Captain Warner

Season 1889–1890

Cub-Hunting should always be understood by the few who go out as a period which belongs entirely to the master and his staff—a rehearsal for the serious business of the season. It is not a time meant for their amusement, and they should be grateful if fortune favours them with a gallop—not look on it as something they have the right to expect. There are many different systems of pursuing cubs and teaching the young entry to hunt, but every master must be allowed to adopt the system which he considers best, without our criticism.

My own opinion is that hounds require education to hunt in the open quite as much as they do in covert, though it should not be forgotten that they very naturally prefer the former to the latter, so that a course of covert hunting is very necessary.

Where there is a litter of cubs, hounds should not be allowed to go away on an old fox, and it should be borne in mind that the old ones have usually a better scent than the cubs.

When, however, the body of the pack concentrate their attention on a cub and force him to leave covert, I think it is much the best policy to let them go, no matter how dry the ground may be or how brightly the sun may shine.

Hounds will always hunt a fox better that they have settled to in covert and driven out. A cub is much easier killed in the open. We seem to have acquired the habit in the Shires of thinking that the hunt servants must always be in the same field with the hounds.

In my humble opinion I think they would often be much better left to themselves with the huntsman watching from a distance, that is, if the young entry have learned to go to the cry. In some rough provincial counties they have to watch the pack at work from a distant hillside, or otherwise follow them entirely by sound.

Riding directly behind hounds, or too close on the flanks, is, of course, wrong at any time of the year; but extra room should always be given during cub-hunting. The master should look on his old foxes as valuable assets for providing sport in the season proper, and should not therefore knowingly pursue them during cub-hunting.

If, however, the pack do get away with an old veteran, and run some distance before they can be stopped, or before it is realized that it is no cub, I think it is best in the interest of hounds to let them continue. When this does happen the early bird feels that he really has captured the worm, and he is rewarded for many mornings of shivering at the covert-side. These remarks were occasioned by turning to my *Field* notes, and finding therein an account of a gallop in October from Cream Gorse to Quenby. Thirty-eight bright and brilliant minutes across the best of Leicestershire, finishing with a kill in the open. I well remember that morning the horse I rode, and nearly every incident in the gallop—I can recall no better at any time of the year. The actual point was five miles, and, of course, as hounds run it was much farther, so that to accomplish the whole in thirty-eight minutes was proof enough of the pace.

The fox picked out an ideal line and, though some of the fences were full of leaf, there was never anything to stop a good horse. Later in the day we had a very fast burst from Thorpe Trussels to Gaddesby Mill, so that, though it was only cub-hunting, we can look on this as a red-letter day of the season.

On the following Tuesday the Quorn had a very remarkable run in the Narborough district, and according to my notes it was an eight-mile point. Foxes had been very scarce in this district, but owing to the efforts of Mr. Rolleston—later to become Sir John—the coverts, though small, were fairly well stocked. I am not familiar with that side of the country, but the fox appears to have been found in Cosby covert and killed in Fleckney village. Firr, unfortunately, had a bad fall early in the run, when, to complicate matters, the whole field, with two exceptions, got the wrong side of the river and never saw hounds again. The exceptions were Mr. Tempest Wade and West, the second whip, and it was due entirely to their efforts that the fox was eventually killed.

Hounds had run for an hour and a half, and would have run into their fox unaided had not a shepherd headed him; but this caused a check at a critical point. However, both the professional and the amateur were determined not to be beat, and persevered for the best part of an hour, when they discovered their fox in a double hedgerow. Two very happy men then escorted the pack to kennels.

Again this season the Prince of Wales' birthday was cele-brated by a good gallop from the covert named after him at Baggrave, which is a curious coincidence, as the master never thought of it when arranging meets. Hounds raced across the grass to Thorpe Trussels, and, though a large field was out, no one was very near them.

There was an interval of bad scenting days, and then, on 23rd November, the Cottesmore had a very smart ring from Stapleford, killing their fox in the open.

This brings me to the 23rd December, when the Quorn met at Wymeswould, and the run of that day was the best I have ever seen. It was my good fortune to be riding an exceptionally stout horse, and was therefore able to keep going when others were obliged to drop out. However good a run may be, you cannot be expected to go into ecstasies over a performance you have not seen, and one is rather liable to add colour to a hunt in which you have held a good position. Even after making allowances for this, I still hold the opinion that it was the finest run that has happened within my experience. More than thirty years have elapsed since that eventful day, but every incident is imprinted on my memory—from the finding of the fox to the finish in the dark. I also number this as the best scenting day within my recollection. In proof of this I witnessed a curious instance, the like of which I never saw before or since. Sometime during the morning we were hunting a very bad fox—probably a recent importation—and whilst hounds were running up the hedgerow on one side of a field he was going the opposite way on the other side. The distance across was well over two hundred yards, and yet, when the pack got the fox's wind, they swung round and raced across the field as if he were in view, though it was impossible for them to have seen him. It was a rough ploughed field alongside of the Fosse road, and not very far from Widmerpool New Inn.

This exceptional scenting day was very near being wasted on trivial things, a fox chopped in one covert, several others blank, and the moderate specimen referred to above. The last chance of the day was Mr. J. D. Craddock's celebrated covert Walton Thorns, and the master had announced should this be blank no other covert would be drawn. I think we all realized there was a great scent, and it was an anxious moment waiting whilst Firr disappeared in the ride—it was about ten to one against finding, as hounds had been there the previous week.

Captain Warner

Let me quote from my *Field* notes: "The day was far spent, there had been no run, and the shadow of despair was gradually settling upon us …"

"These are anxious moments as we wait and listen for a sound that will raise us from the depths of despair to the heights of bliss. Nearly the whole covert has been drawn and we relapse into sorrow, when all of a sudden there is a shrill tally-ho! from Firr that fills our souls with joy. Someone views the varmint across the ride, and the next second Fred's scream tells us he is away."

The run commenced with a ring—thirty minutes at racing pace. I think this was much too good a fox to have indulged in circles if circumstances had not compelled him to start up wind, and with hounds close behind he was obliged to continue on that same course until the Burton Spinneys screened him from view. Here he swung to the left and, after making a wide sweep out by Seagrave village, returned to Walton Thorns: a thirty minutes' gallop with the Quorn bitches flying, and with scarcely a score of men in attendance.

In that half-hour there was not the semblance of a check, hounds just gliding from field to field, and a select little band striving to keep with them. No one dreamt of stopping to open a gate, or could afford even to diverge a yard from the straight line, and, in fact, we were all rather taking liberties with our horses, though enjoying ourselves vastly! Those, however, who entered in the second stage of the run, realized they had dropped in for something out of the common, and it behoved them to husband their mounts' reserve of strength. There was very little time or opportunity for watching what others were doing, but I have an impression of seeing several dismounted men, with glowing faces, discussing the gallop they had just ridden, quite oblivious to the fact that it was not finished.

These men must, I think, have been left behind, for hounds

were barely five minutes in the covert before they were sailing away again up the thorn-studded field beyond—it was a day when scent was better in the open. All Quornites know the line, in and out of the wide road that leads to Burton, and then a perfect hunting country that may land you anywhere. Half a mile short of Ella's Gorse the fox bore round to the right, and then going over Mr. Coupland's old farm crossed the top road near Shoby Lane Ends.

I can distinctly remember passing a small square spinney that is on the edge of the Wolds tableland, and entering the valley that stretches away to Hoby Clump. Shoby Scoles we left wide on the left. It was somewhere about this time that I missed Firr and the rest of the field, and my only companion for the remainder of run was that good sportsman, Mr. "Robby" Muir—he had not at that time won his laurels and his military title in the Boer War.

The pack never once slackened their pace, and I can see them now gliding up the steep rise towards Shoby village, whilst we toiled after them with the unpleasant feeling that we were losing distance. On top of the hill we could afford to put on steam again, and then for a few minutes they were out of sight in crossing the Shoby Lane, but we were able to get in touch with them beyond. My next recollection is a slight check near Mr. Wright's house, Saxelby Park, and then they were off again as hard as ever in the gathering gloom of the shortest day.

Then it was the pack crossed the Midland Railway, and they were only just clear when the express from Nottingham flashed by. We had a choice of bridges to right or left, but either meant a detour of at least half a mile—the right meant going through Grimstone village, and we took the left. This naturally put us two fields behind, but we could still just manage to see hounds, though unable to make up the leeway lost.

On arriving at Welby Osierbeds the pack were skimming up the hill beyond, and looked like dusky ghosts flitting on in the twilight.

At the grass road above Welby village I made a fatal error, and, unfortunately, persuaded my companion to follow me. It was nearly dark, and hounds had again got ahead of us, so that it seemed best to try and cut them off at the Melton turnpike. This would have worked out satisfactorily if the fox had not reached the end of his tether; but, as it was, hounds killed him on the ironstone tramway whilst we were ahead of them. Had we followed them down the little lane which leads by Welby church we should have seen the finish. Thus ended the best run I have ever seen, the best scent, and the stoutest fox.

When Firr came up, "Ruby",* an old favourite, met him with the mask in her mouth.

The Quorn seem to have monopolized the lion's share of sport this season, and they had another good run on 27th December. The fox was found in the Coplow, and after running by Baggrave and South Croxton went straight away to Thurnby station. This part of the run was very fast, and over an excellent country. After this hounds ran down the brookside into the suburbs of Leicester, and killed their fox near the asylum.

This must have been an extraordinary good scenting week, for I see that on the Saturday the Belvoir had a rattling fifty minutes over the best of the vale, and killed their fox in Holwell village. He had been found in Sherbrooke's covert, and by starting out towards Hickling, with a bend by Parson's Thorns, he was able to lead us over an ideal line.

There was rather an amusing scene with these hounds about a week later, though it must have been annoying to the master.

*Ruby by Ranter—Garnish, 1883.

Sport that morning had not been very good, so that when the Harby Hills were being drawn and a halloo was heard in the vale below, every one's idea was to get there as quickly as possible. The field was full of "ride", hounds were for the moment invisible in the covert, and a hundred horsemen set out in the direction of the halloo [*sic*]. We will hope that at least some of them were a trifle ashamed when, after a steeplechase for a mile or more, they found the pack were behind them.

I think this season should rank with those that have been lauded to the skies, as, in addition to many high-class runs, there was hardly a day that hounds did not give us some sport. On 7th February the Quorn ran from Barkby-Holt to a well-known drain at Hoby Rectory, the fox being bolted and killed. This was a most unusual line; but the fox had evidently made up his mind for his ultimate point when he was first found, and ran perfectly straight.

It was somewhere about the close of this season that the Melton midnight chase was run. I cannot remember the exact date, but think it was in March.

Lady Augusta Fane suggested it, and the idea caught on at once, though I believe there was only a day or two between the moment of suggestion and the date of the race. The Fanes then occupied the Old Club at Melton, and they invited the competitors to dine. Unless my memory is at fault, we all sat down in hunting rig camouflaged with nightgowns, and a very merry dinner-party it was.

Shortly before midnight the horses were brought to the door, and their iron-shod hoofs clattering on the cobblestones awoke the vicar from his sleep, which so annoyed the poor man that he took the liberty of denouncing the "unrighteous crew" from the pulpit for disturbing his peaceful slumbers, using as his text, "Have no fellowship with the unfruitful works of darkness."

Captain Warner

Someone must have made a mistake with the almanac, as instead of a full moon, which we had been told to expect, it was a pitch dark night. However this little detail was overcome by the kindness of the stationmaster, who lent us railway lamps.

According to precedent all the competitors were to put on nightgowns over their other clothes; but, as most men wear pyjamas, the articles had to be borrowed from ladies for the occasion.

The course was about a mile out of Melton, and was over some four or five fields, with, perhaps, double that number of fences to jump.

In spite of the shortness of notice, and the fact that until the morning before neither time nor date had been fixed, quite a large crowd had assembled. The spectators could have seen very little, as it was impossible to distinguish anything clearly beyond a radius of about three yards.

It sounds rather silly now, but the race itself was very good fun, and quite exciting. The most noticeable feature to me was galloping top speed across ridge and furrow without being able to see which was the up and the down—it gave you an extraordinary feeling. The most talented racing scribe would have been hard put to it to paint the happenings of either horses or riders, and I can only tell what befell me in the race, as the white gowns of my fellow-competitors was all that could be seen from start to finish.

Being as always very poor, with a limited stud, I did not feel that I was at liberty to risk laming a horse; but Mr. Gordon Wilson very generously came to the rescue and lent me one. This was an old chaser with a "leg"; but I can vouch for the fact that he was sound enough that night, though I was sorry to hear afterwards it was his last gallop. Having the organ of locality strongly developed, and knowing the country well, with, in addition, a fast horse under me, my chances of winning were pretty good. Mr. Edward Baldock acted as master of the ceremonies, clerk of the course, starter and judge. His first duty was to marshal the competitors, and give them instructions as to the lights they had to go round, with other details. The order then was that we were to finish in a gateway, the posts of which were to be the winning posts; but someone pointed out the danger in a close finish, and the order was amended. In the inky darkness it was very difficult to see every one, and unfortunately for me I never received the amended instructions. All with one accord vowed, ere we plunged into the darkness, that we would go at a very steady pace, but at the word "go!" such good resolutions were forgotten, and we dashed off as if it had been a five-furlong scramble in the light.

I arrived at the fence into the country first, and, I think, before the lamp-holders expected us—I could see the light, but it was not shining on the fence. Here my horse refused, but jumped all right on being put at it again, and in fact cleared everything splendidly afterwards.

I was able to catch up the others before we reached the turning point, and then commenced to draw ahead. I knew exactly the location of the gateway, and as the finish was uphill I could send my steed along best pace without fear of his "dicky leg".

Although it was impossible to see, I could hear the other horses, and all were well behind me on my right, so that after pulling up on passing through the gateway I naturally imagined I had won. The whole affair was just for the fun of it, and there was no prize except the cup that Count Zbrowski gave, so that, of course, I did not say anything, but must admit was very disappointed.

Mr. "Algy" Burnaby was the winner, and he is now the Master of the Quorn. I cannot remember all who rode that night, but there was Mr. "Harry" Rawlinson—now a baronet, and one of the most successful generals in this last war. Mr. Gordon Wilson died gallantly at the head of his regiment, of which he was colonel; but both these men distinguished themselves in the South African War. Then there was Count Zbrowski and Capt. Warner—both since dead. I can recall Mr. "Charlie" McNeill and Mr. "Will" Chaplin; but there were several others, though at the moment I cannot think of their names. The supper at Coventry House after the event was a very cheery affair, and to the best of my belief the competitors continued to wear the "nighties" they sported in the race.

February was about the worst month of the season, and even that had many bright spots.

On 7th March the Quorn had a very merry gallop from Scraptoft Gorse, and killed their fox in the stableyard at Lowesby—twenty-eight minutes at racing pace. The same pack met on the following Friday at Brooksby, to bid a sort of farewell to that good sportsman, Mr. Ernest Chaplin. The expenses of a very large family had made it necessary for him to cut down his stud, which from a dozen had been reduced to one. He was going extraordinary [*sic*] well when I commenced hunting, but I think even then he had only a couple of horses in the stable, and the responsibilities of paternity were becoming increasingly heavy. No man enjoyed a hunt more, and he could discuss every detail of a run with his after-dinner smoke. Like the majority of Quornites in those days, he was a great admirer of the huntsman, and when you dined at Brooksby the usual toast was "Tom Firr and fox-hunting."

Another good sportsman now reigns there and, as every one knows, Lord Beatty has made it his home.

The Quorn had a great run from the Prince of Wales' covert at Baggrave on 21st March—a great run, even though it did not finish with blood. The actual finish was close to Hallaton, which is a nine-mile point; but I am very nearly certain that we changed foxes in Tomblin's Spinney—a tiny place on the side of the hill between Billesdon and Lord Morton's.

Hounds raced away from the start, passing Carr Bridge and Lowesby, then bearing to the right, ran straight to Botany Bay. Here they never dwelt a moment, but were out beyond and speeding forward with undiminished pace before half the field had reached the covert. At the Uppingham turnpike they swung to the left, crossing the road near the Billesdon Workhouse, and into the aforementioned spinney.

I had seen the fox several times during the run, and knew he could not have lasted many more minutes, so that when the hunt continued by Skeffington and Keythorpe I felt quite sure there had been a change. It was very seldom that Firr did not get to the head of affairs in the first field, however badly he might have been placed at the start; but on this occasion hounds slipped away out of covert on the back of their fox and ran so fast that he had not a chance of making up lost ground. I don't think he appeared on the scene until we changed foxes, and probably the change would not have occurred if he had been there. Firr was riding that day one of the best horses which has ever crossed Leicestershire—"Revolving Light" by name, and own brother to "Gamecock," a National winner. Capt. Warner had bought him at Lord Manners' sale. He had a very light mouth, but with Firr's "hands" he went beautifully, though I remember Fred Earp was never quite happy on him on the few occasions he hunted hounds, and Fred was by no means heavy fisted. I suppose in his anxiety to reach his hounds Firr must have asked too much of his mount in the early stages of the run, and, being unable to get a second horse, was never able to give him a breather. Whatever the cause, "Revolving Light" died before he could be got back to the stable.

I also that same day killed a horse, which was a serious thing for me. It was a blood mare I had bought the previous

Saturday at Leicester, and I was riding her for the first time. By a stroke of good luck I had managed to get an excellent start, and the mare carried me brilliantly to Billesdon—a bold and free jumper. Having only given a "pony" for her, I was naturally delighted with the purchase, as well as jubilant over seeing such a rattling gallop.

Although I do not remember that she ever touched a fence, she must have just grazed a sharp stake and the mischief was done—I had her shot there and then.

For some unexplained reason a large proportion of the men who were usually in the front rank never saw the fast part of the run, and I don't think they ever realized how good it had been. The time of the whole thing was an hour and twenty-five minutes, with a nine-mile point; but the fast part lasted about thirty minutes.

In referring to the midnight chase I mentioned the names of Mr. "Willy" Chaplin and Mr. "Charlie" McNeill as being two of the performers. Both were first-rate men to hounds, and the former, when on a good horse, can still hold his own. The latter left the Quorn to take hounds, and I hear was a very capable huntsman.

Chapter IX

Captain Warner's Closing Seasons

Season 1890–1891

The ground was so hard during cub-hunting that it prevented us having the usual merry little gallops which we usually expect to relieve the monotony of serious business. The Quorn, however, had a very good run on the last day of October, in spite of hard ground. A fox was found in Walton Thorns, which, after running nearly to Wymeswould, swung round to the right, passing Mundy's Gorse and Thrussington Wolds, crossed the Hoby Vale, and was lost near Queniborough. Truly that was good enough for any period of the season, and the first thirty minutes hounds went so fast that it was all we could do to keep them in sight.

I note that both the Belvoir and Cottesmore put their opening meet off for a week on account of the hard ground; but the Quorn began at Kirby Gate as usual on the first Monday in November. "Fair sport and a moderate scent, but a triumph for Firr in catching his fox under great difficulties," was my summary of the day.

Towards the end of the month the long-expected rain fell, and the Quorn scored an extra good run on Monday, the 24th, after a deluge on the previous day.

They had the good luck to find an old veteran in Shoby Scoles, and with a capital scent ran him to death. His first point was the drain at Hoby Rectory, taking Ragdale on the way; but the master had previously given instructions for the entrance to the drain to be permanently closed for the season. This old fox had doubtless frequently taken refuge there before, and doubtless expected to find sanctuary there on this occasion.

His subsequent wanderings led us over a most unusual line, and I do not ever remember hounds running it either before or since.

The river was crossed below Rotherby, when the pack swung to the left and ran very fast towards Frisby; but on approaching the latter village they turned up the hill and crossed the Leicester main road as if for Cream Gorse. I think the fox knew that covert and had thoughts of going there, but the wind was against him, which doubtless influenced him in recrossing the river and going north. The place where hounds actually crossed was close to the clump of Scotch fir near Asfordby; but as the river was in flood no one seemed anxious for a swim, and the nearest ford was some distance away. I don't think we caught them until they were on the Grimstone tunnel, where they had checked. On the line being recovered the pace increased, and horses that had already begun to flag were asked to face some stiff country in the direction of Asfordby furnaces. The fox then ran the ironstone railway for fully a mile, and until he crossed the Nottingham road; but his many wiles were of no avail, hounds knew he was sinking, and driving on killed him near Holwell Mouth. One hour and forty minutes the run lasted; but it must not be supposed it was a slow hunt, as most of the time hounds were running very fast, and the fox must have been extraordinary [*sic*] stout.

About the middle of December a frost set in that lasted until the end of January, and, of course, cut out a large slice of the season. Although the Quorn were able to hunt the previous week, there was very little sport, and with the ground still hard in places until 2nd February, when that pack had an excellent run from Willoughby Gorse. Seventeen minutes at racing pace to Widmerpool, and down by the brookside towards Bunny, after which the fox took a line of plough by Keyworth, and was eventually killed in Kinoulton village. The pace for the first seventeen minutes must have burst the fox, as the remainder of the run was slow, and probably no other huntsman would have overcome the difficulties encountered. On the following Wednesday the Belvoir had an exceptionally smart gallop—twenty-two minutes from Coston covert to the keeper's lodge at Freeby Wood, where the fox was killed. Hounds ran first of all in the direction of Stapleford, before swinging to the right and rounding the shoulder of the hill on which stand the belt of trees known as the Rickets. Those who are familiar with the country will realize the distance—I made it about seven miles—and to accomplish this in twenty-two minutes meant steeplechase speed all the way. If I remember right Mr. Alfred Brocklehurst had the best of it, though I am nearly certain the "big brother" was in a good position throughout.

This was a typical Belvoir gallop, short, sharp and decisive. Scent that day must have been extraordinarily good, as hounds ran hard until it was dark; but, unfortunately, the foxes found afterwards were of the short running variety.

The Quorn had a very good run on 9th February, though only a ring it embraced such a large extent of good country that it was possible to overlook the fact. The meet was at Wartnaby Stone Pits, the fox found in Welby Osierbeds, and killed close to where the meet had been. Before this was accomplished hounds had run through Old Dalby Wood, passed by Ragdale, and on to Hoby, when they followed the Wreake Valley to Asfordby, and returned to Welby.

The pace was fairly good, without being very fast, and it was this that enabled the fox to carry on for two hours and ten minutes. There are people who will always assert that in a run of this length a change of foxes occurred, and except in the case of a "bob-tailed," or some distinguishable mark, it is not an easy matter to prove they are wrong. This was a case in which I was sure there was no change.

The same pack had an excellent day's sport on 20th February, finding a fox in Barkby-Holt, and killing him near Sileby. The first ten minutes over, the stiff enclosures towards Barkby village and on to Queniborough, hounds were flying, and was, of course, the cream of the run as far as riding was concerned.

The pace at the start was doubtless responsible for the ultimate triumph, because time was lost, and there were numerous difficulties to overcome.

This was a late afternoon affair, the morning having been spent in the neighbourhood of the Coplow.

There were several nice gallops before the end of the season; but the run that scored the longest point was to the credit of the Belvoir. Being short of horses that week, I was unfortunately not there, and can therefore give merely a bare outline. The fox was found in the valley that lies between Melton Spinney and the Waltham road. He was eventually lost near Barrow, close to where the Quorn kennels now stand, which is an eleven-mile point. Shoby Scoles and Ragdale were taken on the way, ensuring a first-rate line of country. Hounds ran very fast part of the time. It would have been a great triumph for poor old Gillard if he had caught his fox, and the run would then have ranked as historical.

In spite of several long stoppages by frost and snow, this was a very good season, and hounds seldom were able to hunt without showing sport.

It was in this season that Lord Lonsdale's much-discussed driving match with Lord Shrewsbury took place—it eventually resolved itself into a match against time. The time and the road had to be kept secret, or there would have been an unwieldy crowd which might have interfered with ordinary traffic.

The *Field* had asked me to report the match, and Lord Lonsdale had promised to let me know where it was to be.

On my return from hunting with the Quorn on Monday, 9th March, I found a wire awaiting me to say that it was fixed to take place at Reigate the following day. I reached London about 11.30, and found a blizzard blowing. The snow, which was like fine dust, found its way through the cracks in the hansom window-flap, so that on reaching Victoria I might have been taken for Father Christmas or an out-of-work baker.

Have no idea what time the train should have arrived at Reigate, but it landed me there about two o'clock in the morning—cold and hungry.

The platform heaped high with snow, and the roads to the station blocked. It must have lain nearly three feet deep on the level.

I trudged through this to the "White Hart" carrying my bag, and on arriving there was told every bedroom was occupied. Lord Lonsdale had gone to bed some two hours previously; but learnt Major "Sugar" Candy had only just retired, and a few minutes later I was banging at his door. In response to a gruff "What do you want?" I told him I wanted the use of his floor to sleep on. Every hotel blanket was in use, but a fur coat is not a bad substitute! Lord Lonsdale arranged matters for me next night, and I spent a very pleasant time until the match on Thursday,

There were several well-known press men, and a very jolly party. I can't remember them all now, but there was John Sturgess, senior, "Pot" Stevens, "Fatty" Coleman, and "Swears". Sir John Astley (the Mate) was there part of the time, but had to leave before the match.

With the *Field*'s permission I now give the article written for them at the time.

"A Sporting Match"

"Disappointment and regret will be generally felt at the unsatisfactory termination to the Shrewsbury-Lonsdale match. Through the past winter the possible time in which each competitor would be able to accomplish the distance has been a topic of increasing interest, and now that Lord Shrewsbury has withdrawn from the contest at the eleventh hour, the public will feel that they have been deprived of a long-standing promised performance.

"The origin of the match has now become a matter of history, so that a full account is rendered unnecessary. A conversation amongst a shooting party assembled at Ingestre last November, commencing on the merits of trotting versus galloping, gradually led up to the wager of the nominal sum of £100 being made between Lord Shrewsbury and Lord Lonsdale. The course was to be twenty miles, equally divided between the four different styles of driving, viz., four-in-hand, pair, single and postilion. Mr. Arthur Coventry was appointed referee, and each competitor was to drive his own team. After several roads had been discussed, Lord Lonsdale chose a fairly level stretch on the Great North Road, while Lord Shrewsbury's choice was a road on the borders of Sussex, close to where his horses were being trained. The referee, probably thinking that either was good enough, decided for the latter, as being the nearer to London. Lord Shrewsbury seems to have been in a strange state of vacillation at this period, and only telegraphed late on Saturday to his opponent to meet him at Reigate on Monday morning at six o'clock. Thereon Lord Lonsdale put horses and carriages in a special train, and went straight to the appointed spot. It was found impossible to run the match on the Monday, and ten o'clock on Tuesday was therefore fixed.

"The morning arrived, and found Lord Lonsdale encamped with all his force at the 'White Hart', Reigate; but there was no sign of either Lord Shrewsbury or the referee. Snow had certainly fallen heavily in the night; but a gang of men and a snow-plough had been early at work, and had cleared away all obstructions. Several well-known sporting men and press representatives had assembled; but, though the road was reported clear, the Shrewsbury party failed to put in an appearance. Telegrams flew to and fro between London and Reigate, and at last, late on Tuesday night, a message arrived from Lord Shrewsbury to say he would pay forfeit. This was, naturally, a great disappointment to Lord Lonsdale, who, however, in consideration of the public money that had been wagered about the time, decided to go the course and make the best record in his power.

"Though the match, by becoming a mere race against time, was shorn of much of its interest, yet a very large crowd was collected at Reigate, and much discussion ensued as to the time it was possible to do the twenty miles in. Another heavy fall of snow had come down the previous night, but the plough had been early to work, and the whole length of road was cleared. The course was a five-mile stretch of road between Reigate and Crawley. At twelve o'clock the sky cleared, the sun shone, and the four different teams filed out from under the archway of the 'White Hart'. It would occupy too much space to give a full description of each horse; suffice it to say they all looked as hard as nails, and fit to run for their lives. Lord Lonsdale had thought if worth doing at all it was worth while doing well, and had taken the greatest trouble that nothing should be wanting to make a record that should occupy a niche in the temple of fame. As far as we in our humble opinion could judge, success had most deservedly crowned his efforts, and look where we might not a flaw or hitch could be seen in either horses, harness, vehicles or arrangements.

"Walking down the road with the easy, swinging gait of the thoroughbred is that speedy horse Warpaint, and he is harnessed to a racing waggon lent by Mr. Fox of New York. Next come a pair of American trotters that have done a very respectable record ere they crossed the Atlantic; but we shall see to-day that they can gallop as well as trot. The machine that glides smoothly behind them is an ordinary road waggon, lent by the Marquis of Cholmondeley. Then, drawing a char-à-banc, the four-in-hand trot jauntily by; bloodlike leaders, and wheelers that look capable of carrying fourteen stone in the front rank to hounds. Last of all comes a hogmaned hunter-like chestnut, carrying the postilion's saddle, and alongside of him is a brown mare, which we understand is Violetta, an animal that was lately racing in France; they are drawing a buggy that was specially made for the purpose by the Hanney Company of Illinois.

"But we must hurry to the scene of operations, or we shall miss some of the fun. A three-mile drive brings us to where a crowd of people are standing about in the snow and the slush, with an air of eager expectancy written on their faces. On each side of the road two little blue and yellow flags flutter gaily in the breeze, and denote that this is the starting-post, as it also is the finishing one. Our drag is drawn up in an adjoining gateway, and a clump of Scotch pines shelters us from the wind. A mile or more of brown road, hemmed in on each side by the white snow, stretches away up the hill and disappears beyond the brow. Some preliminaries have to be gone through; two of the teams have to reach the farther end of the course, and the road has to be cleared. A more good-humoured crowd could not be imagined—lots of chaff, not a solitary policeman to be seen, and never a moment when one is wanted.

"At last everything is in readiness; we assemble round the timekeeper, there is a cry of 'he's off!' and we see Lord Lonsdale in blue spectacles dash by in his 'one-horse shay'. It seems but another second and old Warpaint, settling down in his stride, is disappearing over the distant hill. He is out of sight, and now we have twenty minutes to wait before he can appear again, which time is not ill-spent alongside of the refreshment hamper. A day or two ago very few people believed it possible to do the twenty miles under the hour; but the business-like way in which everything is arranged seems to have altered that opinion, and now we cannot even get a modest sovereign on the event. Watches are consulted, and in a few minutes more we may expect the returning sportsman to appear in sight. Yonder he comes over the brow of the hill! Nearer and nearer come the flying team, scattering with their heels the dirt, which forms a halo round the carriage. There is a cry of 'Clear the course!' a rush to take up positions, and the next second the pair of mares flash by. The mud-bespattered nobleman urges them on until the post is passed, then, with a whoa and a pull at the reins, he has arrested the full tide of their career sufficiently to drop to the ground, and climb the char-à-banc.

" The four horses are well into their collars, and the wheels are spinning round. His Lordship has scrambled to the box, and now, approaching the flags, he seizes the ribbons, and shaking himself into his seat is at it again. Enthusiasm and excitement rise to the highest pitch as we watch each horse laying himself out to his work, all level as a die, and every trace taut. It is a heavy vehicle, but these horses make nothing of it, and the whole thing is soon beyond our ken. We have another twenty minutes to wait, but we see now that, bar accidents, extraordinary [*sic*] good time will be made, and we anxiously watch for the return. Men who had taken up positions along the road are now mustering in great force at the winning-post. A current of feverish expectancy shows itself in a low murmur—it is nothing to do with betting, for hardly anyone here has a farthing on; but it is the genuine interest which the British public always feel in witnessing an extraordinary feat by a thoroughly honest sportsman.

"Now the horses' heads are in sight—they are racing down the hill. The postilion Earl is sitting in the saddle and sending them along at the very top of their speed. Every one gets as near to the post as he can, and in the excitement of the moment is heedless that he stands half up to the knees in snow. Clear the road! The horses seem to fly, and in another second they sweep past the post. Up go hats and caps, real hearty British yells rend the air, and the race is over.

"The twenty miles were done in fifty-five minutes thirty seconds. This is a record that will not be easily lowered. As far as Lord Lonsdale was concerned, he had done everything that human foresight could imagine. Both himself and his horses were trained to the hour, and we may say that neither was in the slightest degree tired or blown by their very severe exertions. Harness and carriages combined lightness and strength, and after the race was over, when it is always easy to criticize and find fault, it was impossible to see what more could have been done to have made better time. The roads after the snow were decidedly woolly, and in places the wheels cut in deep; this would, of course, affect time. Then half a minute was lost by a horseman being unable to pull his horse out of the road, and quite as much when an over-zealous policeman wanted to interfere. The feat will go down to posterity as one of the finest performances in the history of sport."

Memories of the Shires

Season 1891–1892

There was a serviceable scent during cub-hunting, and all three packs were able to blood their young hounds, with the addition of good educational work both in covert and the open. Several enjoyable little gallops were fully appreciated by the early risers; but there was no run of any distinction, though perhaps I should make exception of the day the Quorn ran from Scraptoft to Great Dalby.

This was 16th October, and it is not often a fox makes a seven-mile point at that time of the year. The line included the cream of the Friday country, which means the best in the world. I remember most of the fences were feasible, although they appeared rather forbidding clothed fully in their summer foliage. The brook about midway between Ashby and Twyford obliged us to leave the pack whilst we found a place to cross, and we never really caught them again until they reached Thorpe Trussells. The fox was viewed near Great Dalby, but Firr's horse was beat, and the master very reluctantly gave the order to stop hounds. I had forgotten this run until refreshing my memory with reading the *Field* account, and thinking it over now I come to the conclusion that it was quite one of the best in my experience. Neither the master nor any of the hunt staff had any intention of pursuing an old fox, and it was one of those lucky mistakes by which the field profit. Previous to drawing Scraptoft, a brace of cubs had been killed in Botany Bay, and as hounds had spent a hard morning in covert they were to be allowed in the open as a little relaxation.

Unless my memory fails there was a strong litter in Scraptoft Gorse, and when a cub crossed the intervening field to the Spinney hounds were allowed to follow him. They must then have changed on to the old fox, who was probably lying in the Spinney.

Sport was fair up to Christmas, and then came a long frost accompanied by snow, which cut out nearly two months of the season; but hunting was in full swing again the last week in February.

On 16th March the Belvoir had a very fast gallop from Sproxton Thorns to Freeby Wood, where they changed foxes, and then, after dodging about Brentingby Spinney, they suddenly slipped across the Waltham road and ran smartly to Scalford Bogs.

The majority of the field missed the latter part, and they were presumably changing horse or eating lunch, at the same time discussing the merits of the initial burst.

The Quorn finished the season with a very good gallop on 1st April from Burrough Hill Wood to the Withcote side of Owston Wood, where they killed their fox.

Season 1892–1893

For some unknown reason my *Field* letters for the earlier part of this season are missing, and then there was frost at the end of November.

Hunting commenced again on 16th December, and the following day the Belvoir had a capital run, though as I was not out, the details must remain in oblivion. The Quorn had a very smart evening gallop of forty-five minutes on the Monday; but, unfortunately, hounds had to be stopped through want of light. It was certainly only a ring, but very wide, and embracing a beautiful country.

The end of the month brought a return of frost, and with it came Capt. Warner's resignation of the Quorn Mastership.

Frost had gone by the beginning of February, and I note a very merry spin from Walton Thorns to Prestwold with the

Quorn. There was then a general improvement in scent and some fairly good runs; but from my notes it appears we had a streak of ill-luck, and were continuously just missing having hunts with good foxes by the intervention of the bad.

The fact of two different packs hunting over the same ground on successive days made me sympathize with the farmer, and inspired some remarks which it may not be out of place to reproduce here. "… the unhappy occupant of land whereon these two hunts disport themselves deserves our earnest consideration. The Burton Flat is usually the arena for both hunts, and the farmers who farm there may be excused if they get a little impatient when, having endured the vagaries of a Quorn crowd one day, they are invaded the next by a Cottesmore crush.

"That mad, headlong charge from Gartree Hill, when the crowd is first let loose and before it has had time to expend any of its bursting energy, is a power capable of doing much damage to the fields and fences. Of course, many of those who come out hunting do not pretend to have a knowledge of the sport any further than is necessary to ensure a good fit for their breeches and the right number of folds for their neckcloths. These are very laudable ambitions, and, when attained to perfection, the results are gratifying to every one; but some people think that the education of a fox-hunter should not rest here.

"We cannot very well blame those who are ignorant of the damage they do, but I fear we, who think we know better, give very little thought to the cracking of timber and the brushing through of hedges in the excitement of the run. The same timber and hedge will bear rude traces of our progress, and as the farmer walks round his fields in the calm of the evening, there will be no pleasurable excitement for him in contemplating the gaps."

Captain Warner's Closing Seasons

The Quorn had the run of the season on 20th February, when, finding a fox in Curate's Gorse, they crossed the vale and marked him to ground in the Harby Hills.

The fox was headed near the Parsons, and when the pack swung sharply to the right up the steep sides of Hickling Standard, more than half the field overshot the mark and took no further part in the run. To quote from my article at the time, "This was a run when you were either quite happy or perfectly miserable; when at the finish a flood of generous humour bubbled to your lips, or a sour and crabbed smile closed your mouth in silence."

Have just written of above as the "run of the season," and no doubt it was until the Belvoir capped it with one better on the following Saturday. I do not think that there has ever been anything to beat this in the whole annals of the Belvoir Hunt. This pack had the largest slice of luck during the season, and most of the sport was credited to them.

Unfortunately for a large number of Meltonians, and incidentally the *Field* correspondent, the meet was fixed for Scrimshaw's Mill, which is a fixture beyond the Melton area, and not usually associated with a gallop over grass. The result was the majority who usually attended a Belvoir Saturday did not go, and as my abode was five miles the wrong side of Melton, I also was an absentee, and am still regretting it. The fox was found in Harby Covert, and was killed less than a mile from Brooksby. I am not going to harrow my own feelings over again by going into details which were supplied me by different and reliable men, but will just give you the outlines. For the first twenty minutes, hounds never hesitated or checked, and it was all the first flight men could do to keep in touch with them. At the end of the twenty minutes there was a slight check by Old Dalby Wood, where the fox had been headed, and had it not been for the momentary stoppage, no horse would have had the wind to continue. It had been a veritable steeplechase, in which light weights and blood horses had the best of it. There were several fresh foxes in Grimstone Gorse, but Gillard managed to stick to the hunted one, and running out towards Asfordby swung right-handed and killed him on the banks of the brook that divides Hoby and Frisby.

This run in itself should make the season memorable.

The Quorn had a very hard day on 3rd March, running for three hours and a half without stopping. At one moment they were close to Norton Gorse, and eventually killed their fox a field from Cream Gorse. Of course there must have been a change somewhere, but no other covert was drawn after leaving Botany Bay, though both Baggrave and Barkby-Holt were run through. The pace at times was very fast, so that it is absurd to suppose one fox could have accomplished the whole journey, though the one killed was too tired to struggle into Cream Gorse, only two hundred yards distant.

There was a very good gallop with the Quorn which I distinctly remember, from Brooksby Spinney on 17th March. A very wild morning had been succeeded by a fairly quiet, though extremely cold afternoon. It was getting to the time of year when foxes are difficult to find, and small spinneys are of necessity the most uncertain. We were by no means hopeful whilst watching Capt. "Taffy" Williams' small covert being drawn, and were consequently jubilant when a big handsome fox bounced into the open in full view of the field; but the happiest man was the covert owner.

Hounds were away in a moment, and for fourteen minutes they raced over one of the nicest bits of the Quorn country, although perhaps a trifle stiff except on a good horse. At the end of the burst we found ourselves at Queniborough, and then came two or three fields of light plough which slowed the pace down, but when once across the Leicester turnpike the pack commenced to run hard again.

If I remember aright, four men were down at an Oxer, for though it was only a small field every one was very much on the ride. The country from Syston to Rearsby station is rather intricate, and takes some negotiating. Below Ratcliffe we were between river and railway, but kept to the meadows until reaching the aforementioned station. The fox then decided to cross the Wreake, making a sharp turn to the left. I happened to be with Firr, and for some reason had an idea when hounds swam across that the river was fordable—I knew there was an ancient ford somewhere close. I therefore said, "It is all right," to which Firr replied, "Go on then, sir." It was a beastly cold day, but I had to go then. My horse was bold, and did not hesitate to plunge in, but the ford was not there, and he had to swim. Our difficulties began on reaching the farther bank, and what had looked like a decent place to get out proved a bog. I managed to pull the poor old horse out, and then discovered the landing-place I had chosen was the outfall of the village sewer. Firr watched me until I had crossed, and then galloped round, when, of course, he reached hounds before me. There were some half-dozen men in the field to my left, and what annoyed me was that they found the old ford and crossed without having to swim.

The fox was lost eventually close to Barrow village in a snowstorm, and I believe the master considered I was more than half responsible for the failure of the scent. I do know that every one held their noses when I went near them. My dear old friend Mr. "Bill" Martin lent me clothes to ride home in, or rather I borrowed them without asking; but if he had been there the pages of the *County Gentleman* would have been enlivened by a vivid account of a black and highly scented "Q".

This brings Captain Warner's Mastership to an end, and the period which I have enjoyed most in all the years I have hunted. There were many good runs during his time of office, but what I think more to the point is, that hounds nearly always provided some sport whenever they were able to hunt. Captain Warner was very methodical, and did things thoroughly, so that the business of the hunt was carried on without a hitch. One of the things on which he insisted, and which I consider most important, was that the country should be drawn and hunted fairly. It is a matter that not only affects sport, but is essential in keeping on good terms with covert owners and occupiers of land.

There had been rumours that Lord Lonsdale might take the Quorn, and before the season closed the matter was settled; his brother, Mr. Launcelot Lowther, to act for him in his absence.

Chapter X

Lord Lonsdale

Season 1893–1894

All those who had ever met the new master expected to see men and horses turned out with that perfection of detail for which he had always been celebrated. They were not disappointed. The careless or slovenly man might say that the fit of a hunt servant's breeches would not help sport, but hunting is, in the main, supported by the goodwill of those who never ride, and if the chase is to retain its popularity with the general public, it is essential to make a good show.

The Quorn is the premier pack, and it seems only right that the staff attending them should be rigged out in faultless style, as an example and pattern to less distinguished and poorer hunts.

Although I cannot claim to have been a shining example of neatness in the hunting field myself, I can admire and appreciate it when seen. The hand of a first-class tailor could be seen in the way the hunt servants' coats fitted, and the breeches—spotless buckskin—were perfection. There was nothing to criticize or find fault with. The horses were all clean bred, and had proved themselves good hunters. Every horse was hogmaned, which no doubt made them look neater, but personally I don't like to see a thoroughbred hogged.

The ground was very hard at the beginning of the season,

and before the end of November hunting was stopped by frost.

Up to this point I have given you the best runs of each season, but from now on I shall pick out the days I remember and enjoyed.

That was a very good run on 26th January from Gartree Hill to Burley, the fox being killed in front of the house. Hounds ran very fast at times, but it was not a really good scent, and they were often in difficulties. It was yet another feather in Firr's cap.

Perhaps the fastest gallop of the season was a brilliant burst with the Belvoir from Old Hills, of about twenty minutes.

Season 1895–1896

The earlier part of this season was uneventful, and there was a severe frost before Christmas, but with the New Year we had fair sport nearly every day.

The Quorn had some extraordinary [*sic*] good sport on the forest side, I was told, and a veracious friend who lived in that quarter spun me a yarn—after dinner—of a fox who lived under the shadow of a big rock, and when found would leisurely mount the rock, wet his paw, and hold it up to find out which way the wind blew. That is the story, as I received it, but I cannot guarantee it being true.

I think it was in this season that Lord Lonsdale bought the Brocklesby dog pack, and, bringing them to Leicestershire, hunted them himself on by-days. All those who hunted with him were loud in their praise of the sport shown, but I felt it my duty as *Field* correspondent to stick to the regular days; and though hounds were frequently at my door on Wednesdays, I nearly always went with the Belvoir. I did, however, have a day or two with Lord Lonsdale, and saw some very good sport;

but in my opinion the hounds were too big for an enclosed country where the hedges were thick. It prevented the pack from carrying a good head and getting quickly together.

My first day with the private pack when there was any scent was on 7th March, and with a comparatively small field we had a capital run over the cream of the Quorn country. The morning had afforded a short and pleasant gallop, but the afternoon run from Thorpe Trussells was very good indeed, and hounds were only prevented from killing their fox through want of light.

Season 1896–1897

My first week's letter in this season is missing, and I have no record of the Quorn opening day; but, unless I am mistaken, it was the Kirby Gate that hounds ran from Adam's Gorse to Neville Holt. The following week's issue tells of the fox having been found dead on Wednesday morning after the run on Monday, and it seemed such a tragic ending for a gallant fox that I tried to trace his homeward journey. Here is the story as it appeared in the *Field*, and although I wrote it, that does not ensure the details being true.

"The poor old customer, weary and tired, heard with satisfaction the cry of hounds stop at last, and, stretching his aching limbs beneath the friendly shelter of a haystack, lay quietly down until darkness should make travelling safe. Then, when the last shepherd had gone home to his supper, and the countryside had sunk into the peaceful stillness of night, our friend rose from his hiding-place and prepared to start on his journey back. For the first few minutes his stiffened joints would hardly bear the weight of the body, then the muscles would relax and gradually the condition from years of activity would assert itself, so that he could trot gently on his way. He took things very quietly, as he had many hours of darkness before him. Those cornstacks on the top of the hill supplied him with a light supper in the shape of a fat brown rat who had ventured too far away from home; this, washed down by a hearty drink at the adjoining pond, gave him strength to pursue his journey. Arriving at Launde Park Wood some time about midnight, he sought out a dry patch of grass, and after licking himself clean, prepared to settle down for a good long sleep. The rat, however, had only partially satisfied his hunger; but he was too tired to hunt for food himself. He then bethought him of a vixen whom he had visited in this wood last year, and to whom he had paid marked attention. Sitting down on his haunches, he opened his mouth and commenced a series of blood-curdling howls, which were eventually answered in the far distance of the wood by shrill yap yaps. The cries came nearer, and at last the vixen appeared, which fortunately turned out to be his old love. Explaining the situation to her, and his inability to hunt for food himself, she gave him a hearty welcome, and immediately started off on the desired quest, returning presently with a nice fat rabbit, and half a dozen black beetles to aid digestion. After an amicable discussion on the best way of avoiding hounds the two friends parted, with a promise on the gentleman's part to pay a visit after Christmas.

"All Tuesday the old customer slept soundly on, and though once or twice he woke suddenly with a start as the cry of hounds was borne down from the distant heights of Tilton. At sundown he awoke and stretched himself, prepared to resume his journey. After a roll on the grass in the park, and a momentary stare at the lights twinkling in the Abbey windows below, he jogged quietly on through the Lover's Walk and into Owston Wood, where he stopped some time talking to old friends. He was still very stiff, and he could not get on very fast, so that by the time he neared Burrough the earliest cocks were beginning their morning crow. Here, unfortunately, he came upon an old hen in a hedgerow that had wandered beyond its usual walk, and been overtaken by darkness before it could find its way back. The hen was eaten, and the old customer journeyed on. His home, Adam's Gorse, was little more than a mile distant, and he hoped soon to be having a well-earned rest. The consumption of the fowl had wasted time, and as he entered the valley between Burrough and his home day had begun to break. An early shepherd was mustering his flock to see they numbered right, and seeing our poor friend travelling down the hill, set on his sheep-cur to course him. At any other time the sheep-cur would have been easily distanced but, with stiff muscles and that still undigested hen, the dog gained at every yard. The fence was only a few yards distant, and the fox made heroic efforts to reach it. He thought he was safe, and was already stooping to creep the smeuse, when he felt the hot breath of the dog, and a sharp grip across the loins. Turning round savagely to do battle with his antagonist, the unworthy cur fled, and with tail between his legs returned to his master. The poor old customer had, however, been bitten in a vital part, and he was only able to drag himself to the field at Adam's Gorse, there to lay himself down to die. A few hours later the body was discovered."

Although this was a very great run, and portions of it were quite fast, it was not altogether satisfactory from a riding point of view, at least that was the impression left on me. The mere fact, however, that a twelve-mile point was accomplished, is sufficient in itself to place the Adam's Gorse run amongst the most famous performances in the history of hunting.

I seem to have lost the pages which would have reminded me that this was the year when there were great changes at Belvoir. The Duke of Rutland gave up the mastership, and Sir Gilbert

Greenall was appointed his successor. Frank Gillard retired, and Ben Capell became huntsman to the famous pack, which was lent to the country. In the previous three seasons Lord Edward Manners acted as field master, which had relieved Gillard very considerably, as it is not an easy matter to hunt hounds and control the ardour of a hard riding field.

Capell carried on the traditions of hound breeding on the same lines as his predecessors, and I think with very great success. In fact, the Belvoir blood, which had always been appreciated by other kennels, became in such demand that the stallion hounds were used rather too freely.

It would have been contrary to all precedent to have charged a high fee for the service of the best hounds; but I thought at the time such an innovation would have been of benefit to all.

On 11th November the Belvoir found a fox in Burbidge's covert, and killed him at Ranksboro. This made an excellent beginning for Ben Capell, as it was by no means a good scent.

There was frost at the end of December, and then hunting began with the New Year.

On 16th January the Quorn had an excellent day's sport, and the most enjoyable part thereof was the gallop from Gaddesby Church to an earth at Thorpe Satchville. This is a line of country which to my mind is ideal, every fence jumpable, the enclosures the right size, and the ground gently undulating, so that it is necessary to be in the same field with hounds if you want to see them.

On this particular occasion the fox had been found in Cream Gorse, and circumstances had obliged him to break on the Brooksby side, and he had deemed it advisable to steer for Gaddesby Church before turning to make his point. When, however, he did turn, he never once deviated a hairbreadth from the straight line, which led to the earth, where he eventually found sanctuary. There was a great scent, and hounds flew all the way. I remember the gallop distinctly, and thought it was the fastest gallop of the season, with every element in its favour to make things enjoyable. One little incident, which only concerned myself, took off a little of the gilt. I had been lucky enough to secure a good position, and was first into the road at Gaddesby; but on landing a leather slipped out, and, though I returned it quickly, for the next mile I had to be content to jump fences behind others.

There was another good run later in the day, which finished up in the Cottesmore woodlands.

In my letter of 30th January I mention the fact that the "Quorn Committee have decided to introduce capping non-subscribers," and then go on to speak in favour of what appeared to many old supporters of the hunt as a "dreadful radical upheaval of ancient traditions". At that time I had no idea my services would be requisitioned as the official "capper" or, perhaps, I should not have looked on the custom with such a favourable eye. Let me say now that extracting those golden coins from the pockets of visitors was one of the most unpleasant tasks that has ever fallen to my lot. With very few exceptions did they have the right amount ready to hand out, and the job of searching in a crowd of three hundred for strange faces lost me many chances of getting a start. It was a new departure, and, of course, many visitors had not heard that "capping" had been introduced; but although no one likes being suddenly asked to fork out gold, I never had any unpleasant remarks made whilst getting it. I did, however, notice that when some old friend returned to have a day with the Quorn, he did not meet my greeting of warm welcome in quite the same cheery spirit as of yore. Also, I fear, there were many who avoided me if possible, and who would rejoice if they escaped detection, thinking no shame of not paying for their sport. My task would have been much easier if those from whom a cap was due had sought me out and paid without being asked. One of the very few exceptions who tendered the money unasked was Lord Cecil Manners; but as masters were exempt, and he was representative of Belvoir, I took upon myself to refuse it. In my opinion the Melton Hunt owe a very big debt to the Dukes of Rutland for having provided them with hunting free of cost for so many years, and I should have been ashamed to accept a cap from a son of that house.

In those early days of the "cap" [*sic*] there were many amusing episodes; but there was no foundation for the yarn that I had a fall, stood on my head in the ditch, and spent the rest of the day searching for lost treasure. There may have been some truth in the story that I chased a lady across country, but the lady shall be nameless. My successor had rather a funny experience with a lady—why is it ladies object to pay hard cash? He had pursued this particular fair one all day, and she had managed to evade him until just before the end, when he managed to corner her. Of course she was profuse in her apologies for not having seen him before, and immediately handed over a coin wrapped up carefully in paper. My friend was much too polite to open the paper there and then; but on reaching home that night he found it contained only half the correct amount.

This was quite a good season; but I think the best sport was in March, when all three packs had some very good days.

On the thirteenth of the month the Cottesmore had a rattling good day, hounds running hard until dark. Here is an account of thirty minutes at top speed from Laxton's covert to the Punchbowl, and I can recall every incident of the gallop.

"The whip has galloped on to the lower end of the covert, and his halloa [*sic*] is a signal for us to hurry to the spot. The pack are crossing the little stream that runs below, and are soon flying up the opposite slope. Sticky and holding is that first field, but still we dare not slacken our speed. We top the slope at last, and rejoice to find ourselves on good, sound turf. On we go towards Whissendine, swing right-handed across deep ridge and furrow with the sun shining blithely in our faces. It was somewhere hereabouts that we were with the Belvoir last Wednesday, and the gaps have a familiar look, but in and out a road quickly brings us on to fresh ground. The 'Noel Arms' is, we know, just in front, but something turns our fox sharp to the right. Hounds turn just as sharp, and never falter for a moment. Is it pleasure, is it excitement, or is it funk, that makes the perspiration trickle down our faces? Perhaps a little of all three, but still the result is the most delightful sensation in the world. Each second is a whole volume of a lifetime, and the joy of that second is too intense for words. Hounds race on, their maddening notes rising and falling in perfect harmony. How they twist and turn, but ever driving onwards! What fun it is! Back over the brook we go in the direction of Wild's Lodge, swing left-handed across the turnpike, and check for a second by Wheathill Spinney. Another left-handed turn, and the pack are into the spinney near the Punchbowl. Thirty minutes of real, unalloyed pleasure, and then the best of it is over."

Gillson was a good huntsman, but was a great sufferer from indigestion, and I think with better health would have made a great name for himself. It was, however, in the kennel that he excelled, and I have always considered that his pack were the fittest I had ever seen. Some one has said that more foxes are killed in the kennel than in the field. This is what I wrote on the day of the above run. "Gillson has got together as smart a pack of bitches as anyone can wish to see—full of muscle and the gloss of health shining through their skins. No pack that I have seen carry a better head; they have plenty of music, and can hunt a bad scent as well as race when it is good."

Season 1897–1898

There was not very much sport in November, but the Quorn had a very good hunting run at the end of the month. An outlier was found near Ratcliffe village, and when he went to ground within a few fields, it seemed as if that chapter was closed; but Harry and his terriers turning up, he was speedily evicted. There was a very poor scent, and time was lost by the fox running through Seagrave village; but although it looked hopeless on several occasions, Firr persevered and was rewarded by hounds bowling him over close to Ella's Gorse.

Have I mentioned Harry Houghton before? Masters come and masters go, but Harry is a permanent institution with the Quorn, though it was not until Lord Lonsdale's era that he attained official recognition. Belonging to a well-known and highly respected yeoman family, his love of sport prevented him from devoting his full energies to agricultural pursuits, with the result that a substantial patrimony was early wasted. A passion for fox-hunting, and with no other means of indulging in it, eventually landed him amongst the ranks of the "runners" in some one's faded scarlet coat; but though always ready to do slight services for his mounted friends and earn something to keep the pot boiling, his one great desire was to see the fox hunted and killed. Of late years he has followed the hunt with his terriers in a pony cart, which might indicate prosperity, but I fear that a natural tendency to cheery company and lively evenings have rather retarded his advance to substantial affluence. Perhaps those whom he has assisted in days gone by may give him a pension in his old age.

There must have been a return this season to the custom inaugurated by Capt. Warner, of hunting the south side of the Quorn country on Monday, as I find on Monday, 27th December, the meet was at Brooksby. A very nice run was the result, hounds finding in Ashby Pastures and after taking a turn out to Gaddesby, killed him on the lawn of Little Dalby Hall.

The early part of the run was rather slow, and the field may have become a little slack, so that when hounds suddenly began to run fast at Ashby Folville they were left behind and missed the best part. I can remember the occasion, because I was one of those foolish people, and have a vivid recollection of seeing Lord Lonsdale on his famous grey, cutting out the work over that charming Twyford vale.

On the last day of the year the Quorn had a very good forty minutes from Ella's Gorse, and killed their fox. The run was not straight, but that was forgiven because it was such an ideal line. By Willoughby across the Fosse and then right-handed to the top of Old Dalby and back by Mundy's Gorse to Hoton Spinney—can you imagine a better country?

I have, however, always looked on that as a black day, for in the afternoon Firr had a very nasty fall from which I do not think he ever completely recovered. The following Friday the master was hunting hounds, and we had a good run from Curate's Gorse. The Quorn appear to have had the lion's share of the sport, and a very fine run was the one that commenced near Barkby and ended near Eye Kettleby mill. Lord Lonsdale was then still acting as huntsman.

On 12th March the Cottesmore found a fox in the Punchbowl and killed him near Ridlington, which is a good eight-mile point.

This was a really very good season with perhaps the best of the sport coming after Christmas.

Chapter XI

Captain Burns-Hartopp

Season 1898–1899

When we bade adieu to the Quorn at the end of the last season, we had no idea there would be a change of masters, but Lord Lonsdale was obliged for private reasons to resign at the last moment. A master was required at once, and Capt. Burns-Hartopp came gallantly to the rescue. No man ever worked harder for a hunt or had more misfortunes to contend with than this new master.

It was nearly the first day of cub-hunting on the forest side that Firr had a bad fall, which though it was hoped might only lay him up for a time, proved serious enough to oblige him eventually to retire. The first whip, Fred Gabbitas, was temporarily installed as huntsman; but though very willing I do not think the art of hunting was born in him, and Leicestershire is not an ideal country to acquire knowledge, particularly when the riding over it is also not exactly a labour of love. At the moment I cannot remember how long Gabbitas carried the horn, but he was eventually succeeded by Walter Kyte, who had been whipping-in to him. Kyte was a very good horseman, but had little experience in the kennels, and had acquired his knowledge of hunting through watching Firr when riding second-horse to him.

Of course, every one who goes out hunting considers himself

sufficiently expert to criticize a huntsman, and it seemed a safe thing to comment adversely on a man promoted as it were from the stables. Kyte I feel sure knew he was being criticized, and therefore did not do himself justice. Proof of this was that after he had received notice and knew he was going, he gained confidence, and showed some extraordinary good sport.

However, I am rather anticipating events, but I wanted to show some of the difficulties Capt. Burns-Hartopp was faced with at the commencement of his reign. This season, scent was seldom really good, but we had many pleasant little gallops, and there were few days that we returned without some excitement. The Quorn had a very good run on 7th December from Gartree Hill to Whissendine, where they killed their fox, much to the satisfaction of the much criticized Gabbitas. The earlier parts of the run were of a ringing character and did not promise to blossom into anything better, but at Somerby the fox elected to run straight, and the latter portion was very good.

On Saturday of the following week the Cottesmore had a brilliant twenty minutes from a rough field near Whissendine. That good sportsman and prince of heavy weights, Mr. "Cis" Chaplin, had harboured a fox with such care and nicety that he was able to lead us directly to the exact furrow in which the outlier had curled himself up to sleep. All those who saw that gallop were brimming over with joy, but probably no one was quite as happy as the man who had provided us with the material.

On that last Monday in December, Walter Kyte started as huntsman to the Quorn, and though there was very little scent I thought he made a promising maiden effort.

I think the Quorn run of 23rd January from Welby Osierbeds was the best of the season. Hounds ran straight by Melton and Saxby to Stapleford, which is in itself a six-mile point; but that was only half of the run. I thought at the time there must have been a change of foxes somewhere about this stage, as the pace had been very hot most of the time, and there had been no delays, so that it is almost impossible to conceive one animal making a farther seven-mile point. Near Laxton's covert, hounds were in difficulties; but Kyte recovered the line, when we galloped on by Berry Gorse and Wheathills to Little Dalby. Here there were several holloas [*sic*], but in the absence of any reliable evidence as to which was right, the huntsman very wisely left it to the pack. Some slow hunting then led us by the Punchbowl and Burrough Hill Wood to Thorpe Satchville, where the fox had very considerately waited, and then hounds ran very fast down the valley to Ashby Folville. Swinging uphill again to the Pastures, they drove him through that covert, and killed him two fields beyond.

The huntsman was, of course, entitled to consider that he killed the fox he started with, as no other covert was drawn; but my idea was that we picked up the line of one that had been disturbed somewhere in the neighbourhood of Laxton's covert, though it was extraordinary luck to hunt two such straight-necked customers in one day. Hounds were never touched from the find to Saxby station.

The Cottesmore had an exceptionally good run from Mr. Peake's covert at Burrough on the last Saturday in February, and it was over a beautiful line of country. They ran out as far as Marefield to begin with, then swinging left-handed, kept Owston village to the right. The pace up to this point had been good, but it then increased, and hounds never hesitated a moment until they checked in Pickwell big field. The check was only temporary, and then the pace was maintained through the Punchbowl and Burdett's covert to the Great Dalby side of Gartree Hill. Here the fox turned down on to the Flats and was killed close to Burton Hall. The official time was, I believe, fifty-five minutes.

Captain Burns-Hartopp

The Quorn scored another good run on St. Patrick's Day, finding a fox in Burdett's covert, and going straight away to Prior's Coppice. Hounds carried the line through the latter covert without dwelling a moment, and were pointing for Leigh Lodge when the fox turned back into Launde Park Wood, where several fresh ones brought the run to an end. Except that it lacked blood at the finish, this run would have been considered quite first class.

The close of the season was marked by Firr's resignation, and it was to me a very sad moment when we assembled to bid him farewell—sadder perhaps than when a few years later we saw him buried in the little churchyard at Quorn. Perhaps it is as well to add here what I wrote for the *Field.* Personally I consider that the best sport that I have seen and enjoyed was whilst hunting with Firr, and shall always look back on that as the happiest period of my life.

"Presentation To Tom Firr

"On the lawn in front of Mr. W. Warner's picturesque old house, the Quorn Hunt had gathered on Monday last to say good-bye to the huntsman they had loved so well. Heavy showers in the morning and black clouds overhead, threatened to make the function thoroughly uncomfortable; but as the time fixed approached, the sun came out, and all things were gay. Gay it was to the eye, but our hearts were sad within us. It was an impressive scene, and like nothing else that we are accustomed to see. There was a subdued hush, disturbed only by the flapping of the tent and the gentle murmuring of many voices, whilst the whinings of sixty couples were heard occasionally from the kennels hard by. Beneath an awning on the edge of the lawn, Firr in his unstained scarlet sat in melancholy state, and in a semicircle around him were collected a crowd of those who had often followed him in the hunting field. Beyond the sunk fence, facing the tent, were yet another crowd, and behind a row of horsemen.

"There should be nothing sad in the acceptance of a handsome salver and a substantial cheque*, but every one felt it to be a painful occasion, and there were few who had not only a choky feeling in the throat before the ceremony came to an end. The man we have idolized as a huntsman, and who has served us for so many years was sitting there before us, his health completely wrecked in showing us sport. Little more than a year ago he was riding as brilliantly as ever, and now, by an unfortunate accident, he is cut off from following the profession that had become part of his life. We acknowledge him to have been a king amongst huntsmen, and now, at this moment, we feel the inadequacy of the tribute we pay.

"It was a trying moment for all, and all were glad when it was over. The final parting with hounds, and the sympathy expressed by every one were almost too much for Firr in his weak state of health, but by a marvellous effort of will he succeeded in controlling the emotion which he evidently felt."

Every one had hoped that his health would improve, and he would be able to continue as huntsman; but this was not to be, and it was some time in February that his retirement became an acknowledged fact. When this was finally decided, I immediately wrote an article for the *Field* as some little return, and an appreciation of the eighteen seasons I had hunted with him. Of course I knew nothing from my pen could raise his character as a huntsman in the estimation of those who had been privileged to watch his skill in hunting a fox, but I wanted to draw the attention of old Quornites to the fact that a testimonial was being raised, and to remind them

*See Appendix II.

the opportunity had arrived to contribute in memory of the sport they had enjoyed. I was therefore bitterly disappointed and annoyed when my article was returned. Mr. Blew was at that time the hunting editor of the *Field*, and though I do not think we ever met, I found him very unpleasant in his official capacity—he may have been charming in private life.

"Brooksby" also told me he could not get on with him, and was continually having to complain of his articles being cut up. In my lengthy association with the *Field* I have always been on the best of terms with all the other hunting editors, up to and including the present genial expert. What experience Mr. Blew had actually in the hunting field I have not the slightest idea, but should imagine it was very limited, and like many others with a little knowledge, thought he had nothing to learn.

His work, *The Quorn Hunt and its Masters*, contains many errors, although dates and names may be fairly correct; but I think the most interesting portions of the book are from material supplied him by that good sportsman, Mr. J. D. Craddock.

Season 1899–1900

With a southerly gale blowing on 3rd November, the Quorn had what a hard rider from a neighbouring hunt described as the best run he had seen for ten years.

Custom has ordained that the first Monday in November shall open the real season, and therefore when that month is born a day or two later, the start is delayed.

The occasion of this gallop was the Friday before Kirby Gate. The meets in the previous week had been at 9.30, but the master was an indefatigable early riser, and had gone back to 9 o'clock.

It is the business of the master and his staff to catch as many cubs as possible, for which purpose the early hour is certainly the best. I am a great advocate for hunting early, and believe we should have much better sport with the meets at nine instead of eleven, but all the same should not welcome the change. During cub-hunting we rather expect the first hour or two to be devoted to serious business in covert, and to the killing of cubs, a part of the programme which is not usually very amusing to the onlookers in the Shires. Of course, in a woodland country it is a different thing, but to stand for two or three hours outside a strong gorse covert is apt to become a trifle wearisome, even though you may occasionally see a fox and hear the cry of hounds.

There are people—I admire them—who make it a rule never to be a minute late, however early the meet may have been fixed, but the majority of these severely punctual cub-hunters seldom wait to see hounds go home. For the first hour the consciousness of excessive virtue exudes from them at every pore, but later on want of sleep, insufficient breakfast, and general boredom, reduce them to a state of utter weariness.

On this particular occasion the early bird really did get the worm, for hounds went away with the first fox a few minutes after the hour fixed for the meet. Needless to observe, that bird did not neglect the opportunity of crowing over those who had been less punctual.

Hounds ran up-wind to Beeby, then turned left-handed and marked their fox to ground in the earths at Spring Hill Spinney. For the first twenty minutes there were only about half a dozen men with hounds. I was not there to see it, but honestly believe this was a very great gallop.

Kirby Gate gave us a good run that season, a fox from Gartree Hill making a six-mile point and dying gamely in the Belvoir country.

Towards the end of the month the Quorn ran from Barkby-Holt to Brooksby, and killed their fox on the banks of the river. Then on the following Monday the same pack killed a leash of foxes in the Widmerpool country, so that Kyte was showing good sport in spite of his inexperience.

The last Saturday in November brought the Belvoir a slice of luck in the shape of a rattling gallop from Sherbrooke's covert. Hounds ran over some of the best of the vale, and then ascending the hill killed their fox near Widmerpool—thirty-five minutes at racing pace.

The previous month had been productive of great sport; but December brought with it several days of frost. Hunting commenced again after Christmas, and the Cottesmore had an exceptionally good run from Mr. Peake's covert to Melton Spinney. The first part of this run was at only a moderate pace; but the fox having waited at Gartree Hill a fresh start was made, and then hounds ran very fast on to the finish. From Gartree Hill to Melton Spinney in thirty-five minutes is pretty good going.

Unfortunately the earths were open or they would certainly have caught him in a few more minutes.

The Quorn run of 19th January from Ashby Pastures to Grimstone village, where they killed their fox, is a performance that it would be hard to beat. I had forgotten that this run belonged to the season in which the much criticized Kyte carried the horn, and looking back now I come to the conclusion that it was one of the best seasons within my recollection.

The fox from Ashby Pastures deserved the honours of that day, for he went boldly across the middle of every field, never touched a covert, and after crossing ten different parishes yielded up his brush when he could go no farther. On the following Friday the same pack had another good run, but did not kill their fox. They had been running a twisting fox from Barkby-Holt for some time, and were expecting every moment to kill him, when they struck the line of a cunning old customer who lived in Queniborough Spinney. Hounds then ran very fast over a beautiful country, and after completing an eight-mile point were stopped between Owston and Knossington.

The fastest gallop of the month was with the Cottesmore, when they ran from Berry Gorse to Somerby.

Here I come to 24th February when the Cottesmore had one of the season's best runs. They raced their fox from the Punchbowl to Owston Wood, drove him through the length of the wood and out over Whatborough Hill, then swinging back to the right killed him in the Lake Spinney. Perhaps the most enjoyable part was the gallop to Owston Wood when the close attendants were very limited and select. These are only a few of the good things that I have picked out; but it appears to me there was good sport every day.

Rumours of Mr. Baird's resignation of the Cottesmore had been floating about for some time; but it was about this date that the rumours were confirmed, and I know all those who had hunted with him were sorry he was leaving.

Both January and February were good scenting months, and all three packs enjoyed a long spell of first-rate sport. The Belvoir had a very good day on the first Saturday in March, racing over the vale and catching their fox. Then, again, the same pack had a good day at the end of the month.

Five-and-twenty minutes over the vale with a kill in the open during the morning and an exceptionally nice gallop in the evening, the latter part of which, from Clawson Thorns to Hose Gorse, was first class. For some reason the crowd had grown weary, and when Capell, catching a view of his fox going away from Clawson Thorns, with the pack close at his brush, barely a dozen men followed him. The line at first was along the hillside in the direction of Piper Hole Gorse; but the fox suddenly remembered the earths in the covert he had started from and dropped down into the vale. With hounds racing over the best of grass and no crowd to jostle, that little gallop was to me one of the most enjoyable moments of the season.

The Quorn wound up the season in great style, and the John o' Gaunt run of 12th April I shall always consider to be very nearly, if not quite the best I have ever seen. When on Monday, the 9th, a brace of foxes were killed in the morning, and in the evening hounds ran from the Curate's to the main earths in Welby Osierbeds, we thought an extraordinary season had received its finishing touch. It was a backward spring, the turf was cool and moist, but had not started to grow, so that little harm was done.

Many of the regular Meltonians had left; but the master was desperately keen and granted us one more day. The meet was at Keyham, and several Pytchley men turned up to swell the throng.

By some happy inspiration the master decided to draw John o' Gaunt—there the run began and there it ended. The occupier of the adjoining lands, and who also looked after the covert, told me the fox had lain nearly the whole winter in an adjoining field, and had therefore escaped being hunted. It happened to be a small arable field, and the spring cultivation had driven him to the covert. He was an exceptionally light colour and was probably a seven- or eight-year-old fox; but could hardly have been much older or he would never have stood the strain of that run. He was the stoutest fox that I have ever ridden after in the whole of my hunting experience.

I never enjoyed a run more, and was never better carried. The old horse I was riding was a bad refuser when I first had him; but though he would occasionally revert to old habits in a slow hunt, he was very good when near hounds in a fast gallop.

The run began with a right-handed loop round Marefield, hounds flying and every one having a dart, but never dreaming it was only the preliminary to something much greater.

The season was practically at an end, horses would not be wanted for another six months, and every one meant having a ride.

I have never seen hounds run much faster than they did in that right-handed loop round Marefield, and in fact some of those who had started badly never realized how far the pack had gone before turning. It was on the hill overlooking the Twyford brook that the fox altered his course; but I saw nothing to have headed him. We breasted the hill towards Halstead as far as Sir Richard Button's old farm, and then swung to the left into the valley near Tilton station. Here I made a grievous mistake, which relegated me and all who followed me to positions in the rear. There were two cattle arches, one with an easy swinging gate and the other railed up with stiff railway timber. In the excitement of the moment I found myself confronted with the latter, and the pack more than half-way up Whatborough Hill before we were clear.

Yes. I missed that part of the run, and only saw it from a distance; but perhaps it was as well, for it was the least interesting country to ride over, and I was able to husband my horse's powers for the return journey. Let me say here that the outward course was to the south of Owston Wood, and the homeward to the north.

The big woodlands in this district might have seemed tempting to the ordinary fox, but our hero never touched one, and went straight on. Launde Wood was on the right hand, Launde Park Wood on the left, and the field adjoining Prior's Coppice was the turning point. This was where I managed to get on terms with hounds again, and not having bustled my horse, he was comparatively fresh. I believe the fox went nearly up to Leigh Lodge before swinging to the left and crossing the brook.

If you can find a better line to ride than from Prior's Coppice to John o' Gaunt, leaving Owston village just to the right, you will have found perfection.

Most of the field had rather taken liberties with their horses over those severe hills on the outward journey, and, in consequence, the competition for first go at a fence was not quite as keen as it had been. Walter Kyte was very well mounted, but his horse was getting tired, and when near Owston village I pointed out a hound that had slipped a field ahead of the pack; he gladly accepted my offer to jump some timber and holloa [*sic*] the others on. Rather think that hound's name was "Haughty" and though she had a good nose with plenty of drive, her tongue might have been used more freely. Kyte was always ready to follow his pack wherever they went, and I should not have dreamt of offering my assistance on that occasion if his mount had been fresh.

When we were back within hail of John o' Gaunt, some vigorous holloaing [*sic*] told us our fox was only just in front; but then I felt sorry for him, though a few minutes earlier I had been thirsting for his blood. Like the gallant hero he was he had passed the covert, and was continuing his journey onwards; but on the railway embankment he met a party of platelayers, who, holloaing [*sic*] in his face, obliged him to take refuge in the home from which he started. There he died a few minutes later, and thus ended the great run of 12th April.

Chapter XII

Captain Burns-Hartopp's Final Seasons

Season 1900–1901

Some nice little gallops in October gave promise of good sport later on; but the promise was not fulfilled, and the two first months were barren of anything approaching first class. In the previous season the Quorn had the lion's share of luck; but in this everything went wrong. Capt. Burns-Hartopp broke his pelvis the second week in November, and was in a very serious state for some weeks. No master could have worked harder in the interests of the hunt, and, after a summer devoted to getting things in shape, it was cruel luck to be laid up for the rest of the season. However, he was fortunate to have pulled through.

This season was Mr. Evan Hanbury's first with the Cottesmore, and he is yet another of the good sportsmen who have passed out of this world during the war.

The new master had been one of the regular followers of the Cottesmore for some years, and I had many a pleasant ride with him. His reputation at that time for jumping big fences earned for him the name of "Jumping Josh" and any particularly forbidding bit of timber from which most people turned away he would charge with fearless ardour. In those days he was a bachelor; but that is some time ago, as the war has claimed his son as one of its victims.

On Gillson's retirement at the close of Mr. Baird's mastership, the new master secured the services of Arthur Thatcher, and with very satisfactory results. He was, as every one knew, a first-rate horseman and extraordinarily quick, but he also proved a very capable huntsman. We have it on the authority of "Jorrocks" that a huntsman's reputation is at the mercy of every schoolboy and anyone who has been out hunting half a dozen times, so that it is not surprising Thatcher was subject to some adverse criticism.

It is really very unfair to criticize the methods of a huntsman from the back row, as unless you are in a position to see what hounds are doing, you cannot possibly arrive at a correct judgment of the situation.

Thatcher was so quick that the majority of the field never saw what he was doing and in consequence they accused him of galloping his foxes to death without the aid of hounds.

Those who know anything about hunting, know that if a pack is not allowed to hunt they are very soon spoilt, and I have often seen Thatcher with his hounds persevere on a bad scent to a successful conclusion.

The Belvoir had some very enjoyable gallops in the vale, and Sherbrooke's covert proved a never-failing resort when other places were blanks. The Cottesmore also had some short gallops, but nothing that is worth recalling at this distance of time.

Scent had been provokingly bad all the season; but it improved considerably in March, and on the eleventh of that month the Quorn had a very fast ring from Walton Thorns, and killed their fox. This covert is on the edge of the tableland or wolds, as it is called, and numerous valleys run from it, so that a ring from here may mean compassing a wide extent of country. The ring included Seagrave and Burton Spinneys, which probably meant nearly twelve miles of excellent grass.

On the following Friday the same pack had a smart gallop from Scraptoft Gorse. The start was not very promising; but when hounds turned back from Thurnby station to Scraptoft gardens they settled down to run hard, and never hesitated or slacked till they had bowled their fox over handsomely in the open between Quenby and the Coplow.

The Belvoir had a most enjoyable run from Burbidge's covert on 20th March, the fox just beating them by going to ground in a breeding earth at Thorpe Satchville. I remember the occasion well, and that the deputy master led us to the hill overlooking the covert instead of subjecting us to the usual scrambling start and dash through the ford.

The deputy acting for Sir Gilbert Greenall was Mr. "Ned" Griffiths, and he made a most excellent field master, curbing the too ardent spirits with a firm hand, but doing it with such a pleasant manner that no one could feel hurt. That day was not the sort to expect a scent, a strong wind was blowing, and other conditions were unfavourable; but hounds can generally run a fox which goes straight.

Mr. Griffiths and Capell were delighted with their excursion into the Quorn territory, but would doubtless have been better pleased had they killed their fox.

Season 1901–1902

My *Field* letters for the earlier part of this season are missing, but I don't think there was much sport. The Cottesmore had two capital runs on the last day of November. The first was forty-five minutes, hounds racing their fox to death, and the second was a straight run from Berry Gorse to Barleythorpe.

New Year's Day the Belvoir met at Saltby, and my account reads "the best day of the season thus far"; but what appeared to have raised my enthusiasm more than anything was a flying burst from Sproxton Thorns to Newman's Gorse. On this occasion the time was exactly nine minutes, which, I think, was a record for that distance. Then a twisting fox from Freeby Wood was raced to death, the best part of which was fifteen or twenty minutes in the Chadwell valley. The day ended with a very excellent run from Goadby Gorse to some earths in the Belvoir woods near Stathern.

Sport had been moderate all the season; but there was a great improvement in March.

The Quorn ran very fast from Cream Gorse by way of Barsby to the viaduct near John o' Gaunt station—thirty-two minutes—when they unfortunately switched on to the line of a fresh fox. On the following Wednesday (5th March) the Belvoir had a very nice run from Clawson Thorns, and killed their fox. The same pack had also a very good day on the succeeding Wednesday.

A fox from Burbidge's took a nice line to Kirby Park, and returning by Great Dalby was eventually lost near Wild's Lodge.

In the afternoon there was a still further hunt. A fox found in Freeby Spinney went first of all to Stapleford Park, and then fearing to cross the river again followed its banks until he had passed Melton. Hounds were allowed to do their work without any assistance, when we had the satisfaction and rather unusual experience of seeing them hunt up to within a hundred yards of their fox, and catching a view race into him. Walter Kyte finished with this season his short occupation of the post of huntsman to the Quorn. No man had ever before been pitchforked into hunting a fashionable pack of hounds without some previous experience in kennel and the field. Considering his limited experience, I think he was extraordinarily successful. The knowledge he had acquired was from watching Tom Firr, whilst riding second-horse to that artist.

He was naturally a good horseman, and, with no fear of the fences, was always in the same field with his hounds. I thought in this his last season, that he felt he was being rather severely criticized, and thus lost confidence; but when he knew he was leaving, he did not worry about what people might be saying, with the result that he killed nearly every fox he found.

Season 1902–1903

This was Tom Bishopp's first season with the Quorn, and I remember thinking how well he hunted a fox with a bad scent on Kirby Gate day.

We had found in Gartree Hill, and eventually killed near Freeby Wood. This was the first time I had seen him, being unable to get out cub-hunting.

Bishopp, in his younger days, had earned the reputation of being one of the hardest and quickest men who had ever crossed the Grafton country, but he was getting on in years when he came to the Quorn. Hunting a fashionable pack of hounds is a hard and strenuous life, for which a man must be in vigorous health. Bishopp hunted a fox on a bad scenting day with extraordinary skill and perseverance; but he had lost some of youth's dash, which put him at a disadvantage in a fast gallop amidst the Quorn crush.

November proved to be a good scenting month, and there were several good runs. On the 15th, the Cottesmore found a fox in Berry Gorse and killed him close to Thorpe Trussells.

Then in the evening of the same day they raced another fox to his death from Berry Gorse; but scent must have been exceptionally good that day, for I heard that both the Quorn and the Belvoir ran fast.

A certain amount of frost and snow stopped hunting a few days before Christmas, but sport was good on the whole, though without any run of a sensational nature.

All three packs did well in January until the frost came again. A seven-mile point with the Quorn from Brooksby Spinney by way of Ashby Pastures and across the river near Eye-Kettleby to a kill on the Fosse near Ella's Gorse, was about the best. The Cottesmore run from Stapleford Park nearly to Waltham was, however, equally good, and also ended with a kill.

The Belvoir had several fast gallops, but on Wednesday, 11th February, they had two runs which eclipsed all others for pace. The first one was from Bescaby Oaks to the artificial earth in the valley below Freeby; but nearly the whole field were left, and hardly anyone saw it. The second fox was found in Newman's Gorse, and after an exceptionally fast burst of twenty-five minutes was killed in Annis' Gorse.

The Quorn had an exceptionally fine hunting run on 23rd February, finding their fox in Grimstone Gorse, and killing him at Stathern as he vainly tried to reach the Belvoir woods.

Bishopp excelled himself on this occasion, and I have no hesitation in saying that the run, with its brilliant finish, was entirely due to him. After leaving Clawson Thorn, we descended to the vale, and though scent was only moderate the pace to Stathern was very good. This is a big village, and there are so many places round human habitations in which a fox can hide, that we feared he might escape. I galloped on through the village and down the road to the station, when I was fortunately able to view the fox. He had not seen or heard me, and I did not holloa, but just watched him. To my surprise he went down to the mouth of a pond and was some seconds lapping up water.

I always want to see a fox killed that has been hunted, but I must confess that on this occasion my sympathies were with the weary and thirsty animal.

In spite of this temporary weakness I rejoiced with and congratulated Bishopp when a few minutes later hounds were tearing their victim to bits. The same pack had another run on the following Friday, when, after finding a fox in the Prince of Wales, they ran him round by Gaddesby, Rearsby and Brooksby, to turn back and kill him at Barsby.

It was about this time we heard of Lord Edward Manners' death.

For several seasons he was acting master before Sir Gilbert Greenall took the Belvoir, and very excellently he filled the post. I have already said that Thatcher was a much better huntsman than those who wished to criticize him would believe, and I come now to an extraordinary [sic] good hunting run with the Cottesmore, in which I thought he displayed marked skill. The occasion was on 7th March, when the meet was at Stapleford, and scent was distinctly bad. The fox was found on the Burton Flat and not far from Gartree Hill. First of all, he went towards Melton, and then bearing to the right passed through Burbidge's to Brentingby, after crossing and recrossing the river. He then seemed to change his mind—think he had found the earth closed—and made a bee-line for Somerby, but when within hail of that village swung off to the left.

From this point up to Ranksboro' hounds could only run in spasms in spite of it being a fine stretch of good scenting turf. At this covert the second-whip had galloped on, and was just in time to view our fox away.

Scent, I think, was improving, and hounds ran at a brisk

pace to Whissendine and from thence on to Brentingby; but the fox had not the strength to face the river again, and was killed a few minutes later. I look on this as one of the best hunting runs I have ever seen, in which hounds and huntsmen share the credit between them. Most watches made the time an hour and fifty minutes, though according to my clock it was exactly two hours.

The run of the season was undoubtedly scored by the Quorn, and came in the last week's hunting. To be exact, it was on Friday, 27th March, the day that "Drumcree" won the Grand National.

The fox was found in Barkby-Holt and ran first of all to Mr. Carrington's plantation at Ashby Pastures. From thence on the run was practically straight to the farther side of Barleythorpe, where hounds ran up to their fox and killed. At the time I made the point to be about eleven or twelve miles, but estimated the distance covered to have been at least twenty. There was only one short check in the whole run, and it is therefore due to the huntsman to consider the fox found was the one killed.

A very similar run took place during Lord Lonsdale's mastership, about nine years previously, and that one also started from Barkby-Holt.

My own idea about this later run is that we changed, or may have done, in one of the gullies between Burrough and Somerby. The fox killed was not more than a three-year-old, and I rather doubt the stamina of that age to have stood up before hounds over the distance at such a fast pace. Hounds ran fast enough from Barkby-Holt to Ashby Pastures to have tired an ordinary fox.

There was a fox in Walter Kyte's time that we found on several occasion in Mr. Carrington's plantation and led us a dance into Cottesmore territory. I rather fancied at the time that it was this same old customer who had temporarily taken up his residence in Barkby-Holt. Then there was a very cunning old varmint who inhabited Queniborough Spinney, and was always away before hounds reached the covert. He generally gave us a good run, and was lost in the Cottesmore country. His line was rather similar to the Ashby Pastures customer—possibly it was the same. This finished a very good season.

Tom Firr died at the end of 1902, and the following extract from my *Field* letter of 27th December is my last tribute to that great huntsman.

"My duty as correspondent to this paper would have called me to attend the Belvoir at Harby on Saturday had I not felt hunting that day was out of the question when the great huntsman was being carried to his last resting-place. The little I know and all I have learnt about the 'noble science' has been acquired by watching this wonderful man, and it was a melancholy satisfaction to be able to pay the last mark of respect by following him to his grave. Clad in the sombre garb which custom ordains, a large body of people had gathered in the little churchyard at Quorn to do honour to all that remained of the once famous huntsman. Waiting there in solemn silence, I think most of us recalled stirring scenes in the past, when our pleasure had been due to the efforts of Tom Firr to show us sport. Overhead a dull, leaden sky, a cold, still air, and fences in the distance clearly outlined in black relief—verily a day such as this man has often described to be his ideal for hunting. Without pomp or blare of trumpets, as he had lived, so he passed to the grave. Hunting men are not a class who give much outward expression to their feelings, but as the earth rattled down on the coffin-lid and we turned away they were few who did not feel some emotion and whisper, 'God rest his soul.'"

Captain Burns-Hartopp's Final Seasons

Season 1903–1904

Rain fell heavily in September and October, with the result that there was some good sport during cub-hunting. All three packs had some nice little gallops, but the Quorn run from Queniborough Spinney to Asfordby was perhaps the best.

I notice in my *Field* letter that the Quorn committee decided to start "capping" again, and discussing the question of hunt finances, I ventured to remind readers that subscriptions were due on the 1st of November. People have rather got into the habit of looking on a hunt subscription as a donation, which it does not matter when they pay and is usually left to the last.

There was nothing of a sensational nature up to Christmas, but a general average of good sport, hounds being able to run every day. Perhaps the best scenting day fell to the Quorn on 21st December, when they had three good gallops. The last one was from Ella's Gorse to Melton, a seven-mile point, and most of it being fast. Hounds had to be stopped owing to the failing light, and the fox therefore escaped. This run only wanted a kill at the finish to have given it a prominent position in the annals of the hunt.

Scent was exceptionally good with the commencement of the New Year, but I was unable to take any active part after 28th December. On that day I took a fall, the effects of which lasted for ten years, though finishing the day and riding home fourteen miles.

It was rather a curious fall, and I was never very clear what really happened, but think the horse must have struck me on the head with a forefoot. The horse was one given me by Mr. "Foxy" Keene, and a very bold hunter. I turned him rather quickly out of a road at a small place, but to my surprise he swerved and went sideways into a deep ditch full of thorns, which was also the village sewer. I was head down through the thorns and in some danger of drowning, with my legs sticking up in the air; but the reins having caught in my spurs, the horse plunging pulled me out.

For the next two or three seasons riding was really more pain than pleasure, and this must therefore finish my references to individual seasons.

My last day in 1904 was with the Belvoir on 10th February, when they found a fox in Bescaby Oaks and killed him near Cottesmore village, which was a nine-mile point, My head was troubling me at the time and was not therefore able to see much of the run, but I managed to see the end, and after a fourteen-mile ride home on a bad hack, wrote my account for the *Field* and retired to bed for ten weeks.

Taking it all in all, of the runs that I saw and those my friends told me about, I consider this to have been one of the best seasons within my experience. The ground had been thoroughly saturated with rain, and, as every one knows, provides the best sport when in that state. I am not altogether of the opinion that the difference lies in the improvement of scent, but have always thought that a great deal is due to the sticky nature of the clay, which clogs a fox's brush and handicaps very considerably his speed. We all know that if hounds can keep fairly close to their fox, they will run well with a moderate scent.

Season 1904–1905

Unlike the previous one, the beginning of this season was extraordinary [*sic*] dry, and it was really hardly fit to ride until December. With the exception of a very smart run on the Quorn opening day from Gartree Hill to Wyfordby with a kill in the open, sport was moderate up to Christmas.

Captain Burns-Hartopp's Final Seasons

Capt. Burns-Hartopp continued his run of ill-luck by losing the services of his first whip through a fall in cub-hunting. Will Farmer gave every promise of being a very efficient whipper-in, and it must have been a great disappointment to him to break his leg before the season had begun. There was a slight improvement in scent with the beginning of the New Year; but frost and snow curtailed most of the hunting days in January.

On 17th February the Quorn finding an outlier close to Queniborough village ran him to Ranksborough, where they unfortunately changed. This was a very fine run with only a moderate scent, and the point is over eleven miles. The gallop of the following Friday was, however, better appreciated, for hounds ran very fast, and rolled their fox over handsomely in the open. There was a thick fog that day, and the majority of people had no idea in what direction they were going.

In the same week the Belvoir had a very smart five-and-twenty minutes from Newman's Gorse, when the fox managed to find a rabbit hole big enough to shelter him. Grand National day again provided the Quorn with a good run, and finding a fox in Barkby-Holt they killed him near Ashby Folville; but the distance was much greater, as Carr Bridge, Lowesby and Quenby were included in a wide loop. The next day the Cottesmore had a smart gallop in the morning and a good hunting run in the afternoon; in both instances Thatcher had the satisfaction of handling his foxes.

Every follower of the Quorn regretted that Capt. Burns-Hartopp was resigning the mastership of that pack. No master has ever worked harder in the interests of a hunt, and no man has ever met with such a long series of misfortunes in his endeavour to show sport; but, in spite of cruel luck, he won through in the end. There were occasional lean times, but, on the whole, the period of his mastership showed an extraordinary average of good sport.

I had begun hunting this season as usual, but found that after two hours in the saddle my head would not stand it, and, in consequence, was able to do very little riding.

Some remarks of mine about hunting in "pink", which appeared in the *Field* that season, are here added, as I think It is a point that should not be lost sight of.

"On the occasion of the last day's hunting it struck me that there was a much larger proportion of black coats than I had ever noticed before, and that many regular followers of hounds were clad in sober colours instead of the regulation pink. Now this is all wrong, and not as it should be. All of us who subscribe to hounds or enjoy a stake in the country ought to clothe ourselves in the proper costume out of respect to the hunt and its master, if for no other reason. There are, however, many other good and sufficient reasons which should compel us to wear a scarlet coat when hunting regularly with a pack of hounds. One of these, which is by no means unimportant, is that men over whose land we disport ourselves like to see the scarlet, and that should be quite enough for us. The unconscious influence of brilliant colouring on the minds of those who live amongst sober tints is a fact which is not sufficiently appreciated by men to whom gorgeous displays are common sights. The countryman reaps very few advantages from the sportsmen who invade his district, and we might therefore at least give him the benefit of a respectable show. It is to our interest, and to the interest of hunting generally, that the sport should remain popular amongst those whom circumstances prevent from taking any active participation, and we may be sure that popularity would quickly wane were the scarlet coat to become a thing of the past.

"We are well aware, or should be if we are not, that we hunt only on sufferance, and we accept the privilege of disporting ourselves over the land without making any acknowledgement.

Our forefathers did this in generations gone by, and the tradition of those days enables us to do it now, though the conditions are much altered. This tradition, however, is inseparably connected with the scarlet coat, and the disappearance of one would inevitably mean the weakening of the other. The gaudy garment should not be looked on as an adornment to the figure it covers, but as a badge of honour, which entitles the owner to respect, and at the same time lays on him the duty of universal courtesy to the man who goes afoot."

Chapter XIII

Captain Forester to the War

Seasons 1905–06 to 1913–14

Captain Frank Forester had hunted in Leicestershire from a boy, and no man ever rode straighter to hounds; but his love of hunting was greater than his love for a rousing gallop, so that he graduated early as a huntsman in Ireland and the provinces. I remember him when he came out with a groom and a leading rein; but he is only about a couple of years younger than I am.

Although I was not in England in his last season (1917–18) I hear that when he hunted hounds he was always with the pack, and was going as brilliantly as ever.

It was in this year (1905) that the New Quorn Kennels were finished; but hounds did not move until the following May. For something like a hundred and fifty years hounds had been kennelled in Quorn; but what had once been a tiny village had grown into a town, and was utterly unsuitable for a pack in modern times. The new kennels are near Pawdy Cross roads, and though it is not a very beautiful spot, there are doubtless many advantages to recommend it. A few trees would be a decided improvement, both for appearance and shading hounds in hot weather.

The best Quorn run of this season was from Welby Osierbeds to Croxton Park, where the fox went to ground. It was five-and-twenty minutes to Brentingby Spinney, with a curve out towards Thorpe Arnold to increase the distance, and those who know the country will realize the pace hounds must have run.

The Belvoir dated their best run from Waltham Ashes, though many preferred the gallop from Croxton Park to Wymondham without a check, and a kill at the end.

Capt. Forester lent a portion of the Charnwood Forest country to that good sportsman, Lord Harrington, who in spite of his threescore years and ten was not content with four days in his own country.

A fairly good season, and very few days when you were not able to get a gallop after hounds and jump a few fences.

I am sorry to say that huntsman and masters have got into the habit of complaining about the want of scent on every occasion when they fail in catching foxes; but they seem to forget that such complaints are reflections on their packs. Any cur can hunt and go fast with a really burning scent; but a hound with a good nose ought to be able to drive on when the inferior animal cannot own the line.

I was very severely criticized this season by some of the old Quornites for altering the name of a covert—so they said— though I still maintain I was only reverting to an old name. I must have been guilty of the offence in my *Field* articles for some years; but my critics had only just begun to realize that the name I used had been generally adopted.

I ventured to call the wood which is close to Ragdale by that name, and the majority of people know it now as such. Perhaps I may as well add here the explanation I wrote at the time, but which I fear did not appease the wrath of my critics.

"The alteration of an old-established name would, of course, be an unpardonable offence, but, in this instance, it is possibly merely the restitution of a more ancient title. On a very old map it is plainly marked 'Rakedale Wood,' which proves the existence and use of the name before even the most venerable of my critics was born. Thrussington Wolds, the name by which they wish to describe the wood, was the local term which embraced all the flat or wold land in the parish. Within that area were many patches of straggling, unenclosed gorse, which held foxes, and with the wood became eventually known as Thrussington Wolds; but that is no reason one should lose sight of the original title of one particular portion of the wolds. About the time of Waterloo wheat was making a big price, and all available land was brought into cultivation for the purpose of raising crops. The wolds, which had hitherto afforded a bare existence for a few lean cattle, and a resting-place for the travelling fox, was then ploughed up and made to take its part in producing food for the country. In the process of time the high prices for wheat went down, and much of the poor land reverted to its original state. For generations gorse had sprinkled its seed over the wolds, and these quickly sprung up into robust plants when the plough no longer disturbed the soil. Mr. Charlton then enclosed several acres of this self-sown gorse, which, with the aid of the natural thorn and bramble, grew into an impenetrable thicket, known for a time as Charlton's Gorse, or the New Covert, but which I have always called Thrussington Gorse. Barely 200 yards distant is the wood which has caused the dispute about a name. Those who object to the wood being called Ragdale bring as their strongest argument that it is in the parish of Thrussington. This is correct, but the division of parishes was often made a matter of convenience by those who collected the dues, and, as the wood belonged to the Ferrars family, it should bear the name of the village in which they resided. Thrussington Wolds includes the wood, the gorse and the surrounding land, but the name of Ragdale Wood applies only to the covert in dispute."

On the last Friday in November 1906 the late master of the Quorn, Capt. Burns-Hartopp, was presented with the testimonial which had been subscribed for by those who enjoyed the sport during his reign, and probably the most gratifying feature to the recipient was the fact that a large number of farmers had subscribed.

Mr. Hanbury had given permission for hounds to meet at Little Dalby Hall, which is in Cottesmore territory, and it was there the presentation was made.

Mr. Hanbury must have been then thinking of his own resignation, as a month later he had sent it in, and the Cottesmore country was again vacant. He, with the assistance of Thatcher as huntsman, had shown excellent sport, and the affairs of the hunt had run smoothly, which is always a sure sign of good management.

The Quorn had an extraordinary run at the end of February 1907. They found their fox in Barkby-Holt, and killed him in two hours and twenty minutes at Newbold. Hounds were running fast most of the time, and the fox must have been exceptionally stout to have stood up so long. His point on first leaving covert was Cream Gorse; but foot people and carriages forced him by Baggrave and Lowesby nearly to John o' Gaunt. He was determined to make his original point, and in spite of having to face the wind made a bee-line for Cream Gorse. However on arriving at that covert he was unable to find a substitute, and was obliged to wander down-wind till fate overtook him.

Lord Lonsdale began his reign over the Cottesmore in 1907, and had as huntsman a son of Gillson, who was huntsman in the latter part of Mr. Baird's time. No expense was spared in mounting the hunt servants, and every detail of equipment was as perfect as it could be made. An ill-fitting coat on a huntsman may not spoil his chance of showing sport, but, in the "Shires", a hunt should be as smart as possible and a pattern to the "provinces". Those who knew the new master were fully aware that he would permit no slovenliness in dress.

I can just remember his father having the Cottesmore, and to the best of my belief he rode in a very low-crowned top hat; but being only a small boy at the time am not very certain. At that time Mr. Tailby had a large slice of the country.

The Belvoir gallop from Stonesby Gorse to Wymondham, and thence on to Gunby Gorse, was probably the fastest of anything seen that season. Hounds could have gone no faster, and there was not the sign of a check until they reached Wymondham—a steeplechase with less than half a dozen men anywhere near the flying pack. The second portion of the run was at a more moderate pace, and there was no kill at the finish, so that we may conclude there was a change somewhere.

The best hunting run of the season in my opinion was with the Quorn on 21st February, when they found a fox in the Coplow and killed him at Little Dalby. The fox was probably an old veteran who had found out that huntsmen dislike a railway, and no doubt had often escaped pursuit by sticking close to the metals. On this occasion he dodged to and fro across the line several times before reaching Lowesby station; but finding then that these wiles had not shaken off his pursuers went boldly across the open. Leaving Tilton station to the right, he changed his course on reaching the base of Whatboro Hill, and swinging to the left went straight away to Owston village. The earlier part of the run had not been over a very rideable country; but after the turn it could not have been improved upon. Hounds and huntsman both seemed to realize they were hunting a good fox.

Somerby was left to the right, Burrough Hill Wood to the left, and it was not until the fox had almost entered Great Dalby that he bore to the right and climbed the hill towards

Melton; but his bolt was shot, and hounds ran into him at Little Dalby. This I consider a run that is worth recalling, equally for the stamina of the fox, the perseverance of hounds, and the skill with which their huntsman handled them. Scent was not first class, but it was of a good holding variety, hounds never lost any time and ran very fast occasionally, so that for a fox to stand up for an hour and thirty minutes was a marvellous feat of endurance. A fox of this kind would run hounds out of scent nine days out of ten.

This was Bishopp's last season with the Quorn, and of the many good runs which he brought to a successful conclusion I think he will look back on 21st February as his happiest performance.

According to all precedent the Quorn should have had their opening meet on the first Monday in November; but for some reason it was deferred in 1908 to the following week—it may have been hard ground, though I can't remember. That first of the month was, however, a day to remember, as finding a fox in a turnip field near Thrussington they killed him at Widmerpool after an exceptionally brilliant gallop. The new huntsman, George Leaf, thus made an excellent impression, both in the way he handled hounds and in his quickness in riding across country.

The best sport of that season was in the first month, and the remainder was only moderate, though all three packs enjoyed some nice gallops at end of March 1909.

According to my summary of 1909–10 it was a brilliant season; but, truth to tell, I can remember very little about it now.

One run only has left its impression on my memory, and that was the occasion when the Quorn found a fox in Gaddesby Square Spinney and killed him near Cold Overton. It was the last day of the year 1909, and the meet was at Queniborough. The point was eight miles, and the time an hour and fifteen minutes. It was an ideal line and an almost perfect run.

I did not enjoy it myself, for the reason that I was riding an animal with limited jumping powers, and never went near a fence; but in spite of that was alongside of hounds the whole way by use of either roads or bridle-roads. I was thus able to estimate the qualities of the run although it gave me very little pleasure, except perhaps viewing the fox on several occasions.

At the time Walter Kyte was huntsman to the Quorn there was a fox who lived in Queniborough Spinney, and gave several good runs. It would be hardly possible to imagine that this could be the same; but I had a strange feeling all through the run that we were running the veteran who had repeatedly beaten Kyte. The pace was only moderate at the start, but it quickened up after crossing the road by Barsby school, and from thence I don't think hounds were touched. The stream, which is known when it reaches that parish as the Ashby brook, was kept on the left hand to within a field of Owston village, when the fox crossed, and leaving the valley went on up hill by Somerby brickyard towards Knossington.

I should have liked to have been on the back of a good hunter and to have ridden close to hounds through that run, as it is a line I have always pictured in my dreams.

Both the Cottesmore and the Belvoir had some very good runs that season; but there was nothing that appealed to me at the time to enable me to remember now.

The season of 1910-11 was extraordinarily open, and all three packs had good sport. It will, however, be indelibly associated in my memory with the runs which the Barkby-Holt customer gave the Quorn. He had beaten Leaf and his pack on several occasions; but on 10th February the hunstman had his revenge, and this gallant fox died after completing an eight-mile point. There was only a moderate scent, and in my opinion the hero owed his defeat to having spent his vigour in love-making overnight, so that he was not in the condition to make his usual efforts. Then in the initial burst hounds started away at his brush and gave him a rare dusting for some minutes, which would of a necessity paralyse his subsequent efforts. Yes! and he was strangely out of luck, for he had managed to dodge hounds after that first burst, and they had even gone to draw another covert, then when the veteran thought the coast was clear some one viewed him, and the pack were again switched on to his trail.

After that he never had the strength to get far enough ahead of hounds to give him a chance, and though he struggled gamely on it was all to no purpose. When viewed below Gartree Hill his weariness was plainly evident; but he kept on for another four miles, and was not caught till he reached Kirby.

Of course all credit was due to hounds and huntsman; but I cannot help feeling sympathy for the hunted on this occasion.

We all have to die some time, and he died gallantly as he had lived.

Lord Londsale resigned the mastership of the Cottesmore at the end of this season, and General Brocklehurst was appointed in his place.

The opening chapters of the season 1911–12 were marked by several smart little gallops with all three packs. General Brocklehurst made an excellent start with the Cottesmore in the first year of his reign. It was at the commencement of this season that Capt. Pennell Elmhirst ("Brooksby") retired from the active list.

In my opinion he was the pioneer of modern hunting journalism, and I do not think anyone has yet ever come up to him in writing a readable account of a run. How much the *Field* owe him for having assisted in making their paper the leading sporting weekly, only those who were on the staff forty years ago could tell, and they must be all dead now.

The *Field*, it is true, deals with many other subjects besides hunting; but the "sport of kings" was the chief factor in increasing its circulation, and I think they make a great mistake in relegating the chase to a secondary position. I was paid—very much reduced rate now—to write for them, and it is not my business to criticize their editorial methods; but quite apart from the money question, I took a great interest in doing my best to maintain the standard which "Brooksby" had set up when he wrote for the Melton district.

The doings of the "Puddleshire Hunt" have only a purely local interest, and though they may have equally good sport very few people want to read about them. The tendency of the *Field* nowadays appears to be to give prominence to provincial packs at the expense of the Shires.

There is only one Melton Mowbray, and there is no country in the world that can compare with the district surrounding the town.

It is the ambition of every man with any pretensions to ride over fences to make his pilgrimage to the hunting Mecca, and have at least one day there before he dies.

The doings of hounds in that neighbourhood are therefore of world-wide interest, and should not be hid under a bushel of chaff.

I remember a very fast gallop with the Belvoir on 13th December 1911, lasting twenty-five minutes, and every one said at the time that they had never seen hounds go such a pace. The fox was found in Newman's Gorse, and was marked to ground in Eaton Plantation.

The man who had the best of it all the way was Mr. "Teddy" Brooks. I don't remember mentioning his name before, because he had only risen to the zenith of his riding powers about 1909, and was not born when these memoirs started.

I have no hesitation in saying that he was the best man

to hounds who has ever ridden across Leicestershire. This statement is made without any reservation, and as I have seen all the leading lights for the last forty years my experience should give me the authority to speak.

Mr. "Teddy" Brooks was, I am proud to say, Leicestershire bred, and was a great thruster even as a small boy; but though very keen and ready to ride at anything, it was only in the last four or five years before the war that he rose to the supreme heights. His hands certainly lacked delicacy of touch, and he rather preferred a horse that pulled; but he never touched his horse's mouth in jumping, and I have never seen anyone put a horse at a fence as well. The absolutely perfect horseman should have good "hands"; but "Teddy's" were not what I should call bad "hands" they were merely hard, and in consequence the horse that suited him best was one that had lost some of the sensitive feeling in the mouth.

Why I say that Mr. T. E. Brooks was the best man to hounds I have ever known, is that I have never seen anyone follow a pack religiously field for field, jumping everything as it came, and yet take so few falls. He rode very short, the modern method, which I consider the most effective, both for controlling a horse and relieving the weight on his hindquarters.

I always compare Count Charles Kinsky with "Teddy" as examples of the two different styles

The former was a most perfect specimen of the old-fashioned seat, which is certainly more graceful than the modern hunched-up position.

Count Charles was not only an ornament in the saddle, but was also a first-class man to hounds, with lots of nerve and splendidly mounted. On first coming to Leicestershire he rode gallantly at everything; but the Leicestershire bottom is very deceptive, at one spot it may be only a few feet in width, and yet ten yards away on either side it becomes a yawning chasm. Zoedone's pilot rode straight ahead, and never stopped if hounds were running fast to gauge the probable width, with the result that he not only took a good many falls, but broke several horses' backs. "Teddy" rode at these places with equal confidence, and when they happened to be extra wide would get over with a scramble; but as there was no weight on the horse's hindquarters there were never any broken backs. Thirty years ago I should have laughed at the idea of a man being able to ride across country with his knees up to the pommel of the saddle; but we "live and learn", and experience has taught me that the modern method is correct.

Poor "Teddy" lies out somewhere in an unmarked grave not far from Menin, where he fell when the Leicestershire Yeomanry made such a gallant stand in the early part of the war. At the same time Colonel Evans Freke was killed, and many other good men from the Shires.

I am not going to bore you with any more runs, as we have now reached the spring of 1912, and I cannot recall anything very sensational in 1914. In the September of that year I joined the army, and was only released in March 1919. One solitary day's hunting is all I had in that time.

There have been many changes since then. Lord Lonsdale took the Cottesmore at the outbreak of war and carried on practically at his own expense—at the moment of writing he is still the master of that pack.

Capt. Forester resigned the Quorn in 1918, and after a short period of a committee, Major Burnaby and Mr. W. E. Paget became joint masters. Their huntsman, Wilson, is, I believe, a great success; but have not yet seen him hunt hounds.

Major Bouch has the Belvoir now in his own hands, and I understand is hunting hounds himself.

How much hunting I may be able to do in the future—

writing in autumn 1919—I am unable to say, as, after having acted as hunting correspondent to the *Field* for nearly thirty years, they now say that they can pay me less than a third of what I formerly received. It therefore appears likely that I shall have to follow hounds on foot, as I shall not be able to keep a horse with hay and corn at its present price.

In addition to this I have taken unto myself a wife, and the necessary expenses attached thereto.

I will conclude this volume with an apology for giving undue prominence to my own doings, and to the runs I myself enjoyed; but I was writing memories of things that affected me personally, and not the second-hand stories of others.

Like Whyte-Melville [*sic*], the best of my fun I owe it to horse and to hound.

Chapter XIV

Reflections: Old Friends, Men and Horses

The man who left the strongest impression on my mind in early days was Mr. Little Gilmour, though I was only a boy at the time, and he was then on the shelf as far as hard riding was concerned. He was a contemporary of my father's, and their lights were probably brightest from 1835 to 1855, whilst my arrival into this world did not occur till 1860. Whyte-Melville I can also recall, an occasional visitor to Melton, with a kind word for a small boy. A figure that is associated in my mind with the same period is that of Sir John Fludyer. I managed with his assistance to get to the end of a run from Little Dalby to Owston Wood, and ever afterwards when able to have a day with the Cottesmore he took me under his wing. Much water has flowed by since that time, and I have met men of all sorts; but "Sir John" still remains my ideal of a gentleman, both in appearance and manner—kindly, courtly and considerate.

Capt. "Puggy" Riddell and Capt. "Tom" Boyce were both regular visitors to Melton before I emerged from the chrysalis of boyhood. The latter was with us up to a few years ago, and to the last looked much as I remembered him forty years earlier. No one knew exactly how old he really was, and he was always rather touchy on the subject. It was said he had been gazetted a cornet before Queen Victoria came to the throne; but that was doubtless a slight exaggeration. His age was always a joke with friends who wanted to pull his leg, and hence the point of the story.

Some stranger seeing the tall chimney of Asfordby ironworks in the distance, asked Mr. Pennington what it was, to which that genial humorist replied, without a moment's hesitation: "Oh! that's a monument to the old fellow called Tom Boyce, who used to hunt here years ago." The said "old fellow" being out hunting that day, and very much alive; but the chimney was known thereafter as "Tom Boyce's monument", much to the disgust of its godfather.

I cannot remember Captain Boyce in his best days; but he was very quick, rode blood horses, and have seen him go well when past his "three-score-and-ten".

Mr. Pennington emigrated from Yorkshire, when after trying South Leicestershire and the fringe of the Cottesmore, he eventually settled down in the Quorn country. Having married a sister of Capt. Hartopp, he foreswore his Yorkshire birthright and became identified with the county of adoption. Ever ready to see the humour of a situation, and to crack jokes at the covertside, his wit enlivened many a dull moment, and his power of repartee was only excelled by the eccentricity of his remarks.

This reminds me that I have omitted mention of a very good run with the Belvoir, which finished close to Ragdale, where the Penningtons then lived. The account of the run is missing from my *Field* cuttings, and I can only make a guess at the actual date, but believe it was Wednesday, 13th March 1889.

Where hounds had met or what had happened in the morning I have not the slightest idea now; but a much reduced field accompanied Gillard to see him find the afternoon fox at Melton Spinney.

On the previous Saturday I had bought a horse at Leicester just over from Ireland, and it was his misfortune that this occasion should have been chosen for his introduction to Leicestershire. It was my usual custom to ride a new horse first, and have an old friend second, but I rather think the first horse that day was also a new purchase.

A fox was away at once and with hounds equally quick after him, they ran a "cracker," nearly up to the Waltham road, and back to within a field—the Melton side—of the starting-point. My youngster—rising five, but at the time I thought he was a year older—had carried me brilliantly, and, of course, I was delighted with him.

The fox had, I suppose, just made this preliminary circle to find out if it was necessary to exert himself further, and then realizing scent was too good to dawdle about, he set his head for a distant point.

Having secured a good position, I meant seeing the best of the fun, and incidentally trying still further the abilities of my new purchase. The pack were streaming away downhill and putting on the pace. I managed to get first cut at the brook, which my young Irishman flew in his stride. There is always a certain amount of satisfaction in jumping open water, however small; but the pleasure is considerably enhanced by getting over first

The railway gates at the level-crossing were flung open by plate-layers who had seen us coming, and we sailed on uphill to the Scalford road.

My young horse had carried me so satisfactorily up to this point, that it was with the utmost confidence I launched him at a foot-stile, both high and stiff. Timber in any shape or form must have been unknown in that part of Ireland responsible for his education, as he appeared to think it was a species of fence he could brush through. I hit the ground somewhat heavily; but he had such extraordinary good shoulders that he only came on his head, and in a lightning-like recovery put a foot through my top-hat. There was a smaller stile into the road, but the first one had taught him a lesson which he never forgot during his sixteen seasons in Leicestershire.

There was a slight check in the road, and then hounds settled down again to run hard. The Nottingham turnpike was crossed near Sysonby, and from there we went straight on to Welby, where, I think, the fox was headed, as he bore right-handed for a field in the direction of Ab-Kettleby before resuming his original course.

Hounds at this time were running on continuously and running fast, though not racing. I cannot now recall every field we went into, but Saxelby Wood, Lord Aylesford's and Shoby Scoles were all left to the right.

The fast part of the run came to an end at the main earths in the Hoby Vale, and from there hounds hunted on to a stick heap near Thrussington Grange. The majority of horses that were left could barely raise a gallop at this period, and though we should have liked to see the fox killed, the pack would have run away from us in a few more fields.

This was an exceptionally fine run, and of those who reached the end there are probably not many now living; but the survivors will not easily forget that day. The point from where hounds turned back in the preliminary ring is rather more than nine miles.

Only a fox of extraordinary staying power could have lived through it, and still carried on. My own idea is that this was the same fox the Quorn found the following season (23rd December) at Walton Thorns, and running him the reverse way killed at Welby. That is the run I have already alluded to as the best I have ever seen. Besides several other features which were very similar, both runs began with rings. It was this gallant fox's bad luck to have been found on this latter occasion, when scenting conditions happened to be quite perfect and hounds were glued to the line.

After the Belvoir run the hunt servants, and the few who had struggled to the finish, went to Mr. Pennington's to refresh. I remember poor old Gillard, in his courtly manner, thanking his host and hostess for their hospitality, and also the final remark with which he bowed himself out, "I will inform his Grace on our return of your very great kindness to us." This, of course, amused Mr. Pennington vastly, and he quoted it for many years afterwards.

Amongst Gillard's numerous duties was a report to the Duke of each day's sport, and I believe he never failed either to write an account or to give the details personally.

After a feed of gruel my youngster went home apparently none the worse for his severe day; but when I sold him by auction the following autumn he was returned as a whistler, which was probably the result of his exertions. I subsequently sold him to a lady, who rode him in Leicestershire for many seasons. He was a horse of extraordinary character, knew more than most men, could open any box door not fastened on the outside, and would kill rats as quick as a terrier. Like many other good hunters he was a shockingly bad hack, and though he never came down he had an alarming way of stumbling over trifling obstructions. I had named him Shylock, and by that name was known to his death.

Talking of Mr. Pennington reminds me of Capt. "Chicken" Hartopp, who was probably one of the best known characters of the "eighties". He was hunting in Leicestershire regularly when I first commenced; but subsequently went to Ireland, where I think he had the Kilkenny hounds for one or two seasons, and unless I am mistaken Fred Earp whipped in to him. His father, the squire of Little Dalby, was alive then, and he doubtless found "the Chicken" an expensive luxury to maintain.

"The Chicken" never lost an opportunity of playing a mad

prank, and a history of his numerous practical jokes would fill a volume. He was always ready for a fight, and could hold his own in a scrap; but his great delight was to blow up something with dynamite, and he had some very narrow shaves of killing himself with that explosive. Popular with every one and beloved by those who knew him intimately, his comparatively early death cut short a career, which might have accomplished something, when attaining years of sober discretion.

Capt. Hartopp had a very powerful voice, was very fond of singing, and in great request at village concerts. He and his friend Major "Sugar" Candy had an argument as to which could sing the best, and with a small wager on the result they competed against each other on the stage at the Aquarium. At the time that building, amongst other entertainments, ran a sort of variety show, and was under the management of a well-known character "Fatty" Coleman, who was asked to act as judge.

"Fatty" told me about it many years later, and in the presence of Major Candy. Neither of the competitors would have made a fortune at a concert hall; but it was a good race, and "the Chicken" was eventually placed first. Both men usually treated life as a joke and tried to get the maximum of fun out of it; but on this occasion they were desperately in earnest and very serious in their efforts.

The competitors and judge have all three now left the stage of life, but none of them will be forgotten by friends who are still alive.

I think Major Candy has already been mentioned as a very good rider, with excellent hands; but in his younger days I believe he was very successful "between the flags" and have heard on one occasion in Ireland he won five races out of six.

Captain "Doggie" Smith was probably in his prime before my riding days started; but I never remember to have seen him anywhere, except in the front rank with hounds. When he left Leicestershire he retired to Sussex, and is still hunting there; but, as lately as Capt. Forester's mastership, he paid his old haunts a visit, and was jumping everything, though well over seventy.

With beautiful hands, good judgment and splendid nerve, he always got the best out of his horses without overtaxing their powers.

I cannot recall anyone with whom it was such a pleasure to ride a run as Captain Smith, for he had not a spark of jealousy, and was invariably in a good temper, or if not, had the tact to hide it. He is one of the few men of whom I have never heard anyone say an unkind word.

Mr. Arthur Coventry it was always a pleasure to see on a horse, and his abilities in race riding are well known. Mr. George Lambton was a familiar figure in Leicestershire at one time; but he forsook Melton for Newmarket, and we seldom see him now.

There have been many changes in the hunting visitors to Melton since I first started hunting regularly in 1879, and there are few of the old lot left.

Mr. Arthur Pryor is still at Egerton Lodge, which house will always be associated in my mind with Lord Wilton—"the old Earl"—and his son, Lord Grey de Wilton.

It was some time in the "eighties" that the "Bell" sheltered a very hard-riding crew, the best of whom were Mr. Alfred Brocklehurst, Mr. "Buck" Barclay and Count Charles Kinsky.

Lord Cowley did not hunt with us regularly, but paid frequent visits, and was always in the first flight, though like others he was rather inclined to press the pack too closely. Lord Cholmondley was also an occasional visitor, and a very fine horseman, not afraid to gallop; but it was as Lord Rocksavage he was best known at Melton.

I think it must have been in the early "nineties" that "the

Tenth" were quartered at York, and there were always some of them at Melton. Good men to hounds all of them, and in a fast gallop you might be sure of seeing them in the front rank. There was Mr. Joe Lawley, Mr. Kavanagh, Lord "Bill" Bentinck, Mr. Bryan and many others, who I can't remember now; but, unless I am much mistaken, Mr. Ned Baird belonged to that regiment.

They were a particularly nice and cheery lot of men, as well as exceptionally fine riders.

Later on Count Zbrowski came to Coventry House, and inaugurated the American invasion; many of those who stopped with him in his first season became regular visitors in succeeding winters.

I remember my first meeting with Count Zbrowski was a morning cub-hunting at Gartree Hill, and I think Major Candy introduced me to him with the remark, that I would ride some of his new horses over Leicestershire for the benefit of their education. However, Zbrowski was a very fine horseman, and could do that equally well himself; but he had at the time a horse they called the bone-breaker, which he said he would be very pleased if I would ride, supposing I did not mind the risk of a fall. He had apparently earned his name by breaking the collar-bone of those who had ridden him; but I was short of horses then, and could not afford to be too particular. The first time I rode the horse he was sent on to the meet for me, when I noticed his mouth was bleeding. Afterwards I always rode him on myself, and found he had a very light mouth. The cause of his falling was being ridden by heavy-fisted men, and he carried me brilliantly without ever making a mistake, until his owner realized what a first-class hunter he was.

A few seasons later I used to buy horses during the winter and spring, selling them by auction the following October.

It, however, rather spoils the pleasure of hunting when you

have to consider the damage you may do to your mount, and the risks of laming him.

I had a few fairly successful sales; but the horses were nearly always bought by people from a distance, as my known reputation for extreme poverty in Leicestershire made those who knew me think it impossible I could have a good horse. The only horse ever bought by anyone who had seen me riding them was a chestnut Lord William Bentinck gave about a hundred and twenty for at my sale. I had not recommended him, but he had noticed him carrying me well, and the horse was certainly a fine performer. Unfortunately his new owner took him up to Yorkshire, where the heavy plough found out his weak point—a very pronounced "dishing" with one foot. This did not affect him on the grass; but in the deep "going" it rendered him helpless, and I fear proved a disappointing purchase.

The best horse I ever owned, and the only one on which it seemed a waste of time to jump small fences, I bought from a farmer for twenty pounds. He originally belonged to Mr. H. T. Barclay, and having broken down was given to the farmer. Being fired and allowed a year's rest with occasional work in the plough team, he was quite sound when he came to me. Doubtless he would have carried me for many seasons had I not aspired to win a race with him; but in addition to being a wonderful jumper was very fast, and was only cantering when most hunters were galloping. It had long been my ambition to win the Ladies' Purse at the Melton Hunt meeting, and this seemed my opportunity. Unfortunately that spring the ground dried up very quickly, and it was as hard as a turnpike road. The result was that I was unable to give him a winding-up gallop, and in the race itself dare not press him to keep his place on that part of the course which was slightly downhill. Later on he made up lost ground, and was close up fourth in a large field, finishing up without being the least bit distressed, but I have always thought that with the "going" soft I should have won easily.

The race went to a very good horse belonging to Mr. Nathaniel Gubbins, ridden by that excellent rider and first-rate sportsman, Capt. Fritz Amcotts.

I do not think the original owner, Mr. "Buck" Barclay, ever realized what an exceptional horse he had owned, and if only he could have been kept sound the highest honours of steeplechasing were within his grasp. He was named Baa-baa, and was by Last of the Lambs, though what his dam was I never heard, but am quite sure she was clean bred.

Another good horse I owned was bred by Mr. Barclay, who gave him to me as a four-year-old, when he was small and seemed unlikely to grow. He however developed later, and eventually reached sixteen hands.

I was very fond of the horse—christened Buck after the donor—and hated parting with him; but was offered a good price and had to sell. He was very clever, and I had taught him to jump into his stride with the first sound of "gone away", so that I was nearly always sure of getting a good start, and as I generally rode him with the Belvoir in the days when that pack were famed for their lightning bursts, being "quick off the mark" was all important.

I bought a black horse at Leicester one autumn that I rode for many seasons, and he never left my hands until I had him shot. He was a great favourite and a brilliant hunter, but had some peculiarities, one of which was a great objection to allowing another horse to jump a fence in front of him. Bone spavins, which grew worse with age, prevented him flexing his hocks, and in consequence he liked to take his fences at a hand-canter. Like every other horse, he knew at once the place you had picked in the next fence, however distant it was, and nothing annoyed him more than if circumstances obliged you to change your mind. The only falls he ever gave me were on those occasions when I was obliged to pull away from the place and seek another. Yes! I had forgotten he gave me a fall jumping some timber out of the grass roadway under Borrough Hill. It was rather a drop and I had steadied him, when just as he was taking off, a man, who should have known better, jumped alongside of me, touched my horse, and he rolled over into the ditch. The ditch happened to have a very sharp bank, and the horse was on his back with the whole of his weight resting on my knee. It was an absurd position, but very painful, and the man who was the cause of it never turned his head to see if I was free.

Luckily for me a lady riding by noticed my predicament, and went for assistance. There was a small ladder close at hand, which, being used as a lever under the horse's quarters, speedily set me free. Mr. "Cis" Howard, an occasional visitor to Melton, was the good Samaritan who came to my assistance.

That black horse I called Liberty, from some connection with his reputed breeding, which was Irish, as was also his education, and he was a made hunter when I bought him. I usually rode him with the Quorn, and he seldom missed his two days a week.

Another very exceptional horse was one I bought from Mr. Edmund Leatham called "Brigadier" by "Old Victor". He had earned a big reputation in the show ring under the ownership of that well-known Yorkshire dealer, Mr. Andrew Brown, and I believe had won the championship in London.

Up to great weight, and with lots of quality, he was, of course, worth a good deal, and I think Mr. Leatham gave three hundred for him, which was considered a big price then. As I have already said, my friend Edmund Leatham was one of the best and boldest men who ever crossed Leicestershire, but he had undeniably heavy hands. Now "Brigadier" had really a very good mouth, but having gained a reputation for pulling, his new owner put on him a heavy, long-checked bridle, with the result horse and rider were always fighting, usually finishing up their day, one with aching arms and the other with bleeding mouth. I gave fifty pounds for him, which was more than he was really worth at the time, as he had ricked his back, was supposed to be a whistler, and might never be sound again. However, a summer's run put him right, and when he found his mouth would not be hurt, he never pulled an ounce. I rode him several seasons, and finally broke him down one day with the Belvoir.

Amongst the many horse-dealers I have known, the majority of them were good fellows and first-class horsemen; but the one who I have always said rode to hounds like a gentleman and not like a horse-dealer was Will Gale. I use the word gentleman in this instance to indicate a man who rides hunting for the pleasure of being with and seeing hounds—the selling of his horse being a secondary consideration.

I have had the pleasure of riding to hounds in the company of Gale for many seasons, and I look on him as one of the best men I have known.

Mr. "Sam" Hames I consider is one of the finest horsemen of my acquaintance; but if he will forgive my saying it, I think with him the horse comes before the hound.

I have written of men and horses in this garrulous style as they have occurred to me, but will worry the reader with no more. Of all the good men herein mentioned, I again repeat that Teddy Brooks was far and away the best—there will never be another.

Epilogue

In 1932 I attended the boarding school of Langford Grove in Essex, a beautiful house once owned by Lord Byron. My father had selected the school after consulting his many friends, not least the Norfolk landowner, Harry Birkbeck, who was enthusiastic. This greatly eased my introduction to a new way of life, since the parents of my contemporaries already knew my father or knew of him, and I was readily invited to their houses in the holidays.

All told, there were about sixty girls, all carefully chosen by Mrs. Curtis, the founder and headmistress, many drawn from her circle of writers, musicians, and painters; and though no one could assert an academic education was in the offing, the art school benefited from the monthly visits from Duncan Grant and Vanessa Bell. Vanessa's daughter, Angelica, by an illegitimate union with Grant, was a classmate, who was kept in ignorance of her true parentage at that time. Not surprisingly, our otherwise routine schooldays were enlivened by early exposure to the racy goings-on of the Bloomsbury set whenever members chose to visit. Angelica, who was my senior by a year, swiftly adopted their bed-hopping antics after leaving Langford, famously losing her virginity in H.G.Wells's spare room to David Garnett, a "rusty, surly old dog with amorous ways and a primitive mind" according to her aunt, Virginia Woolf.*

Although I had only a passing acquaintance with Angelica, whose intellectual bent I found somewhat patronising, there

*Angelica Garnett obituary, *Daily Telegraph*, 8th May 2012.

was another senior girl whose company I much preferred-the Hon. Claudia Betterton, who invited me to stay from time to time. Claudia later married Major Derek Allhuesen, the equestrian rider, who later still, won gold and silver medals at the 1968 Montreal Olympics.

All of a sudden, my education was rudely interrupted when, unbeknownst to me, I caught a touch of blood poisoning, and was taken on a stretcher to Chelmsford Hospital, where I was treated for septicemia. My parents, of course, immediately came down to visit since I had a life-threatening condition, which was ameliorated by a handy combination of good medical care and strong genes.

Back at Thorpe Satchville for the holidays, and with no less than eight large bibles in his library, my father sometimes read me stories from the Old Testament. At other times, we would read from Surtees' *Handley Cross*, laugh at the jokes, and admire the Leech drawings. When he was not away to visit fellow sportsmen, Otho gained a reputation for being very careful with money, habitually inviting friends to the house between breakfast and lunch, or in the afternoon before teatime; a system borne of necessity since he was reliant upon his books and articles to finance his days out hunting; rates were good before the Great War, but fell thereafter.

On one of my term breaks, I recall my father reminiscing about Frank Forester; apparently, he was so proud of his daughter, Mary, that he escorted her round the congregation at her wedding in 1914 to Sir Arthur Fitzgerald, so that everyone could admire her beautiful complexion! The service was held in Melton Mowbray and was further enhanced by a youthful Malcolm Sargent who played the organ. By the time of the Heywood Hardy painting of Mary in 1917, she is evidently relied upon by her father to assist and is seen riding 'point' to stop the fox bolting back as the huntsman draws the covert. Frank hunted on his steeplechasers at a pace that astonished the hardest Quornite, and woe-betide any member of the field who broke ranks to ride ahead of him. When the full season started the foxes went away across country as if the devil were after them.*

Frank Forester resigned his mastership of the Quorn on 1st February 1918, and thereafter, the hunt was kept ticking over by committee until the Armistice was signed that November. He shared with my father a distaste for the showmanship exemplified by Lord Lonsdale, of whom my father privately disapproved, but rightly, in my view, refrained from criticising in his memoirs.

But I digress. Returning to my days at Langford Grove, though the school never sought to scale the heights of academia, Mrs. Curtis- we called her Curty- took the unusual step of forging educational links and cultural exchanges with a number of German families, who had immigrated to England in the early 1930s, and who sought to send their children there. I remember one gifted girl called Angela Brugelmann who had no particular artistic talent, but was highly intelligent. Her father, a prosperous businessman from Cologne, had written to Mrs. Curtis requesting an English girl to stay, and I joined her family for about two months in 1936. Afterwards, I went to stay with a delightful family called Schulz at their house on the Ammersee, a lovely mountain lake, 1710 feet above sea level, in Upper Bavaria. And it was here that an excellent Russian teacher gave me my grounding in the German language and the essential grammar.

It was during my stay with the Schulz family that I attended a term at Heidelberg University; and before I completed my studies, an unexpected episode took place. Frau Schulz's sister, Lise-lotte, happened to be married to von Ribbentrop;

* *Leicestershire & The Quorn Hunt* by Colin Ellis

an encounter was in the offing. Sometime late in 1938, Lise invited me to stay for the weekend at the Henkell's, the proprietors of the champagne house of that name. They had organized a party to attend an opera at Darmstadt; and it was at this gathering that Lise introduced me to the then German ambassador to the Court of St. James, Herr Joachim von Ribbentrop, a sinister man whom I recall being alarmingly cold and polite at our short meeting.

After a brief sojourn in France, and upon my return to England in the spring of 1939, I was presented at Court as a debutante, one of the last occasions where full dress was worn, my hair adorned with Prince of Wales ostrich feathers. We dined at Buckingham Palace afterwards, off gold plate, before going on to a dance; a few months of fun before Europe disintegrated, and more sombre events shook the world.

Determined to make a contribution to the war effort, I wrote to an elderly retired admiral, whose daughter I had met in the Deb Season. And to the surprise of both my mother and myself, I was invited to come to London and join the newly formed Ministry of Information. My role was to eavesdrop on foreign journalists, in particular, the Italians, who were very anti-British. If they diverted from a pre-agreed script, we simply cut the lines so they would miss their deadlines.

Some six months later, in April 1940, with the 'phoney war' well and truly over, and with my newfound fluency in German in hand, I gained an immediate passport to Bletchley Park where work began in earnest to break the German Enigma codes. I suspected, though never asked throughout a lifetime friendship, that a well-connected soldier/diplomat whom I knew, had facilitated my transfer. And curiously, I benefited from not being mathematically inclined, since I found myself placed in Hut 3, the nerve centre of the entire, top secret, operation. Meanwhile, I was fortunate enough to find comfortable accommodation in the village of Little Claydon, the only draw-back being a lengthy drive to BP.

Bletchley Park is some fifty miles northwest of London, near the new town of Milton Keynes in Buckinghamshire. Situated on land formerly belonging to the manor of Eaton, according to the Domesday Book of 1086, Sir Herbert Samuel Leon erected the current structure in the 1880s; it holds all the charm you might expect from a neo-gothic mansion built by a Victorian magnate. Nevertheless, the house survived demolition in 1938 when Admiral Sir Hugh Sinclair, director of Naval Intelligence and head of MI6 bought it for the government as war loomed. The property was quickly made fit for purpose, although the first government visitors rather amusingly adopted the Woodhouseian cover as members of Capt. Ridley's shooting party. By the time of my arrival in spring 1940, BP was fully operational.

Our contribution to the war effort was deemed crucial enough to exempt us from the exigencies of petrol rationing: for us, it was freely available. So there was an early recognition by the authorities that our work might make a crucial difference in winning the war, or at least foreshortening it, as is now generally accepted.

For my part, I was not interested in any of the Bletchley social gatherings, my preference was to save my days off and drive to London for parties at the Four Hundred club or Quaglino's, where I met many dashing young officers. Such excursions were invariably tinged with sadness when so many failed to return; whether in the Army or RAF, they were so determined to fight for King and Country. Their resolve put iron into my soul: we were fighting for survival.

Returning to Bletchley for an early morning duty round, I would hurriedly change out of my Worth dress, out of sight of my colleagues, and report back for duty in my uniform;

yet, my mind was etched with images of the London skyline littered with barrage balloons, and even Claridges was obliged to serve rook pie.

Hut 3 was set up as the Intelligence Hut in January 1940; we dealt with primarily Luftwaffe and Army decrypts from Hut 6, and later on, Mediterranean Naval decrypts. The Hut was headed by Commander Malcolm Saunders, assisted by an ex-diplomat, Sir Herbert Marchant, and two professors from Cambridge, Prof. F. Norman, and Prof. F. L. Lucas, the latter confusingly known as Peter. Peter Lucas was a Greek scholar, who entertained us in the coffee break with stories about Greece, the Greek islands, and mythology. For that reason, I generally opted for the 8am to 4pm slot whenever I knew he was going to be there; otherwise, I preferred the 4pm to midnight rota. I have retained many fond memories of him, and he, in his turn, indulged me whenever I needed time off.

Within days of my arrival, the work in Hut 3 had escalated dramatically, following the German invasion of Norway on 9th April 1940, and the invasion of France on the 10th of May. I would receive the intercepts 'in clear' and it was my task to make sense of the different messages coming in from the code-breakers in order to identify the imminent threats posed by the enemy. Nigel de Grey had just arrived; a dull offshoot of an interesting family, whose ancestor was the tragic Lady Jane Grey, the nine-day Queen beheaded by Mary Tudor. His colleagues were wont to refer to him as 'the dormouse.' De Grey, however, had earned his spurs, having shot to fame in breaking the Zimmerman telegram in 1917. Immediately upon arrival, he recognized the necessity to have an organized file if we were not to be overwhelmed.

Thus was born the 'Index', a massive file of intelligence, the messages kept on cards in shoe boxes, the text displayed in telegram format. As I set about organizing the Index, it was essential to ensure it was relatively easy to retrieve material whenever the need arose. Across the room sat a red telephone, which was used to pass vital intelligence on to the Chiefs of Staff and Winston Churchill. The Premier was fond of referring to Bletchley as the 'golden goose' and telephoned Hut 3 for his daily reports. Being 'open plan' there was a perpetual air of excitement in Hut 3.

It was from de Grey's Index that the decoded material was assembled to comprise BP's 'Ultra' intelligence reports, which made a critical contribution in Montgomery's offensive against Erwin Rommel in the two battles of El Alamein in North Africa. Intercepts of Italian enigma material also helped Admiral Cunningham sink their navy at the battle of Cape Matapan, a two-day naval engagement which took place between the 27th and 29th March 1941. Of this latter action, a certain midshipman, Philip Mountbatten, operated the searchlights to disclose the whereabouts of enemy battleships. This distinguished gentleman is, of course, better known to us all as HRH Prince Philip, Duke of Edinburgh.

Two months later I played a small but exciting part in one major incident- the attack on the *Bismarck*. Our intercepts indicated her position in the Bay of Biscay on 22nd May 1941, and we knew the ship would steam back towards the French coast once alerted. Time was short. With the intelligence to hand, our reports were swiftly passed on to the Royal Navy, as well as the RAF, who confirmed the initial breakout. Battle honours would go to the Fleet Air Arm and the Swordfish pilots on the aircraft carrier, HMS *Ark Royal,* who set off to strafe the battleship. Four days later, at 8.47 pm. on 26th May, swordfish torpedoes struck home, one disabling the *Bismarck*'s rudder; it was enough, and she was sunk the following day. Admiral Lutjens managed to send a message to Group West immediately after the night attack: 'Ship unable to manoeuvre. We will fight to the last shell. Long live the Fuhrer.'

Epilogue

Alas, I missed the excitement of D-Day as I was heavily pregnant with my daughter, Annette, and needed the necessary period of confinement. I did not return to Bletchley after standing down in May 1944; so I never expected official recognition or a pension since we were not supposed to exist. It was made very clear to me at the outset when I signed the Official Secrets Act, that if I divulged any information about my work there to anyone, I would be shot. Consequently, neither my husband nor my family knew about my wartime work until a book about Bletchley, by Wing Commander Fred Winterbottom, was published in 1975. It is fortunate for posterity however, that Churchill's order to destroy the machines and paperwork linked to 'Colossus' after World War II did not prevail, though it took long years before the State recognized the significance of the centre's preservation. Colossus was the forerunner of the modern computer, the key to breaking the Enigma codes.

In the spring of 1950 I so nearly missed meeting my wonderful second husband, Bill Jaffray, grandson of the Victorian newspaper magnate, Sir John Jaffray. We met at a cocktail party thrown by Lady Portsmouth. Espying me across a crowded room, Bill asked Sir Robin McAlpine to introduce him, only to receive the rebuff: 'Oh, no! You can't meet her, she's a nice girl!' Bill was relatively new to Hampshire at that time, having sold his family estate of Skilts, near Redditch in 1946. He was an outstanding sportsman and keen rider to hounds with the North Warwickshire, irrespective of the loss of his right arm in the Great War; and by some marvellous completion of a circle, his own father, when a young man, had hunted with the very same pack shortly before Tom Firr left in 1872 to join the Quorn.

Anne Jaffray

Appendix I

Masters and Huntsmen of the Quorn

Seasons	Masters	Huntsmen
1696-97 to 1751-52	Thomas Boothby	Edward Chesterton (alias Parsons)
1753-54 to 1799-1800	Hugo Meynell	John Raven
1800-01 to 1803-04	Earl of Sefton	John Raven and S Goodall
1804-05	Earl of Sefton and Lord Foley	?
1805-06	Lord Foley	J Harrison
1806-07 to 1816-17	Thomas Assheton Smith	The Master
1817-18 to 1820-21	George Osbaldeston	The Master (Tom Sebright occasionally)
1821-22 to 1822-23	Sir Bellingham Graham	?
1823-24 to 1826-27	George Osbaldeston	The Master
1827-28 to 1830-31	Lord Southampton	Dick Burton, G Mountford
1831-32 to 1832-33	Sir Harry Goodricke	G Mountford
1833-34 to 1834-35	Francis Holyoake	G Mountford
1835-36 to 1837-38	Rowland Errington	G Mountford
1838-39	Lord Suffield	C Treadwell
1839-40 to 1840-41	Thomas Hodgson	Webb, Tom Day
1841-42 to 1846-47	Henry Green	Tom Day
1847-48 to 1855	Sir Richard Sutton	Tom Day, Jack Morgan, R Robinson
1856-57 to 1862-63	Earl of Stamford and Ben Boothroyd, Warrington	John Treadwell
1863-64 to 1865-66	S W Clowes	John Goddard
1866-67 to 1867-68	Marquis of Hastings	Charles Pike, Thos Wilson

Appendix I

1868-69 to 1869-70	J C Musters	The Master and Frank Gillard
1870-71 to 1883-84	J Coupland	F Gillard, J MacBride, Tom Firr
1884-85 to 1885-86	Lord Manners	Tom Firr
1886-87 to 1889-90	Capt W P Warner	Tom Firr
1890-91 to 1892-93	Capt W P Warner and W B Paget	Tom Firr
1893-94 to 1897-98	Earl of Lonsdale	Tom Firr
1898-99 to 1904-05	Capt J Burns Hartopp	Tom Firr, Walter Keyte, Tom Bishopp
1905-06 to 1917-18	Capt F Forester	Tom Bishopp, George Leaf, The Master (N Capel assisting)
1918-19	Committee	Walter Wilson
1919-20 to 1927-28	W E Paget and Major A E Burnaby	Walter Wilson
1928-29 to 1929-30	Major A E Burnaby	Walter Wilson (1918-19), George Barker
1930-31 to 1931-32	Major A E Burnaby and Sir Harold Nutting	George Barker
1932-33 to 1939-40	Sir Harold Nutting	George Barker
1940-41 to 1946-47	Committee (Major W P Cantrell-Hubbersty Acting)	George Barker
1947-48	Mrs Cantrell-Hubbersty and F Mee	George Barker
1948-49 to 1950-51	Mrs Cantrell-Hubbersty, F Mee and Major the Hon R Strutt	George Barker
1951-54	Major the Hon R Strutt	George Barker (1929-59)

Memories of the Shires

1954-60	Lt Col G A Murray-Smith	Jack Littleworth (1959-67)
1960	Mrs Ulrica Murray Smith	
	Lt Col T C Llewellyn-Palmer	
	and Capt E O Crosfield	
1962-65	Brig R G Tilney	
1965-72	Capt J J A Keith	Michael Farrin (1968-98)
1972-85	Capt F G Barker	
1975-83	Mr A J M Teacher	
1985-91	Mr J Bealby	
	Mr E R Hanbury	
	Mr W B Hercock	
1991-94	Capt F G Barker	
1992-94	Mr A R Macdonald-Buchanan	
1992-95	Mrs D E H Turner	
1992-2000	Mr C H Geary	
1992-2000	Mr R T Thomas	
1994-95	Mr R G Henson	
1995-96	Mr R S Morely	
1995-96	Mr R Carden	
1996-97	Mr R C Smith-Ryland	
1997-2003	Mr A R P Carden	
1997-present	Mr E R Hanbury	
1998-2000	Mr A W R Dangar	The Master
2000-04	Mr R Hunnisett	Richard Mould (2000-02)
2000-present	Mrs K M J Madocks Wright	
2002-05	Mr W Cursham	Peter Collins (2002- present)
2004-present	Miss P K Turner	
2006-present	Mr J K Mossman	
	Mr T R Hercock	
2012-present	Mr A Bealby	
	Mr A C G Shields	

Note: For season 2012-13, there are seven MFHs.

Appendix II

Personalities of the Day.

Masters.

John Coupland. MFH 1870-1884.

John Coupland was Master of the Quorn for fourteen seasons. His resources from a family shipping business in Liverpool enabled him to bring to the Quorn a pack of foxhounds purchased in the Craven country. By his second season, he found the ideal huntsman in Tom Firr, whom he brought from the North Warwickshire hunt in 1872. He gave Firr the chance to prove himself a superb huntsman and sent him off to a flying start with the finest hunters he could find. This Master's perceptiveness and tireless dedication to the sport earned him the highest praise from Otho Paget.

John Coupland was described by those who knew him as "an unfathomable man- very smooth manners, but you did not know what was in his mind." Nevertheless, by the time of his resignation, he was accepted almost as an institution, as a song of the time pays tribute.

> Here's Coupland the master, so natty and neat
> So courteous his tone and so faultless his seat
> You would swear that our Coupland as Master was born
> All booted and spurred at the head of the Quorn.
> (*Leicestershire and the Quorn Hunt* by Colin D.B.Ellis, 1951)

Lord Manners. MFH 1884-1886.

At the sudden resignation of John Coupland, Lord Manners came forward for just two seasons until a more permanent replacement could be found. He was known as "Hoppy" Manners on account of his unusual gait, and acquired fame when he won the Grand National in 1882 on his own horse, Seaman, a bay gelding. The consensus of opinion that day was for Seaman meriting much longer odds than the 10 to 1 cited, but Lord Manners won by a head, in the teeth of a blinding snowstorm.

Capt. W.P. Warner. MFH 1886-1893.

The appointment of Capt. Warner was announced in April 1886, at about the same time that 'Brooksby' handed over his duties as hunting correspondent to *The Field* to Otho Paget; henceforth, articles were insightful accounts about hounds and hunting, in sharp contrast to the society tone adopted by Brooksby and relished by those who liked to see their names in print.

Capt. Warner was very popular, and his tenure marked the happiest period of Tom Firr's time. According to Lady Augusta Fane, "everything ran smoothly, and sport was far above the average, especially in the Monday country, where in one season we had as many as nine good gallops from Walton Thorns across the Vale, ending up either at Little Belvoir or one of the coverts near by."

The Master was blessed with a lively sense of humour. When Firr's horse stumbled, catapulting the huntsman into Twyford Brook, he emerged with a jovial grin, saying, "I could hear you laughing, captain, while I was still under water."

The Captain appreciated his good fortune in his huntsman however, and to avoid unnecessary mishaps, took pains to ensure he did not participate in the Midnight Steeplechase in March 1890, much to Firr's chagrin.

The Earl of Lonsdale. MFH 1893-1898.

For Hugh Lowther, the 5th Earl of Lonsdale, assumption of the Quorn mastership was a matter of prestige; for the Quorn field it was an entirely different matter. Whereas Capt. Warner had run the Hunt establishment economically, Lord Lonsdale demanded the utmost magnificence in every department. He spent his own money lavishly and expected everyone else to do the same, which, not surprisingly, irked the field considerably. Lonsdale upped the subscription rate to meet the higher expenditure, though when he discovered some people were wearing a hunt button but not subscribing, he adopted an amazingly tactless solution. A new Hunt button was introduced bearing a large coronet with a small Q beneath it. A number refused to wear the new button, and criticised the Master for trying to change the Quorn into Lord Lonsdale's Hunt, declaring they were "not his Lordship's lackeys."

Although Lonsdale was notably successful in clearing the country of wire, and was a great sportsman in his own right, his dictatorial methods inevitably meant he was outwearing his welcome. Then, in 1898 a crisis forced him to resign the mastership, namely two scandalous affairs, the former with Lillie Langtry, snatched from under the nose of the Prince of Wales, later King Edward VII, the latter with a famous married actress, Violet Cameron. Queen Victoria's tolerance was exhausted, and she let it be known he was no longer welcome in the realm. Lonsdale abruptly resigned the mastership and departed for Canada, where he embarked on a gruelling 3000- mile polar expedition. He returned two years later, but not to the Quorn.

Capt. J. Burns Hartopp. MFH 1898-1905.

After Lord Lonsdale's sudden resignation in June 1898, the Quorn committee pressed Capt. Burns Hartopp to become their next Master. He accepted "because he loved hunting and loved the Quorn country." His tenure was dogged by a series of misfortunes. At the close of his first season, March 1899, Tom Firr retired, his health broken by a terrible fall. By the following season, the Boer War had broken out, which 'left some sad gaps amongst the first flight and caused a serious shortage of horses.' In November 1900,

Burns Hartopp suffered a heavy fall and broke his pelvis, which was, in his words, "screwed together again with bits of iron." A motorcar accident followed in autumn 1902. As if this was not enough for any man to contend with, the hunt finances were under pressure: significant sums of money needed to be raised for new kennels, a huntsman's house, and other cottages. The site was chosen in 1903 and occupied by the end of 1905, the total cost coming in at £14,000. Notably, Lord Lonsdale generously lent the committee £5,000 interest-free for ten years.

Capt. James Burns Hartopp, (not Tommy, as he has been mistakenly called) was also known to his contemporaries as "Chicken" Hartopp for his penchant to place bets on what his chickens would do next! An inveterate gambler and frequenter of Crockfords, his fascination with gambling nearly led to a humiliating confrontation with the Hunt committee. In the end, Capt Frank Forester came forward with an offer to take up the mastership.

Despite his mishaps, Burns Hartopp exuded a magnificent imperial confidence, ringing his bell one morning and shouting to his manservant: "Hey, Johnson! Bring me my shaving water at once and order me a train. I'll hunt with Sir Bache!"* A year after resigning the mastership, he was painted astride a magnificent grey hunter by Sir Arthur Stockdale Cope RA.

Capt. Frank Forester. MFH 1905-1918.

Unlike Lord Lonsdale, Frank Forester loathed any kind of self-advertisement or pretension in any man, a view shared by Otho Paget in private, but eschewed in *Memories of the Shires*. The field found Capt. Forester a rather terrifying man in the early stages

---

* Capt. Burns Hartopp ordered a train to hunt with Sir Bache Cunard when the latter was MFH for the Billesdon Hunt, in former times Quorn country. Sir Bache, who retired from the mastership in 1888, was the grandson of the founder of the Cunard Line.

of a run, according to Colin Ellis. "Utterly fearless, he rode his steeplechasers across High Leicestershire at a pace that astonished the hardest Quornite. The fences were his and his horse's business and it was the business of the field to keep out of his way. When the full season started the foxes went away across country as if the devil were after them-and Captain Forester's hounds came out at the sound of his voice like a pack of devils to a sorcerer's summons."

Frank Forester was immensely proud of his beautiful daughter, Mary, who happily supported her father, as can be seen from Heywood Hardy's 1917 painting depicting her riding point to head off a fox. The Great War had not stopped hunting, but made it immensely difficult to carry on, since the majority of Hunt horses were requisitioned for service. Capt. Forester is due no small tribute for his determination to "keep things going" and hold out the hope that life would return to normal once the war was over.

When he resigned the mastership on 1st February 1918, the Quorn committee temporarily took matters into their own hands for the following year. Forester was subsequently photographed on one of his steeplechasers in circa 1910 for the volumes on distinguished *British Sports and Sportsmen*.

Huntsmen.

Tom Firr, April 1841 to December 1902. Quorn huntsman from 1872 to 1899.

Arguably the most gifted huntsman of all time, Tom Firr holds centre stage in Otho Paget's *Memories of the Shires*, a legend in his own lifetime. At the age of just 28, he was appointed huntsman to the North Warwickshire, a first-rate pack, where he carried the horn for three seasons. Firr already enjoyed a high reputation when John Coupland, an astute judge of ability, brought him to the

Quorn in 1872. Tom Firr possessed at their highest all the physical and mental qualifications that go to make a successful huntsman. He was gifted with a beautiful voice and a marvellously quick eye for a country; he knew always what his hounds were doing, and trusted them, while he had them under perfect command. Impatient crowds never flurried him, and his coolness under pressure was proverbial. Firr never seemed to be in a hurry, but his quickness of decision at a critical juncture was unfailing, for he possessed an almost intuitive knowledge of what his fox would do. Indeed, contemporaries remarked that Firr looked like a fox and thought like one too. He was a splendid horseman, and a more daring rider never took a straight line over the Quorn pastures; and his quiet, self-respecting manner made him universally popular among those with whom he was brought in contact.

Unusual among huntsmen generally, Firr sounded a number of different notes on his horn: a gay note when hounds were breaking covert, a sad one when the fox was lost, a steadying note when drawing a wood, and a most dismal note, only heard on the last day of the season; small wonder his hounds adored him.

It was during the 1897/98 season that Firr sustained a serious accident when his horse jumped a fence into a pond on the landing side, and trod heavily upon him in getting up again. In October 1898 he took another very bad fall at a wall, sustaining injuries so serious that he was never again able to carry the horn. Paget described the poignant ceremony, which took place on 10th April 1899, when Lord Belper presented Firr with a purse of £3,200 in the presence of perhaps the most distinguished persons in the hunting world; it was the largest testimonial given to a retiring huntsman; although Firr, at an instant, would have traded the tribute for the recovery of his health. His grave and its prominent position in Quorn churchyard reflect the high esteem he drew from his admirers and countrymen.

Appendix II

Frank Gillard. Belvoir huntsman, 1872-98, whipper-in, 1860-72.

A gentleman's huntsman, Frank Gillard enjoyed an extraordinarily long reign in service for the 6th and 7th Dukes of Rutland. Gillard paid the utmost skill and attention to improving the bloodlines of the Belvoir pack to a concert pitch of excellence. Acknowledged the premier pack of the day, twenty-five masters of foxhounds paid a yearly pilgrimage to the ducal kennel at Belvoir throughout one summer month. Hounds were bred to a height of twenty-three inches, and to a colour combination of rich black, the purest white, and bright tan, known as "the Belvoir tan." Therein lay Gillard's renown.

With a keen eye and iron-gray hair, Gillard invariably set about the day's work in good cheer, taking to heart Rutland's advice: "Make as many friends as you can, Frank, and as few enemies, and then life is sure to run smoothly with you." Contemporaries observed that no day's sport was too long for Gillard, who would continue drawing coverts as long as daylight permitted, regardless of the distance back to kennels; though perhaps one accolade went too far in noting that his musical voice was so 'inspiriting' (inspiring) that his horn was warranted to charm the very foxes from their earths!

Although Gillard could not match Firr's astounding flair, he held his own in those fiercely competitive times when the Melton Hunts vied with each other in showing the finest sport. A classic instance of rivalry was sparked on Monday 22nd December 1884 when the Belvoir and Quorn Hunts met in the middle of a run, and their respective packs joined forces. Gillard had roused his fox in Harby covert when his quarry headed for Curate's Gorse in Quorn country before being turned to a small plantation by Widmerpool. Whilst Gillard was standing in the central ride cheering hounds, Tom Firr galloped up with his hounds just as the fox crossed the ride sight unseen behind Gillard. "Tally-ho!" shouted Firr, "Tally-ho! That's my fox!" "Now, Tom, behave yourself," replied Frank, "I shall be very angry directly, Tom, if you don't let my fox alone, for you know you had no line into this covert!" The argument was settled however, when both packs took the line after the fox.

Gillard elected to retire in the spring of 1896 at the same time as the Duke of Rutland resigned the mastership. From all over the country, many of the huntsman's peers came forward to pay their respects. "It is sad news the Duke of Rutland (is) giving up the Mastership of the Belvoir" wrote another MFH to Gillard, "and I can well realise what you must feel at the change that is coming after being such a long time with the Belvoir. I quite think that is a national calamity . . .". A testimonial of £1,300 and a silver ink-stand were presented to Frank on his retirement by Sir William Gregory at the Grantham Show.

Ladies in the hunting field.

Riding to hounds provided young ladies with an opportunity to escape their chaperones, an early form of emancipation. As early as 1844, *The Sporting Magazine* hailed their advent at the Melton Hunts. "Let too, the fair and amiable – to wit the Countess of Wilton, Mrs. Colonel Wyndham, and other ladies – shed by their presence a chastening influence over Melton, and it will always be, as it is now, the resort of Fashion, and the place *par excellence* for the votaries of the Chace." Another lady, a certain Miss Walters, also known as 'Skittles,' defied the conventions of the day that only married ladies – with permission from the MFH – were allowed out.

In 1860, Mrs. Russell Clarke published *The Habit and the Horse,* a handbook of advice for young ladies on how to ride, how to dress themselves, appropriate conduct in the field, and so forth. Skittles ignored such advice: in one incident she lost her riding habit altogether, and was found by the field in nothing more than top-boots and a white petticoat!

As the 19th century wore on, ladies a-hunting became increasingly numerous, with the increasing availability of independent means. Some displayed excellent horsemanship, and some were to be found in the first flight or at the end of a fast run. In Otho Paget's day, Lady Augusta Fane, Lady Gerard, and Mary Forester** were keen riders to hounds, who made a real contribution to the sport, and seemed consciously aware of the privilege to live in historic times in the long annals of our Nation's hunting tradition.

** On 19th February 1914 Mary married Sir Arthur Fitzgerald, fourth baronet of Valencia and 22nd Knight of Kerry.

Appendix III

Mr. Reynal's Beagles
By Peter B. Devers
Reproduced by kind permission of the author

America seems to suffer from a lack of eccentric sportsmen, the type of character found in Britain in the novels of Surtees, Nimrod and Somerville and Ross. In these novels of the British and Irish countryside are found some of the most bizarre, entertaining, and almost unbelievable characters imaginable. People like Soapy Sponge, Jorrocks, Colonel Thornton and John Mytton make us gasp with pleasure, dismay and astonishment at their exploits. Their activities in hunting a pack of hounds were universally superb, but their relations with their fellow man were mainly abysmal. In Eugene Sugny Reynal of Millbrook, however, we find a true-to-life eccentric to rival any born in Britain.

Eugene Reynal was the quintessential 19th-century gentleman. He was very aristocratic, autocratic, and most conscious about whose company he kept. Despite his arrogance, he was quite shy. Proper dress and deportment were the supreme virtues in his life. God help the man or woman who came hunting with him who was not correctly and immaculately turned out! Woe betide the employee who did not offer him the proper deference his status demanded! He viewed life only in black and white with no middle ground. Were you of his class, you were either his friend or his enemy. If you were not of his class, your existence was noted only if you served him in some useful way. His life was lived by an extremely rigid code which could have been drafted whole from early 19th-century

Appendix III

Britain. There were gentlemen, gentlewomen and then there was everybody else.

Reynal was born in New York City in 1877, a direct descendent of Count Eugene Sugny, aide-de-camp to General Lafayette during the Revolution. He was a lackluster student at several private schools, and as far as we know did not attend college. His family was quite wealthy, and Reynal was born into the gilded age, a heady and dramatic time of conspicuous wealth and consumption. The industrial and mercantile fortunes that had built up since the Civil War blossomed, and America's first leisure class looked to Great Britain for inspiration. In New York and elsewhere, Americans entered into the great sports of foxhunting, racing, and polo in greater numbers than ever before. Country estates, emulating the manors of Britain, sprung up all about the metropolitan regions. Liveried servants acres of greenhouses and formal gardens, and hunting establishments were founded by the wealthy. Reynal shot into this life full bore.

Hounds and hunting captured Reynal's soul at a young age. For the first time he found something he was good at, could be successful at, and would become renowned for. His passion was a true one, based not on show but on a deep love of the sport itself. This passion was infectious, and Reynal and two of America's nascent premier houndsmen – Fletcher Harper and Ned Carle – bound themselves together into a tightknit clan of adventurous young sportsmen. Through Reynal both these men eventually found their way to Millbrook, playing an important part in laying the foundations of the Millbrook Hunt.

In 1898, at the age of 21, Reynal became master of the Fairfield & Westchester Hounds, quickly discarding the harriers and replacing them with English foxhounds. These foxhounds were hunted until the pack disbanded in 1911. He held the mastership through 1901, and returned as a joint master in 1905. The following year, again being reelected master, he moved the hunt kennels to his estate,

Rocky Dell. He resigned the mastership in 1909, being replaced by Julian Day, and sent the hounds back to the old kennels. Harper and Carle signed on as whippers-in. After a fire destroyed the kennels in 1910, hounds were moved back to Rocky Dell. An even greater tragedy awaited. Seven weeks after being brought back, the entire pack came down with rabies and had to be put down. Luckily, the small pack of beagles he was developing was spared that fate.

In early 1908, while on a hunting trip in Britain, Reynal became captivated by the boundless joy and drive he saw in several of that country's beagle packs. The small hounds drove their quarry with the greatest vigor, and he admired their plucky spirit and cry no end. His friend and equally good hound man Ned Carle writes, "Eugene S. Reynal, that truly great hound man, brought out a few couples of beagles to his estate at White Plains, Westchester County, NY from the Thorpe Satchville, kenneled at Burrough, Melton Mowbray, England in the famous Quorn country. Another truly great hound man, the late J. Otho Paget, was master and owner of this pack, and as he was having financial troubles at the time, Mr. Reynal was able to bring a few couples back to America. This was the beginning of a truly wonderful pack of working hounds. Mr. Reynal aimed to keep his beagles at 13 inches or under. They had wonderful noses, a good cry, and, above all, tremendous drive – hence Mr. Reynal tired a bit of 'shank's mare' and often turned out mounted. These little hounds were able to kill now and then, and were known to have taken four hours to pull one down."

Even in 1910, Reynal could see that the Westchester area was developing, and that hunting on the scale he wished to practice it was fast becoming more and more difficult-Casting about for some new country, he was told of the great expansive farms of Dutchess County, and of Millbrook in particular. On the 18th of October he shipped his beagle pack to Millbrook by the Dover train, having heard that the European hare population was in need of some hounds to keep them in line. He was met at the train by James Cooley, a sporting correspondent for the *New York Herald,* who was also secretary of the Millbrook Hunt. Cooley often stayed at Thorndale, so the hounds were brought there and put up in a stall. The next day, records Cooley, they had "great sport by a magnificent pack, much regretted darkness calling it quits. Reynal said he would like to take a hunting box up here another year and hunt with us. Wish he would."

The following day hounds met again on the lawn of Thorndale at 7:15 AM. Cooley writes, "Great run! Quit at 12 PM. Reynal and Carle left this afternoon, both enthusiastic about the sport we are having here." Carle was also enthusiastic about young Miss Margaret Thorne, a beautiful and independent spirit, the daughter of his host. He lost his heart to her as they scrambled up Cardiac Hill in pursuit of the pack. On the train back to Westchester, Reynal waxed enthusiastic about Millbrook. There was no pack of foothounds anywhere near, so the best of the countryside was open for him. Carle waxed enthusiastic about Miss Thorne... (and the hunting).

It did not take Reynal long to make his move. In 1911 he bought the Germond farm, a 300-acre tract of land halfway between the villages of Millbrook and Verbank. The farm had a lovely hilltop site with magnificent views of the Catskills, and a late 18th-century home that had been built by the Germond family. It was much less pretentious than his magnificent Westchester Tudor manse, but it fitted his idea of what a "sporting squire" would live in. While he retained a handsome townhouse in New York City, Germond Hill Farm was to be his principal residence for the rest of his life.

Kennels were quickly built and Reynal fielded the first foot pack, Mr. Reynal's Beagles, to call the Millbrook countryside home. He consulted with the great British hound man and hunting author J. Otho Paget about the type of beagle he wanted. For many years Paget sent him the best hounds he could find, hounds suitable for the rolling hill country of Millbrook. These drafts decreased with the years as Reynal, having enough variant bloodlines, commenced his own breeding program. Hounds were bred for drive and nose. Looks were secondary, and he detested houndmen like Dicky Gambrill of the Vernon Place who, he thought, bred solely for them.

The hunting historian and bon vivant J. Blan van Urk wrote admiringly of Reynal's breeding philosophy. Reynal "was something of a perfectionist and a particularly expert hound man. He once owned a beagle named Dairymaid for whom he had high hopes as a brood bitch, but after hearing her babble a few times in the hunting field, Mr. Reynal commented, 'I wouldn't breed to her under any circumstances. It would take six generations to breed that lie out of her.'"

The beagles were usually hunted on foot and occasionally on horseback. Roadwork commenced in early July, at the quiet hour of 4 AM, and hounds were worked for about an hour. In August cubbing started, at 5 AM, and lasted for two hours. This was promptly followed each and ever)' day by his unvarying breakfast of a quart of ale and eggs. September saw cubbing moved to 6 AM, lasting for precisely three hours, with a formal opening meet the first Sunday in September. Until he acquired a harrier pack in 1924, he hunted the beagles seven days a week. So no time was wasted getting to hunting on Sundays, he and his daughters Jeanne and Roxanne attended Mass at Saint Joseph's Church in full hunting kit.

Reynal brought with him his two closest compatriots, Ned Carle almost immediately and a bit later Fletcher Harper. Carle was for many years his able and trusted first whipper-in. His great love of hounds and hunting gave him a common language with Reynal and enabled him to overlook many of his friend's disastrous habits and failings. Carle's courtship of Margaret Thorne commenced in earnest, and in 1913 they were married. Carle played an enormous part in setting the course of the Millbrook Hunt, then a mounted harrier pack. He knew how to panel and trail a countryside, and with his friend D.U. Sloan set about making Millbrook into one of the finest hunting countries in the world. His legacy is still apparent to all who take to the field each autumn. Carle's marriage, however,

Appendix III

fell apart in 1924. Tabloid headlines in the New York press blared, "Man Prefers Dogs To Wife, So Loses Her." Divorce in the early 20th century was the scandal par excellence, and all in Millbrook were mortified by such unwanted publicity. In truth, Carle loved Margaret very much and sought a way to mend their marriage. It was not he, but rather she, who left home. Oakleigh Thorne, Margaret's father, privately sided with Carle and urged his daughter to reconsider. Such was not to be, however, and in 1924 Carle left Thorndale and Millbrook forever. He went on to assume the last mastership of the Westchester Hunt, then went to the Smithtown Hunt on Long Island. With his second wife, in a much happier marriage, he sired Jake, master of the Keswick Hunt in Charlottesville. The young family developed its own small pack of beagles, The Raeburn. Carle wrote a fine article on early beagling in Millbrook and America in D.W. Prentice's book, "The American Beagle" (1916).

Fletcher Harper, later to become the legendary master of the Orange County Hunt, had been severely injured in a hunting accident in White Plains in 1909. He had been attempting to jump a farm gate which wasn't quite latched, and which gave way, tripping his horse. It was a long slow fall, in the slowest of slow motion, and there wasn't enough of a jolt to throw him off. Consequently he fell under the gate, with his horse landing on top of it. He was carried from the field on a ladder which was strapped to Reynal's Stanley Steamer. Jeanne Reynal remembers being horrified when the car turned in the drive, thinking it was her father. She was even more horrified to find it was Harper. He was operated on in Reynal's house, and spent 11 months there recuperating. Reynal bore much of the expense of his friend's recovery, and urged him to come to Millbrook. Through Reynal's intercession with Oakleigh Thorne, Harper was hired as Thorndale's estate manager. Fie was one of the grandest of people, a man everyone felt drawn to and comfortable with. When he married Flarriet Wadsworth, cousin of Major Austin Wadsworth, master of the Genesee Valley Hunt, Reynal and his other friends presented him with a lovely old home and farmstead on the Verbank Road. He named it Friendship Farm, a name it keeps to this day. In Millbrook, Harper hobbled out with hounds when he could, but his leg was never really strong enough for the arduous cross-country running Reynal's pack required. When time allowed he followed as best he could in a small buggy. One hunt he was dismayed at having to miss occurred on December 12, 1912. The Reynal pack had a hunt of 4 hours and 18 minutes to a kill in the open, a run calculated at almost 30 miles as hounds ran!

Reynal was short in stature but possessed of a terrier's courage. He was incensed that America was leaving Britain to fight alone, and took a steamship to France in 1914 hoping to enlist in the Lafayette Escadrille. When they wouldn't have him due to his eyesight and age, he joined the Morgan-Harjes Ambulance Corps for 1914-1915, seeing much action at the front. With America's entry into the fighting in 1916 he switched to the Remount Corps, procuring horses for the army in Spain. He suffered an acute attack of appendicitis in 1918 and was shipped home for an operation. The delay almost killed him. At a critical point in the operation his heart stopped for three minutes, and the doctors literally had to pound him black and blue to get it started again. This episode was later recounted to his hated enemy, the illustrious American hound man Joseph B. Thomas, when Thomas was hunting the Millbrook country. Thomas was heard to comment, "Christ, I knew he was egocentric, but to try and imitate the only man who did that trick - and succeed - well if that doesn't beat all!" Before going overseas Reynal deputized his daughter Jeanne as acting master, and the hounds were hunted as always.

The hare population in Millbrook was enormous at the turn of the century. Charles Dietrich, founder of a company that evolved into Union Carbide, had fenced in 2,000 acres of land on the edge of the village in the late 1800s. He attempted to re-create a bit of Bavaria, his native country, within the confines of this preserve. All sorts of European game was imported, including the hare for which Millbrook became famous. Also imported were families of Italians to build and work the great estates. Poaching, a national pastime in Italy, was thoroughly enjoyed as the Italians cut holes in the fencing and liberated numerous hare for their stewpots, allowing others to escape and prosper in the rich open terrain of Dutchess County. For Reynal, though, there was always the worry that farmers would shoot and extirpate hare from his hunting country.

In order to make sure there were always enough hare for his beagles, and later harriers, in 1925 Reynal started giving a farmer on whose land he found a hare $5, and on whose land he killed $2. This was later increased to $10 and $5. In the early 20th century, this was significant money to a farmer who was fortunate to make $30 a month. In addition, he gave an annual gift of money to each landowner in his hunting country, helped maintain all the panels, and paid damage claims immediately. Roger Hall, a coon hunter and former groom to the McQuade family that lived at the bottom of Germond Hill, remembers a delightful incident of Reynal's payments:

"One day Reynal met at our place and asked where the hare was that I told him about. I showed him the area and he took his hounds down there and ran all around and came back mighty mad. There's no damned hare there at all, he said. Well, I went down and sure enough there was the hare just a-laying all squished in a huddle where she usually was. I told him to come back, and he had to almost step on her before she got moving. Well he put her up, and they ran all around and around and then the hounds stopped at a burrow, and he thought she went in. Now he had a chauffeur to dig these things out, but as he wasn't there, I was told to do it. I pushed a stick down the hole to see how it went and dug for an hour. Well it wasn't there, and I told him he was properly fooled by an animal with half the brain of his own. Mr. McQuade, who was there, said I was doing the hare a great injustice, and Mr. Reynal huffed and puffed and huffed and puffed and gave me $10 for my trouble and rode away."

Victor McQuade was probably very lucky that day that his friendship with Reynal was a close and valued one. A retort like that would probably have earned most men Reynal's eternal enmity. For all his prowess in handling hounds, his ability to deal with people, including his family, was virtually nonexistent. His daughter Jeanne recalls, "Father, though a hunter and gentleman, was also a bully, taking offense at imaginary slights. But though he was a bully he was not a coward - so much for moralists. He was reasonably popular with his cronies, and perhaps even with the staff in the early years as they too were a product of his age. His most violent disputes with his men were petty in origin, springing from his refusal to lose face before his subordinates over petty questions of authority. But as times changed he did not. He was an anachronism in his own day."

"Most men can put up with so much," recalls Percy Ferris, Reynal's farm manager, "but Reynal - he couldn't put up with so much." Of all the staff only Ferris and Reynal's devoted housekeeper, Elizabeth York, "Bithy" managed a long tenure at Germond Hill Farm. This was probably due to the fact that Reynal viewed his staff with an attitude of noblesse oblige and saw that they were "his people." Even so, whenever the loyal Bithy was in his presence, she was required to stand while he sat. The chauffeur Ward Wilkins's main job seems to have been driving discharged staff members to the Dover train, and bringing back those to replace them.

Reynal's feuds could be legendary. Joseph B. Thomas, an outstanding proponent of American foxhounds, came in for particular enmity. This great hound man, author of the classic work "Hounds and Hunting Through The Ages," was invited to hunt the Millbrook country by Oakleigh Thorne in 1925. Thomas's hounds had the great effrontery to run their fox though a field that Reynal was drawing with his beagles. In Reynal's eyes this was a regrettable though not terrible event. What got his ire up was a letter from

Appendix III

Thomas stating, "I will let you know where I am drawing next so your hounds won't interfere again in the field." Reynal frothed at the mouth over this discourtesy from a parvenu visitor to Millbrook. That Thomas championed American hounds over English was heresy enough, but this incident was the nail in Thomas's coffin. When Thomas rented the Vail farm in Verbank – in Reynal's country – Reynal became virtually apoplectic. Bithy was ordered to draw the curtains on the south side of die house whenever the hour approached when Thomas would be coming by. It grew so intolerable that when the 5-year lease was finally up, Reynal bought the farm to keep Thomas out of the country, and renamed it "Craven Lodge Farm, after a famous sporting house in Britain - and also as a sly swipe at his enemy.

The worst feud, however, was a short-lived one which almost split the hunting community of Millbrook in two. When the divorce of Margaret Thorne from Ned Carle was announced, Reynal's loyalty to his friend Carle was so great that he wrote a letter to Oak-leigh Thorne withdrawing from the Thorne family and their guests all invitations to hunt with his packs. Thorne was the squire of Millbrook, master of the Millbrook Hunt, and a man of immense integrity and generosity who was liked by all. The hunting community was horrified at being asked to take a side, for many hunted with and liked Reynal as well. Alter a few months of this Carle was apprised of the situation and, aghast, went to explain things to Reynal. Thorne had actually taken Carle's side on the question in private, but when all was said and done, with Margaret resolved to have her way, her father supported her in public-

Carle was definitely not stabbed in the back by his father-in-law. Reynal apologized for having misunderstood the situation and reinstated the invitation. Thorne was out with him the next day, and peace was restored to the Millbrook valley and hunting fields.

Reynal's relationships with his children, three daughters and two sons, were equally trying. Jeanne, Adele, Roxanne, Louis and

Memories of the Shires

Eugene were every bit their father's offspring, as tough and single minded as he in many respects. Nice things each did for the other were often callously disregarded. When Adele returned from a long stay in Paris, Reynal hoped she would stay in Millbrook. To prepare for her he bought three new Nash Lafayette autos and put in a tennis court, as he understood she had become enamored of the sport. When the chauffeur brought her to Germond Hill, Reynal pointed out the car and said it was hers. She flippantly said she'd be damned if she was going to live in Millbrook and stalked away. Reynal was so hurt he went on a drinking binge for a week.

When youngsters Jeanne and Roxanne scrounged together $400 to buy Hannibal, an important stallion hound from the Western, this birthday gift was received without so much as a pat on the head. They also poured money into paneling parts of the Verbank South Country as a surprise present, and this too was received without acknowledgment. In all likelihood there were few gifts which would so please a huntsman as dedicated as Reynal, but his fear of expressing feelings kept him silent, and his daughters believed for many years their gifts – and love – a failure.

Reynal had a severe drinking problem. It was probably used as a crutch to make up for his inability to forge or acknowledge deep-rooted emotions of love and compassion. His childhood was seemingly devoid of affection, and throughout his life he was haunted by a feeling that he was loved by no one. When drunk there was no one meaner or more selfdestructive. After a fierce row with daughter Roxanne he sold three of her ponies, vowing she would never hunt with him again. At the end of another drunken row with Roxy she called him an old son of a bitch. To her amazement, instead of lashing out with a knifelike cut of his own, Reynal broke down in tears saying his mother "was a saint, not a bitch."

Dr. Howard Collins, master of the Millbrook Hunt in the '30s, vainly attempted to get Reynal to curb his drinking. Collins was one of the few men for whom Reynal had total and absolute respect, but even this was not enough to get him to heed the advice. Reynal almost killed himself in a car accident in the early '30s.

After a day's beagling in August 1931, and after wining and dining his friend Henry Perry, Reynal decided to drive to the city. He reportedly took both hands off the wheel to light a cigarette – as he was accustomed to do on horseback after a hunt – and his Nash Lafayette flipped over on its side. His arm was pinned beneath it, broken in five places. People stopped and tried to help, but he would have none of them. "I can park anywhere I want," he exclaimed irritably. Finally Ferris, Reynal's farm manager, came, and Reynal didn't want him to help either. Ferris ignored Reynal's ravings, pulled the back seat out of the car, and placed it on top of the damaged auto. He then extracted Reynal and laid him on this makeshift bed. People gathered to watch, among them John Place who declared loudly that the bleeding Reynal was about to die. With that, Reynal got off the seat, belted the man in the mouth, said "You first," and got back up on the seat again. A young surgeon arrived and proceeded to cut off Reynal's shirt. Reynal protested, exclaiming it was a mortal sin to do this to a Brooks Brothers shirt. The effect of the alcohol was such that no sedative would take hold, so the loyal Bithy grabbed several bottles of champagne, and off they went together in the ambulance, Bithy plying him with the bubbly all the way.

In 1924 Oakleigh Thorne decided to switch from harriers to foxhounds, in large part due to the fact that the Millbrook fields were becoming larger and the fox provided longer and more active sport. He turned over the "South Country" to Eugene Reynal. Reynal decided at this time to start a harrier pack of his own, and so imported twelve-and-a-half couples of hounds from the Dunstan and North Norfolk. The following year he bought eight-and-a-half more couples from them, two couples from the Aske Court, and a stallion hound from the Western. In all he usually had 75 couples of harriers and 40 couples of beagles in kennels.

Memories of the Shires

One ton of oatmeal was bought each month to feed Reynal's hounds, and several horses were bought at $10 to $25 each to be boiled for meat and gravy. Feeding time was generally at 3 PM. A horse would have been lugged up earlier from the below ground cold storage room to the cookhouse above. The meat was boiled off the bones into a soup in one container, and in another kettle the oatmeal was drawn. The meal was then poured into a long wooden trough on the kennel floor and the gravy ladled over it. A specially constructed chopper/cutter designed by Reynal was used to mix the broth and meal together uniformly. Reynal would then appear each day just as this operation was completed and check it to see if it were right. He then would go first to the eight lodging rooms that held the harriers and look them over. Hounds that were thin, weak, or slow feeders would be called out first and given a head start. Then the others would be allowed out. He would call them away from the trough by name when he thought they had eaten enough. Each hound knew it's name and followed the order implicitly or received a quick crack of the whip on it's back. The same routine was followed with the beagles. Hugh Collins, MFH of the Millbrook Hunt, recalls watching Reynal feed his beagles one day. The dog hounds were let out into the feeding room, and Reynal stood between them and the trough. The hounds stopped and looked at him expectantly. He then stepped over the trough, faced them, and called them one at a time to dinner. For a boy used to seeing the Millbrook Hunt's hounds devour their dinner in a feeding frenzy, this example of discipline was astonishing.

Every Monday the hounds were turned out into the yard and the kennels thoroughly scrubbed top to bottom with lye and water. The lodging rooms were aired out and fresh wheat or rye straw was placed for bedding. The outside Hags had to be kept immaculate as guests were often invited to see the hounds no matter how many times they'd been there before. Reynal himself somewhat humorously acknowledged his passion about exhibiting his charges: "You may be invited to see hounds on the flags, which can be somewhat boring to the uninitiated. If you look closely, however, you will notice two things. Some of the hounds are dogs. The rest are bitches."

Reynal did most of his own medical work on hounds and horses. He knew as much as any vet of the period about ailments and treatments, kept a better stock of medicines for his animals than for his family, and had all the equipment necessary for a neat workmanlike operation. If another hand was needed he called for that wonderful Irish foxhunter, raconteur and fellow whiskey lover Middleton O'Malley Knott. After an operation Knott would pronounce it a "three-shot bit of work" or "four-shot" if it took a bit longer, and the two would repair to the house to work off their reward. Between them the Irishman and the Anglophile managed to keep the Reynal quadrupeds in fine shape.

Hunting was carried on each and every day. The packs, harrier and beagle, were private and people were only allowed to hunt upon invitation. This was generously accorded most people who evinced a serious interest in the sport – if they were the proper sort. Henry Higginson, in his book "Hunting in the United States and Canada" wryly hints that most shouldn't ask. The harriers and beagles each hunted three days a week, with Sunday hunting given over to whichever pack Reynal thought might provide the most fun on that day. Reynal usually hunted a pack of 20 couples. Sometimes as many as 50 people hunted with him, but usually the field was confined to only a handful.

Reynal was a hound man, and the ability of his charges to work a line was more important to him than racing and chasing. He would let hounds puzzle out a check themselves, though he might already have seen in which direction the hare went. He only came in with a helping hand when he felt they were at a complete loss. He was the alpha male of the pack, and hounds would actually turn and look at him when completely puzzled. Whether out with the beagles or harriers, four to six hours would be spent in the hunting field.

Reynal meticulously noted each hound's strengths and weaknesses. He cheered them on enthusiastically in their successes. If he received true love from any living creature it was from his hounds. They adored him.

Proper appointment and deportment in the hunting field were demanded by Reynal of all who wished to hunt with him. Hunt servants could not be less than perfectly turned out. Guests would be politely (for Reynal) asked to leave the field if they showed up improperly turned out. One day Reynal decided to take Jeanne and Roxy down the bill to hunt with the Millbrook Harriers. D.U. Sloan, a hated enemy, was there as well. With him he brought Percy Rockefeller and his five sons. To Reynal's absolute horror the boys were dressed in cowboy outfits, packing sixguns, wearing stetsons, and riding western saddles. This blasphemy was too much for Reynal and he immediately sent his daughters home, telling them not to look back. He was so livid he could barely speak. Rockefeller immediately joined Sloan on Reynal's list of undesirable elements. When Rockefeller called asking to hunt with the Reynal Beagles he was met with a stream of such loathing that he thought he had called an insane asylum. So great was Reynal's interest in proper attire that he wrote a quirky little book, "Thoughts Upon Hunting Kit," that was published by the Derrydale Press. A great many of these books were thrown away after Reynal's death, so it has become one of the scarcest and most sought after works by collectors of American sporting literature.

Of all his children, Roxanne was the one most bitten by a love of hounds and hunting. She was a feisty independent spirit much like her father, but though she loved him, she put up with little of his abuse. One day, after showing off his hunters in the training ring, he called a groom to bring out Roxy's little pony William. As usual Reynal was half sober or half drunk, depending on whether you liked him or not. He straddled the pony – in fact he could walk while the pony went along – and pointed it at a 4-foot fence. The pony was always willing to give his best but this treatment infuriated Roxanne.

Appendix III

As Reynal made ready to cuff William with his crop Roxy mounted the fence and gave her father such a belt he was knocked off the pony into the dusty ring. Wendell Blagden, a sympathetic friend, shouted out, "Good show, good show, well done the little one!"

Despite the fact that the love/hate relationship swung back and forth from day to day, nothing impaired the union that was wrought over a love of hounds. Reynal had developed this pack to the nth degree of perfection, and now, with the new challenge of doing the same with harriers, the hunting of the beagles was turned over almost completely to Roxanne. Hugh Collins, a former MFH of the Millbrook Hunt, recalled Roxy as being "a tough kid, very keen on the beagles, very, very good with her hounds." He spent many a happy Sunday afternoon following her across the Millbrook hills.

Roxanne was often left to work and hunt the beagles herself, and, according to Collins, did so with great skill and intelligence. Perhaps the greatest triumph of father and daughter occurred at Madison Square Garden, at the Riding Club Show, at that time the premier hound event in the country. For many years Reynal's beagles were beaten on the flags by those of Dicky Gambrill. Reynal thought this unfair as Gambrill bred for looks, whereas he bred for hunting qualities. Discovery of a way to top him in public occurred somewhat by accident

Early one morning Reynal was walking his pack of harriers south down Route 82 when he encountered Roxy walking the beagles north. The hounds started mingling and each huntsman shouted the roading call, "Hounds, side over" used when a car approached. In a flash the beagles swept to Roxy's side of the road, and the harrier's to Reynal's. They each proceeded on a few rods until it dawned on them what had happened. Both stopped, looked at each other, and let out a whoop of pleasure.

At the Riding Club Hound Show in New York Reynal was asked to exhibit his harriers, they being the only such pack then in existence in the states. Before all the premier hound men in the country

Reynal brought his pack of hounds into the arena, and Roxanne followed with the beagles. They were allowed to mix and mill about the floor in a great mess. Then, with a nod, both Reynals from either side called out, "Hounds, side over." They called only once. Like the parting of the Red Sea the beagles flowed dramatically to Roxy and the harriers to Reynal. The applause was thunderous!

With the passage of time, however, when Reynal realized he could no longer hunt his beagles and harriers to the utmost, he decided to give them up rather than continue on in a haphazard fashion. The beagle pack was sold to his friend Dean Bedford, and the harriers went to Amory Haskell, of the Monmouth County Harriers, in New Jersey. The harriers were sold with the proviso they never be used on a drag. Reynal thought this beneath them. A fitting close to this illustrious hound breeder's career was marked by the grand champion win of "Mr. Reynal's Monarch," in the American Kennel Club Dog Show, where this hound was declared the most perfect dog of all breeds in America. A portrait of Monarch by Edward Megargee hangs in the AKC offices in New York City.

Many people who knew Reynal have remarked on his faultless and courageous horsemanship. In the saddle, man and animal melded into one being. In 1906 and 1912 he played on a team that won the Open Polo Championship of the United States. In the winter of 1928 he went with Roxanne and Adele to Britain to look for hounds. He came home with no new ones – but did bring back 22 horses. Amongst them was one previously owned and ridden by the Prince of Wales. John Miller, Reynal's last horseman, recalls, "He was one of the best ever. He feared nothing, and where others aimed for the low spots he always looked for the toughest. He would look through the crook of his arm while galloping onwards to see if anyone fell off, and laugh like hell if they did." Hugh Collins recalled, "Eugene Reynal would, when mounting, grip his reins once and that would be it for the day. He always had very good horses, excellent horses, and beautifully schooled. He trained them himself, always."

Appendix III

All of the horses were exercised before daylight. Each groom had only three horses that were his sole responsibility. One would be ridden and two led, alternating the horses throughout the week. The circuit traveled was 10 miles from Germond Hill across his fields to the Camby Road, thence to the Flint's gates, and back to Reynal's in time for breakfast. Reynal attended to much of their training himself. The tack room at Germond Hill was a showplace. Reynal had seven saddles for himself and more for family members and guests, all of the highest British quality. Each horse had its own fitted bridle.

Reynal was generally kind to other people's children. In South Millbrook there was a farmer who had a son who was an epileptic. This boy loved seeing the beagles go by, and would often become so excited he'd go into a fit. On several occasions when this happened Reynal whipped off his hunting tie and used it to tie the boy's tongue down till the fit abated. He would mutter, with great concern, "Hurry boy, hounds are moving on..."

Possibly, though, the boy whose attention he caught the most was young Morgan Wing. Wing's father said he thought the boy was born in a whelping pen, and supported his frequent forays to Germond Hill to meet with Reynal. Reynal probably found in young Wing a protégé, a substitute son who picked up the baton after Roxy moved on to other things. Wing found a mentor, an adult who treated him like an equal, and who was delighted to teach him all he could about hounds and hunting. The old master made him do every little thing connected with running a hunting establishment: cleaning kennels and tack, grooming hounds, pack breaking them, whipping-in to them, blowing the horn. The only thing Reynal would not let Wing do was hunt the pack. That was reserved for the Reynal family alone.

Wing found Reynal a fascinating man and visited him as often as he could. On forays to Germond Hill while on breaks from Pomfret and Princeton, Wing would partake of Reynal's time and hospitality at every opportunity. Wing recalled his tutelage in hound work with awe, amazed at how natural and easy it seemed to Reynal. He was also amused to be introduced to a new niece on every visit, countless numbers of them over the years. After about the fifth introduction to a niece he began to catch on. Indeed, Reynal's reputation as a ladies' man was lifelong. He was a handsome man in youth, and stayed that way. After the car accident he pestered the young nurses sent to attend him so badly that one after another quit. Eventually the family had to hire an old harridan to care for him just so Reynal would leave her alone and get on with the business of recuperating. His wife Adele rarely visited the country. Jeanne recalls that, "though my parents were not legally separated, in truth they were. A rapprochement was made toward the end of their lives, and they died in a somewhat happy state, within a month and a half of each other."

Through Morgan Wing, Reynal's excellence as a hound man passed into another generation. His lifelong love of hounds, all the knowledge he painstakingly gleaned in over 40 years of a hunting career, were given with great generosity to the young teenager who would eventually found the Sandanona Beagles. When Reynal died on January 31, 1939, he left one of his prize hunting horns to Wing. No, not the sterling silver one, nor the one from Elizabethan England, but the old copper piece that he had carried in the field. That was the important one.

Index

Index